LECTURES ON LATIN POETRY

LATIN POETRY

LECTURES DELIVERED IN 1893 ON THE PERCY
TURNBULL MEMORIAL FOUNDATION IN
THE JOHNS HOPKINS UNIVERSITY

BY

R. Y. TYRRELL

REGIUS PROFESSOR OF GREEK IN THE UNIVERSITY OF DUBLIN

KENNIKAT PRESS, INC./PORT WASHINGTON, N.Y.

LATIN POETRY

First published 1895
Reissued 1969 by Kennikat Press

Library of Congress Catalog Card No: 68-26294.
Manufactured in the United States of America

TO THE PARENTS OF

PERCY GRAEME TURNBULL

𝔗𝔥𝔦𝔰 𝔙𝔬𝔩𝔲𝔪𝔢

IS DEDICATED WITH SENTIMENTS OF THE SINCEREST

RESPECT, ADMIRATION, AND ESTEEM

BALTIMORE, MARYLAND.

δίκᾳ ξεναρκέϊ κοινὸν φέγγος.

PINDAR, *Nem.* iv. 12.

Oh for red flowers of fire from Pindar's hand,
  To weave with warp of legendary lore
  That pictured woof, the tale of Baltimore!
O fairest daughter of old Maryland,
O lordly town on whose inviolate strand
  Burst the loud shock of war that overbore
  The tyrannous Atlantic's imminent roar!
Long to its scabbard her reluctant brand
  Clave: and when, weeping — those were gracious tears —
At last she drew it, then with force tenfold
The huge third wave of battle ruining roll'd
  And thunder'd on, till from the frozen meres
To sun-bathed Florida, from main to main,
Man cast from off him Race's galling chain.

R. Y. TYRRELL.

PREFACE.

THESE lectures form the third course delivered on the Percy Turnbull Memorial foundation in the Johns Hopkins University of Baltimore in the spring of 1893. The first course was given by Mr. Edmund Clarence Stedman in 1891, on "The Nature and Elements of Poetry," and was followed in 1892 by "The Growth and Influence of Classical Greek Poetry," by Professor Jebb. I will not deprecate in vain the (alas!) inevitable comparison with these two masterly volumes, but will hasten to put before my readers the general scope and aim which I proposed to myself, and in doing so I will use the words which formed the opening paragraphs of the introductory lecture as delivered in Baltimore : —

"In the first of the lectures I take a very rapid survey of Latin poetry as a whole, never pausing to consider at all closely any particular poet, except in the case of one or two literary personages whose influence on the course of Latin poetry seems to have been generally underrated, and to whom I shall not have an opportunity to recur in subsequent lectures. I fear the imperative necessity to generalize on this first — to me most welcome — occasion of making your acquaintance will render it hard for me to avoid trying your patience.

The next lecture, too, dealing with the early Latin poetry, must still be of a somewhat general cast. After that we shall be able to confine our attention mainly to individual poets, or to compared or contrasted pairs of poets, until the consideration of the Poetry of the Decline again makes it necessary to abandon the microscope for the field-glass, and to accommodate our vision to a wider prospect. I will endeavor here briefly to describe what will be my scope and aim.

"It is plain that I should not have sufficient time, even supposing I had sufficient audacity, to construct a kind of catechism of what we should believe about Latin poetry, or even to attempt to give an exhaustive summary of its contents. Still less would it be possible or profitable to try to set forth a *conspectus* of what other people have thought on this subject. It comes, then, to this : I must aim at putting before you what I think most interesting in connection with Latin poetry, sometimes describing how certain masterpieces (for, of course, we shall be brought to consider some masterpieces) have affected myself. I hope, therefore, that if I do not constantly pause to explain that I am only giving what is in my own mind, and not at all claiming any right to speak *ex cathedra*, you will not for that reason suppose that I am putting forward for your acceptance views which I am really submitting to your judgment. This University has invited an expression of my opinions on a subject which has been for many years most attractive to me, and I regard such an invitation on your part as a very distinguished honor done to me and to my University. I hope to gain your assent to most of my views, and, even when I do not gain assent, I shall be glad if I succeed in stimulating the play of consciousness on important and fascinating topics, even though it should take the form of a criticism which even if dissentient will, I am sure, be kind. I shall not attempt to give a life of each poet who may be under consideration, except in so far as the incidents of his career have left a distinct impress on his work. It will be more in accordance with my own tastes, and (as I believe) with the scope of the Percy Turnbull Lectures, to devote the hours during which it will be my pleasant task to address you, not to biography or literary history, but rather to analysis and literary criticism ; and to endeavor to set before you rather studies in the different poets and periods than chapters in a history of literature. I shall have to ask, not what were the works of each poet, but what was his work ; how he looked out on the world, and what was the world on which he looked ; whether he had a message to society, and how far he succeeded in delivering it.

"I shall be by no means an unvarying eulogist of Latin poetry. Indeed, in the case of some of the poets I fear I shall run the risk of being called a harsh and unsympathetic critic. I shall have to put before you many things which have often been said before. I have, however, endeavored as much as possible to avoid tracks that are too well beaten,

and to dwell in preference on points of view which
may seem to have been comparatively neglected.

" To attempt, it may be said, to say anything at
the same time true and new on such a theme as
Virgil or Horace, really seems out of the question.
But it is a characteristic of philological and historical inquiry that the same subject admits of being
viewed from very diverse points, and this is pe-
culiarly true in dealing with poetry. Each actor,
each musician, has a different way of rendering
Shakespeare or Beethoven, and there is no final
interpretation of the work of a great artist. Literature can do no more than give us the opinions
and sentiments of particular persons at particular
times. To estimate — even to understand — these
opinions and sentiments, we must know something
of the times and circumstances in which they were
expressed. It will be requisite, therefore, now and
then, to invade the domain of history and biography, and thus diversify our more purely literary
studies."

Such, then, broadly, was my aim. But here I
must make my acknowledgments to the writers
who have throughout been my guides and inspir-
ers. Many of them will be at once recognized as
indispensable : for instance, every writer or lecturer on Lucretius must owe infinite obligations
to the great work of Munro ; and the same remark
applies to the best editors of the other great poets
of Rome : I mean to that editor who (like Conington and Mayor and Ellis) has in each case been

acknowledged to have made a particular poet his
own peculiar province.   Then the historians of
Rome — Mommsen, Merivale, Gibbon — often help
the lecturer, as well as histories of literature, like
the excellent work of Mr. Crutwell, and the late
Professor Sellar's acute and eloquent studies in
Roman poetry.   The German writers, especially
Bernhardy and Teuffel revised by Schwabe, are,
of course, very valuable.   But I have found the
French school most helpful and stimulating.
M. Patin's volumes entitled "Études sur la Poésie
Latine" have been invaluable to me, especially in
the earlier lectures, and, though I have often expressed my obligations to him, I owe to him many
debts not specifically acknowledged, in the way of
suggestion and point of view.   An equal or greater
debt I would own to another charming French
critic, M. Constant Martha, whose eloquent study,
" Le Poëme de Lucrèce," is as fascinating in style
and as profound in insight as his " Moralistes sous
l'Empire Romain," which works have both been
largely used by me in the third and seventh lectures.   Nisard's "Les Poëtes Latins de la Déca-
dence" was the basis of the last lecture.   Often,
too, the masterly essays of M. Gaston Boissier have
been helpful and inspiring.   Indeed, for breadth of
view as well as charm of style, the French writers
on Latin literature seem to me quite unrivaled.

In the case of other writers who have not been
so largely used, acknowledgment is made to each
in his own place.   Among them I would mention

especially the late Professor Nettleship's essays, and the tract of Hartman, " De Horatio Poeta."

Though my obligations to previous writers are so large, my own opinions will be found to be a very pronounced ingredient in the book : I fear they will seem too pronounced to some, especially to the uncompromising and indiscriminate *fautores veterum.*

Many of the lectures appeared in English and American magazines either before or after they were delivered as lectures ; and I have to thank the proprietors and editors of the several magazines, especially those of the " Quarterly Review " (London), and the " Atlantic Monthly " (Boston), for permission to use them in this volume. In hardly any case, however, does the lecture appear in exactly the same form which it had as an article. Nor are the lectures printed precisely as they were delivered. To some (especially V., VI., VIII.), considerable additions have been made. The Appendix on Recent Translators of Virgil formed no part of the lecture as delivered in Baltimore and Chicago ; neither did the remarks on Petronius in the eighth lecture. I have not printed in the lectures certain expressions called forth from me from time to time at their delivery by the uniform courtesy and friendliness of my hearers in America, at Baltimore, Richmond, Chicago, and New York, — a courtesy and friendliness which upheld me at a time when my state of health made me apprehensive lest I should be quite unfit to show myself at all worthy of the high distinction which the invitation of the several learned bodies conferred on me. I therefore ask leave to express here my deep and abiding sense of the true kindness and generosity of which I was the object in America. Dull indeed would be the lecturer who should not feel, in such audiences as I had the good fortune to meet, a source of sustaining inspiration and of a comforting conviction that, whatever failings there might be on his part, one thing at all events would not fail, — the encouraging kindliness and genuine sympathy of hearers as sincerely warm-hearted as keenly intelligent.

CONTENTS.

I.

INTRODUCTORY.

II.

EARLY LATIN POETRY.

III.

LUCRETIUS AND EPICUREANISM.

IV.

CATULLUS AND THE TRANSITION TO THE AUGUSTAN AGE.

V.

VIRGIL.

VI.

HORACE.

VII.

LATIN SATIRE.

VIII.

LATIN POETRY OF THE DECLINE.

LECTURES ON LATIN POETRY.

I.

INTRODUCTORY.

POETRY may be regarded and estimated from two points of view, — the *à priori* and the *à posteriori*. The former rests on principles which are very likely to be arbitrary and incomplete. It will always be found to be more satisfactory to ask ourselves what a thing is or has been — provided, of course, an answer is possible — than to decide what it ought to be according to certain principles laid down by ourselves. The *à priori* method has manifest disadvantages in a review which extends over many centuries. For, as regards poetry at least, abstract principles must of necessity be vague and shifting. Just as a great traveler makes our old maps worse than useless when a lake takes the place of a Sahara, and a mountain ridge that of a prairie, so too in literature, sometimes a new planet swims into our ken, and the main principles of artistic construction are revolutionized. What would Pope have made of Browning, or of Walt Whitman? Would Edgar Allan Poe have thought

Different points of view from which Poetry may be regarded.

of describing as a novel that delicate study in psychological analysis, "The Lady of the Aroostook"?

It is in her Prose rather than in her Poetry that Rome has really expressed herself. For a long time the Roman people were exclusively devoted to agriculture and war. Their sole care was to defend themselves and preserve their existence, to devise for themselves some kind of constitution in the constant struggle of patrician and plebeian, of rich and poor, and to discover a *modus vivendi* with their external and intestine foes. To these problems they devoted all their energies, and their efforts in these directions were crowned with conspicuous success. Their laws have survived the Roman Republic to this day, have afforded a model to the civilized world, and bid fair to last as long as Western civilization endures.

Chief bequest of Rome to the civilized world.

Poetry came to the Roman nation late, after the conquest of Italy, Carthage, and Greece, and formed part of the plunder of the world which began to pour into the Imperial treasuries. Hence the first and broadest distinction between Greek poetry, which developed naturally, and Latin, which was transplanted; and this is the reason why Rome succeeded best in didactic poetry, because that product of art best bears removal to another soil. When the Greek nation became a province of Rome, the Latin

Rise of Latin, as distinguished from Greek, poetry.

Testimonies to its foreign origin.

literature became a province of the Greek. This fact is oftenest expressed in the terse but trite Horatian verse which tells how —

" Captive Greece captured her conqueror rude ; "

but not less apt, and certainly less hackneyed, are the words which Livy puts into the mouth of Cato in the Senate, — " Therefore the more I fear that these things may prove our conquerors, not we theirs." [1] The same rather obvious truth is expressed with characteristic rudeness by Porcius Licinus, a poet contemporary with Cicero : —

" During the second Punic War, to Italy's rude land
   The Muse repair'd with winged foot, and there she took
      her stand." [2]

Equally characteristic of its author is the elegance with which Ovid describes the early struggles of Rome, which left her no time for the cultivation of literature.

" Not yet had Greece, the home of words not deeds,
  On her rude conquerors imposed her creeds ;
  Who best could fight, his was the highest art,
  And he most learn'd who best could launch the dart." [3]

[1] " Eo plus horreo ne illae magis res nos capiant quam nos illas. " — XXX. 4.

[2] " Poenico bello secundo Musa pinnato gradu
   Intulit se bellicosam in Romuli gentem feram."

[3] " Nondum tradiderat victas victoribus artes
    Graecia, facundum sed male forte genus ;
   Qui bene pugnabat Romanam noverat artem,
    Mittere qui potuit tela disertus erat."

Fast. III. 101.

When we refer to Latin poetry before the Greek influence, we are either talking of an assumed and hypothetical literature like that of which Macaulay has given us such ingenious and eloquent specimens in his "Lays of Ancient Rome," or else of writings and documents which have nothing but the name in common with poetry as we now understand the word. Cicero, indeed, tells us that Appius Claudius Caecus wrote a poem of a gnomic character which he calls Pythagorean. If he did, it is interesting to find that didactic poetry was not only Rome's greatest success, but her earliest attempt. But for the rest, early Roman poetry, which was then called *scriptura*, was used only for state documents, lists and records, and the poets were called *scribae*. The poems, *carmina*, were laws such as those of the Twelve Tables, treaties of the kings with Gabii and the Sabines, pontifical books, and such like, and were written in Saturnian verse. Beside these there were rustic litanies, and those chants at festivals and funerals in praise of ancestors and founders of families, of which Cicero speaks, and on which Macaulay based his theory of a lost Latin ballad poetry. To these must be added the Fescennine strains in which peasants bantered each other at rustic merry-makings, and from which more or less directly rose three kinds of composition in which Roman writers achieved high success, — comedy, satire, and amoebaean pastoral poetry.

Pre-Hellenic Latin poetry.

But all these pale dawnings of art faded into mist before the sunburst of Greek literature. To apply to it the eulogy of Lucretius on Epicurus, Greek literature extinguished everything on which its radiance burst, —

Effect of Greek literature.

"E'en as the Sun uprisen quenches the fires of Night."[1]

The first and greatest debt to Greece was the Drama, the popularity of which at Rome has been greatly underrated. It is true that it had to struggle with certain difficulties which it did not meet in Greece, and to which in modern times it is not exposed. The Romans unquestionably looked on the expression of grief as unmanly. Cicero condemns Sophocles for allowing Philoctetes to utter cries of pain, and for suffering Heracles to give voice to his agony in the death scene in the "Trachiniae;" and commends Pacuvius for putting no lamentations into the mouth of Ulysses when dying of the wound inflicted by his son Telegonus. Pacuvius expresses the Roman feeling when he says that

Difficulties which beset the rise of the Drama.

"A man may rail against the strokes of Fortune,
But not bewail them: that were woman's part."[2]

Attius tells us that the best comfort in affliction is the hope that we have concealed our wound. In the "Telamon" of Ennius, the father, hearing of

[1] "Restinxit stellas exortus ut aetherius Sol."
[2] "Conqueri fortunam adversam non lamentari decet;
Id viri est officium; fletus muliebri ingenio additust."

the death of his son Ajax, says that, when he sent him to Troy to fight for his fatherland, he knew that he sent him

> " To deadly strife, not to a festival." [1]

Such a theory as to the limits within which the expression of grief ought to be confined would of course be adverse to the production of genuine tragedy, and would rather favor the rise of those so-called tragedies which Seneca under the Empire wrote for the arm-chair, not for the stage, and in which he surfeited even the Romans with stoical dignity and superhuman impassibility.

Again, comedy suffered from the fact that Rome would tolerate no invasion of private life, as is shown by the fate of Naevius, who expiated by his death in African exile an attack on the powerful family of the Metelli, and an allusion to the private life of the victor of Zama. Besides, these importations from Greece were supported only by the taste, perhaps the affectation, of the rich and noble; the people preferred rope-dancers, as we learn from the Prologue to the " Hecyra " of Terence. Hence we find that the actors despised the verdict of the masses, and were ambitious to appeal to the classes alone. Arbuscula in Horace [2] is indifferent to the hisses of the populace if she can only secure the applause of the Knights.

---

[1] " Ego cum genui tum moriturum scivi et ei rei sustuli.
   Praeterea ad Trojam cum misi ob defendendam Graeciam
   Scibam me in mortiferum bellum non in epulas mittere."
[2] *Satires,* I. 9. 76.

However, that, in spite of these very serious dis advantages, Tragedy at least was held in no mean estimation at Rome, we gather not only from the great wealth and posi- *Early success of Tragedy.* tion attained by the tragic actor Aesopus, but also from the distinct testimony of Horace, who tells us [1] that houses thronged with spectators of high position witnessed the reproductions of the works of the Attic dramatists in Rome, where the classes, not the masses, seem to have been able to make or mar the fortunes of the stage.

One of the strongest arguments against the au- thenticity of the early history of Rome is that, though the duration of the mon- archy was about two hundred and forty *Difficulty in the history of Latin Tragedy.* years, yet this period is said to have embraced only seven reigns, an average of about five and thirty years to each reign. The history of Latin Tragedy presents a similar difficulty : three names, Ennius, Pacuvius, and Attius, stand to represent a period of more than a hundred years, from the first Africanus to Sulla. Comedy, not being so distinctly an imported and transplanted novelty, but having a somewhat congenial soil in a coun- try where Fescennine interludes, masques, and Atellane plays were indigenous, would doubtless have taken deeper root but for the stern prohibi- tion of those personalities without which the comic drama can hardly become truly popular or racy of the soil.

[1] *Epistles*, II. 1. 60.

The Graeco-Roman drama of Plautus and Ter-
Plautus and ence was really sad under its superficial
Terence. gaiety. The complete separation of political from private life, the isolation of women,
the dullness of home, the consequent craving for
coarse excitement, the demoralization of the slave
into his master's pimp, — all these traits are common to the Rome of Plautus and Terence and
to Greece in her decline. The two playwrights
felt this. Terence dealt with the phenomena presented to him after the manner of Horace, with a
smile and a shrug ; Plautus, in the fashion of Juvenal, with fierce indignation and disgust. The *fa-*
Their *bulae palliatae* of Plautus and Terence
successors. were succeeded by *fabulae togatae*, dealing with a lower stratum of society ; and finally
by *tabernariae*, which went lower still, until the
trabeatae were introduced under Augustus, and
took in hand a very high class of society again.
This whole distinction between plays vulgar, mid-
dle-class, and aristocratic betrays a want of that
dramatic sense which ought to tell the playwright
that in the true drama of life these classes are
mingled and fused, and not distinctly ticketed and
kept apart. Hence Rome produced no Euripides,
no Shakespeare, no Molière.

The so-called *togatae* are represented by a num-
Verses ber of names more or less obscure, —
ascribed to Luscius, Attilius, Titinius, Turpilius,
Trabea. Trabea. As we shall not have occasion
to return to these shadowy personalities again, it

may be interesting to quote here the extremely clever verses which Muretus wrote and submitted to Joseph Scaliger, who pronounced them to be by Trabea : —

> " Here, si querellis ejulatu fletibus
> Medicina fieret miseriis mortalium,
> Auro parandae lacrimae contra forent.
> Nunc haec ad minuenda mala non magis valent
> Quam naenia praeficae ad excitandos mortuos.
> Res turbidae consilium non fletum expetunt.
> Ut imbre tellus sic riganda est mens mero,
> Ut illa fruges haec bona consilia efferat." [1]

The manner is perfect ; but it is no disrespect to Scaliger to point out what modern scholarship has observed, but what in his day was unknown, that the modern origin of the verses is betrayed by several violations of the proper caesura in dactyls and anapaests, and by the fact that a writer of Trabea's time could not have made the first syllable of *lacrimae* long.

After them came the remodeled Atellane plays under Sulla. In them originally the place Atellane was Campania, the persons were con- plays. ventional types, and the language even is said to have had a tinge of Oscan. The scene was not

---

[1] " Sir, if by cries and groans and floods of tears
Mortals could minister to human ills,
Then every tear were worth its weight in gold.
But tears no more can mitigate man's woes
Than keens and dirges can bring back the dead.
Affliction asks philosophy, not tears.
Moisten your clay with wine, from which will spring
Sound sense, as from the rain earth's kindly fruits."

Rome, but some municipal town, and the dialogue
was mainly improvised.   Sulla turned these Atellane interludes into regular plays like the comedies of Plautus and Terence, and is said even to
have composed some Atellane farces himself.
The chief authors of these were Pomponius and
Novius, in whose time circumstances rendered
attacks on provincial oddities more *piquant*, because Italy, having saved Rome from the Cartha-
ginians and the Cimbri, began then to ask from the
Imperial City something more than the privilege
of shedding her blood in Rome's defence ; and nothing pleased the Romans more than to be reminded
how absurd were the pretensions of these provin-
cials, these rustics, these *inurbani*, to be on a foot-
ing of equality with Rome.   In the hands of Pomponius and Novius the Atellane passed from half
Oscan *patois* to Latin, from prose to verse, from an
improvised sketch to a written play, from a cast
consisting of amateur young aristocrats to a company of regular actors.   In these plays Pappus,
Bucco, Maccus, and Dorsennus were used as stalk-
ing-horses for the ridiculing of certain social
types ; for instance, *Pappus praeteritus*, or " The
Disappointed Candidate," dealt with the humors
of elections, and to some extent foreshadowed the
Harlequin, Clown, and Pantaloon of modern pan-
tomime.   They were followed by the mimes of
Laberius and Publilius Syrus.   When the mimes
fell into disrepute, as if to illustrate the sensible
admonition of their creator, Laberius, —

"I 've had my day, and so will my successor.
None have a property in public favor," [1]—

the Atellane play was revived by one Mummius
under Tiberius. It became disgustingly coarse and
licentious. We learn from Martial [2] that undei
Domitian a real crucifixion was introduced into
such a play.

The mimes were interludes, like the Atellane
plays, but no longer dealt with the con- The mimes.
ventional personages of whom Rome had
become weary. The virtue of the Roman lady, so
jealously guarded (as we shall see) in the comedies
of Plautus and Terence, was no longer maintained
in the mime. Valerius Maximus tells us that the
town of Massilia showed her regard for morality by
prohibiting the mime, and Ovid [3] points out how
absurd it is to allege the licentious tendency of his
poetry in an age when that form of the drama was
patronized.

You are no doubt familiar with the story how
Caesar, offended by some independent Anecdote
verses of Laberius which seemed to be about
Caesar and
aimed at himself, compelled the veteran Laberius.
mime-writer, though a knight, to take part as an
actor in one of his own farces ; and you are ac-
quainted with the manly lines in which, in his prologue, Laberius expressed his sense of the affront
which had been put upon him : —

"I, who 've lived sixty years without a stain,
Who left my house this morn a Roman knight,

[1] "Cecidi ego, cadet qui sequitur, laus est publica."
[2] *De Spect.* VII. [3] *Trist.* II. 497.

> Go back a player!   Certes, I have lived
> A day too long." [1]

But I may be permitted to remind you of an anecdote handed down by Macrobius and
others touching an amusing exchange
of words between Laberius and Cicero.
When Laberius, on the occasion just referred to,
was about to resume his seat among the spectators
after playing his part, he found no room in the
places reserved for the Equites. "We should be
glad," said Cicero, who was present, "to make room
for you, if we were not so much crowded." "That
must be a strange sensation for you," replied Laberius, "seeing that you are so accustomed to sit
on two stools at once." This little incident perhaps accounts for Cicero's disparaging allusion to
Laberius in a letter to Cornificius : [2] "I have grown
so inured to boredom that I can sit out the pro-
ductions of Laberius and Syrus." Horace's well-
known sneer at Laberius is perhaps only a sign
that the court poet did not forget that Laberius
had offended the founder of the Empire by such
free speeches as : —

And about Cicero and Laberius.

> "Many he needs must fear whom many fear." [3]

It may amuse us here to recall a few of the
maxims ascribed to Publilius Syrus, as we shall not

---

[1] "Ego bis tricenis annis actis sine nota
Eques Romanus a lare egressus meo
Domum revertar mimus.   Nimirum hoc die
Uno plus vixi mihi quam vivendum fuit."

[2] *Fam.* XII. 10.

[3] "Necesse est multos timeat quem multi timent."

again return to this subject. Perhaps among the best are, "The beggar's wants are few, Publilius the miser's countless;"[1] "Good com- Syrus. pany's the best lift on a journey;"[2] and a very ingeniously expressed sentiment which cannot be Englished, as we have no words answering to the distinction between *cuivis* and *cuiquam*. The meaning is little more than "What has happened once to one man may happen again to another." The expression is very deft, —

"Cuivis potest accidere quod cuiquam potest."

Trimalchio, in the "Satyricon" of Petronius Arbiter, estimates the respective merits of Cicero and Syrus, and decides that Cicero has the greater power of expression (*disertiorem*), but that Syrus has greater distinction of style (*honestiorem*). It is uncertain whether the very elegant iambics in condemnation of Roman luxury, attributed there by Trimalchio to Syrus, are really by him, or are a clever parody by Petronius.

Before this epoch, epic poetry had taken its rise with Naevius and Ennius, who, succeeded Poetry of the by Lucilius, also laid the foundations of Caesarian Satire. But it was in the Caesarean age epoch. that the yield (*proventus*, as Pliny calls it) of poetry became really copious. That period was marked by a mania for writing verses, in spite of the civil and political disorders of the time. Caesar himself,

[1] "Desunt inopiae pauca, avaritiae omnia."
[2] "Comes facundus in via pro vehiculo est."

on his way to Spain, wrote an *Iter,* or "Impressions of my Journey." Many of the orators mentioned in the "Brutus" were poets also. Hirtius chronicled in verse the Istrian War. Furius Bibaculus essayed the task, which Marcus Cicero abandoned and his brother pursued, of describing the campaigns of Caesar in Gaul. Calvus, whom Horace to his lasting disgrace couples with Catullus in depreciating both, sang Quintilia in rivalry to Lesbia, and strove with an "Io" to emulate that divine poem, the "Peleus and Thetis." Helvius Cinna for nine years touched and retouched his poem entitled "Smyrna," dealing with an unpleasant theme like that of Shelley's "Cenci" until the work became unreadable, and his conduct proverbial through a verse of Horace's. It is but fair to add that the "Smyrna" won the pronounced approval of the coming poet Catullus.

But of all the writers in verse, save only those two, Lucretius and Catullus, who from the time of Nepos down to the present day have been recognized as the "bright particular stars" of the Caesarean epoch, by far the most important and interesting, not only for his real poetical ability but for the influence which he exercised on subsequent Art, is the great orator and consummate man of letters, M. Tullius Cicero. As both his powers and his influence in this department of literature have been very greatly underrated, I may be excused for dwelling a little on this phase in the genius of a man who might almost have

Cicero's poetry.

been called "myriad-minded." If Cicero does not
deserve the name as well as Shakespeare, at all
events he has a far better title to it than that
unknown bishop to whom the term μυριόνους was
originally applied by Photius. Plutarch describes
Cicero as having been alike the first poet and the
first orator of his age, — a criticism which startles
us when we remember the gibes of Juvenal and
Martial, and the unfavorable comments of Seneca,
Gellius, and Tacitus. It is true that as a poet he
was eclipsed by Lucretius and Catullus, but he had
first been eclipsed by a greater than these, — by
himself. He was his own greatest rival, *supposti-
cius sibi ipsi*, in the phrase of Martial. The glories
of the advocate, the orator, the philosopher, the
unrivaled essayist and letter-writer, made his poetic
bays pale. Before the rise of Lucretius and Catullus, there is little doubt that Cicero was the poet
of his age. Even in his early works, "Marius" and
the "Phaenomena" and "Prognostica," we find a
new and very noticeable polish and harmony of cadence, which must have had a great effect on the
nascent muse of Lucretius and Catullus. In the
poem on his consulate, whence come the unlucky
verses which in the minds of most people stand by
themselves for the poetry of Cicero, —

"O fortunatam natam me consule Romam !" —
and
"Cedant arma togae, concedat laurea laudi," —

we find an expression on which Virgil himself
could not have improved when he calls the comets

claro tremulos ardore, "quivering with lucid fire."
The jingle for which the first of these verses has
been condemned can hardly have been due to want
of ear.   The writer who is so fastidiously sensitive
to euphony that he will not allow words which
might conclude a hexameter, as forming a dactyl
and spondee, to stand together in his prose works,
is not likely to have fallen inadvertently into the
collocation of *natam natam.*   Indeed, Quintilian
quotes a similar assonance in a letter of Cicero's
to Brutus,[1] and we find *pleniore ore* in Off. I. 61.
Moreover, one must remember how easy it would
have been to transpose *natam* and *Romam.*   If
Cicero deliberately accepted this assonance, one
would be disposed to think that his authority
might well be set against the judgment of Quintilian and Juvenal, not to speak of later critics.   The
vanity of the verse is but a vice of the age in
which the austere Caesar could send such a piece
of fustian as *veni, vidi, vici* to the senate, and escape the ridicule with which such a dispatch from
the seat of war would now be received.

As regards the second of the verses so generally and so inconsiderately condemned, it may be
remarked that the expression, *cedant arma togae,*
would not have seemed ridiculous to Cassius, who
uses a very similar phrase in a letter to Cicero,[2]

---

[1] "Ciceroni in epistulis excidit *res mihi invisae visae sunt,*
Brute." — Quintil. IX. 41.

[2] "Est enim tua *toga* omnium *armis* felicior." — *Fam.*
XIII. 13. 1.

nor to Pliny, who writes of *togae triumphum lin-
guaeque lauream.* Caesar thought highly of the
poetry of Cicero, who sometimes betrays some of
the characteristic traits of the " fretful tribe."
He is very anxious to know what people think of
his verses, especially what Caesar thinks. In a
letter to his brother he says of the poem which we
have been discussing : "What is Caesar's opinion
about my poèm ? The first book, I know, he deems
excellent, — not surpassed even in Greek literature ;
the rest, up to a certain point, he seemed to
think — what shall I say ? — slipshod. Find out for
me, is it the style or the subject he does not like ? " [1]
We read with pleasure in another letter [2] that
Cicero abandoned his intention of collaborating
with his brother Quintus in a poem on Caesar's
" Gallic Wars," because he " feels no heart for the
theme," *abest* ἐνθουσιασμός. He is too good a republican to enjoy strewing flowers on the path of
Caesar to the throne. The Augustans felt no want
of heart for the praise of Caesar, nor did Cicero
show any lack of enthusiasm when he eulogized Cato
or thundered against Antony. A passage from
the same unlucky poem, too long to quote, challenges comparison with the splendid verses in the

[1] *Q. Fr.* II. 15. (16.) 5. The words *reliqua ad quem-
dam locum* ῥᾳθυμότερα may mean " the rest of his expressions
were not so enthusiastic," but the broad meaning of the passage is not affected by the interpretation of the particular
words.
[2] *Q. Fr.* III. 4. 4.

18   *INTRODUCTORY*

first Georgic in which Virgil recounts the portents
which presaged Caesar's death. It is true that
there is in Cicero an excessive illustration of the
same point. This is a characteristic of the early
style, and shows him inferior as an artist to Virgil.
But it is one thing to be inferior as an artist to
Virgil — a proposition which may be predicated
of nearly every poet who has ever written — and
quite another to be, as Juvenal describes Cicero,
so wretched a poetaster that, if in eloquence he
had been on the same level, he might have regarded with indifference the dagger of Antony,
since he would have been too insignificant to excite
the resentment of any one.

But by far the finest poems of Cicero are those
Cicero's
translations
from the
Greek. splendid translations from the Greek
with which he has embellished his rhe-
torical and philosophical works. There
is in the "De Divinatione," II. §§ 63, 64, a very
fine rendering of the portent from which Calchas
inferred the duration of the siege of Ilium — the
devouring of the little birds by the serpent; [1] and
the song of the Sirens [2] is translated with great
taste in "De Finibus," V. § 49. But conspicuous
above the rest are the speeches of Prometheus on
the Caucasus, and of Hercules dying on Mount
Oeta [3] — versions from Aeschylus and Sophocles
which used to be ascribed to Attius, as being quite
beyond the unhappy author of —

[1] *Iliad*, II. 299–330.   [2] *Odyss.* XII. 184–191.
[3] *Tusc.* II. §§ 19–25.

"O fortunatam natam me consule Romam,"

but which are now rightly attributed to Cicero, and which no judicious critic can read without recognizing a dignity and even splendor of diction not surpassed in Latin literature. With these we would couple a beautiful rendering from the "Cresphontes" of Euripides,[1] in which Cresphontes declares that —

"When a child's born, our friends should throng our halls
And wail for all the ills that flesh is heir to;
But when a man has done his long day's work,
And goes to his long home to take his rest,
We all with joy and gladness should escort him."

These vigorous and admirably tasteful renderings from the Greek drama by Cicero possess a further and unique interest as standing midway between the roughness of the old Latin drama and the far less powerful — almost feeble — elegance of Varius and Ovid.

But now appear two great geniuses who would have eclipsed Cicero as a poet, even if he had not already eclipsed himself. Lucretius and Catullus. Lucretius gave the world a philosophical poem which has never been surpassed, and Catullus showed for the first time what truly epic Latin hex-

[1] "Nam nos decebat coetu celebrantes domum
    Lugere ubi esset aliquis in lucem editus,
    Humanae vitae varia reputantes mala;
    At qui labores morte finisset graves
    Hunc omni amicos laude et laetitia exsequi."
    Tusc. Disp. I. § 115

ameters were, in the divine poem of "The Marriage of Peleus and Thetis." Catullus is sometimes described as the forerunner of Lucretius, but he is not so either chronologically or psychologically. The great work of Lucretius has been well called "an improvisation of genius;" and it has all the merits, together with some of the defects, of its high-engendered origin. Catullus, on the other hand, weighs his words, sometimes holds himself in, and, as Horace says, plays the part of the polished talker who husbands his powers, and sometimes deliberately forbears to exercise them. Catullus is in fact already an Augustan, and leads us by an easy transition to the Augustan Age.

Augustus encouraged poetry with political views. The so-called Augustan poets were almost a college, or at least a select literary hierarchy like the French Academy. Valerius Maximus speaks of "a College of Poets" (*collegium poetarum*), and its president seems to have been Spurius Maecius Tarpa, of whom we hear in Cicero's letters and in Horace. Patronage was not a 'new thing in the time of Augustus. Scipio, Laelius, Memmius, were the forerunners of Maecenas, Pollio, Messalla. But Augustus encouraged it not only by private hospitality, but by making it a guild, by multiplying copies of standard works, and by establishing libraries and encouraging the sale of books: we learn that there was a bookseller at Utica. It has been said that the Bourbons forgot nothing and learned nothing.

The Augustan College of Poets.

The first Roman emperor, unlike them, was an
apt pupil in the school of life, and ever ready to
learn and to apply its lessons.   But, like them, he
forgot nothing.   Least of all did he forget that
there was once a young man called Octavius and
afterwards Octavian.   He remembered that young
man too well to neglect any means of obliterating
his memory.   Poetry, it struck him, not history,
was the screen that lay most ready to his hand.
History could not but hint at least at the unscru-
pulous treachery of that young man's triumvirate,
the cruelty of his parricidal massacres, the inglori-
ousness of his military career, his domestic infamy.
Poetry could leave all these untouched and dwell
on the reign of peace, the restoration of religion
and morality, the standards of Crassus retrieved, and
the boundaries of the Empire enlarged.   Among
all his Academicians he met none so skillful to
harp on this string as Virgil and Horace, as that
worshiper of Nature whom he drew reluctant
from his rustic retreat, and that grandson of a
slave whom he found content with a small clerk-
ship in town.   To quote the expression of M.
Taine, Roman Poetry first passed under the yoke
of Greece, then under the yoke of Augustus.

The Augustan Age, strictly so called, as regards
poetry, may be said to run for us from Lost Augus-
Virgil to Ovid, who had just seen Virgil tan poets.
and no more.[1]   But a multitude of Augustan poets
have perished, and are revealed to us only by

[1] "Virgilium vidi tantum." — *Trist.* IV. 10, 51.

grammarians, who quote from their works to establish some usage. Cornelius Nepos gives us a sad example of how contemporaneous renown may fail to make any impression, even the slightest, on posterity. He points, in emphatic and carefully weighed terms, to one of whom he writes, "I think I can well assert that he is our most brilliant poet since Lucretius and Catullus." To whom is he referring? To one L. Julius Calidus, of whom we know nothing, except that there was once such a person. Tibullus [1] assures us that no one came nearer to the immortal Homer (*aeterno propior non alter Homero*) than one Valgius. Paterculus places beside Virgil a certain Rabirius, of whom we know only two things, that he composed a poem on the Alexandrine War, and that Ovid [2] gives him the praise of being "mighty-mouthed" (*magni oris*), the very epithet which Tennyson bestows on Milton in the fine experiment in Alcaic verse beginning : —

> "O mighty-mouth'd inventor of harmonies,
> O skill'd to sing of Time or Eternity !
> God-gifted organ-voice of England,
> Milton, a name to resound for ages !"

We are told, too, of others who at least chose fine themes, and themes neglected by their betters. Some one named Cornelius Severus, in a poem on the Sicilian War, rendered due homage to the greatness of Cicero, who is not mentioned by Virgil, Horace, or Ovid, or even alluded to, unless

[1] IV. 1, 180.   [2] *Pont.* IV. 16, 5.

we are to see an allusion, which would not be very flattering, in a passage in the sixth book of the "Aenëid."[1]   We also read that a Pedo Albinovanus related before Tacitus the voyages of Germanicus in the Northern Seas; and that a certain Cotta wrote a "Pharsalia" under Augustus, in which we may infer that he embraced the cause espoused by the gods, not that which found favor with Cato, and glorified the winning side.

But of all these once eminent poets and poems we know next to nothing; and still less about the tragedies of Pollio and Varius, the comedies of Fundanius, the elegies of Gallus, the epics of Varius and Rabirius.   What little information we do possess we owe to chance allusions in Virgil, Horace, Seneca, Quintilian, Velleius, and the Grammarians.

Thus Time scatters about his poppies of oblivion, and poets who in their own time had the reputation of a Milton or a Tennyson have now become a mere name, — so many letters in a certain order.

These considerations invite a reference to an ingenious speculation of the brilliant French critic, M. Patin.   We are far from sure, he points out, that we possess in our so-called Augustan poets a type of the poetry which really was most characteristic of that age.   Nay, more, there are reasons to believe that time has spared to us what was rather

M. Patin's view of the extant Augustan poetry.

[1] Line 849, *orabunt causas melius.*

a recoil from the prevailing genius of the time. These reasons may be classified under two heads. First, *our* Augustan poetry is remarkable for its carefulness. Now, Horace is never tired of urging the necessity of careful writing. We have often heard that "easy writing is hard reading," and that "Time will have nothing to do with anything produced without his aid." These may be called the favorite texts of Horace when he preaches on Art, and undoubtedly his protests are directed not against his predecessors but against his contemporaries. It was because they were written without any real carefulness and *limae labor* that so many of the poems of his time were ephemeral, and resembled the garlands in the elegy of Propertius [1] which withered on the brows of the revelers, and shed their bloom into the wine-cup as it went round. Now Horace often speaks of his own assiduous care, and rests on it his hope of immortal fame. Propertius foretells Virgil's deathless renown as the guerdon of the same quality. We know that Virgil thought that he had not bestowed nearly sufficient care on his epic, and wished to destroy it; and Ovid tells us [2] that with his own hand he burned the "Metamorphoses." Afterwards, on learning that the work still survived in other copies, he begs his readers to remember that it had not received from him the last touch (*summam manum*), and announces that he craves not praise but pardon (*et veniam pro laude peto*).

[1] II. 14, 52.   [2] *Trist.* I. 7, 15.

Thus it would appear that the poets whom we especially denominate Augustan in one important quality represent not the spirit of their age but rather a recoil from it. And, further, we learn from various hints in *our* Augustans that there existed under Augustus and his immediate successors a court poetry which was official and conventional, and was devoted to the laudation of the Emperor and his exploits in commonplace and mythological fashion. *Our* poets more or less ironically protest their inability to rise to the height of such an argument. Horace declares that such a theme is for a Varius. Propertius tells how Apollo touched his ear and admonished him to beware of strains so ambitious. Virgil opines that we have had enough of Pelops and his ivory shoulder, of the relentless Eurystheus, and of the altars of the infamous Busiris.[1] *Our* Augustan poets betake themselves to the Alexandrines, Theocritus and Callimachus. The elegy of Propertius [2] to the court poet Ponticus, author of a dead and buried " Thebais," is an excellent expression of the relation of *our* Augustans to the court poetry of the Augustan Age.

It seems, then, highly probable that what we call the Augustan poetry was really not the poetry characteristic of that epoch, but even a recoil from it, and a timid but decisive protest against it. The more credit to *our* Augustan poets, who taught their countrymen what was true *urbanitas*. The expression *urbanitas* always has a very definite

[1] *Georgics*, 3, 4.   [2] I. 7.

meaning in the mouth of a Roman, to whom the City was as supreme as to a modern Parisian. *Urbanitas* was the essential condition of literary acceptability. But its meaning changed in every generation. Lucilius is called *perurbanus* by Cicero, and *inurbanus* by Horace, yet each of these critics knew exactly what *urbanus* meant, and applied it correctly according to the view of his age.

It may be said that Virgil wrote to order. So Virgil and he did, but the theme suited the poet as Ovid. well as the time. The court of Augustus was as corrupt and *blasé* as that of Ptolemy, for which Theocritus sang the delights of rural life. And Virgil had a personal interest in the old stock from which "stout Etruria grew" (*fortis Etruria crevit*). In his epic Virgil succeeded in producing, in an age no longer epical, a brilliant reflection of the poetry which characterizes the epoch of childish belief and *insouciance*. Virgil has borrowed much from Homer, but he has taken from him nothing that he has not made new. He is the cloud which receives the light of the sun, and gives it back with the colors of the rainbow. Victor Hugo has said that Virgil is the moon of Homer, and truly there is in him a tender melancholy which takes the place of the dazzling brilliancy of the Greek. His pious reproduction of the age of childish belief has suggested to critics a comparison of Virgil with Tasso. Ovid was the Ariosto of the Augustan age, who took mythology no more seriously than Ariosto took chivalry.[1]

At Rome it seemed as if the stream of epic poetry would never run dry.   On it rolled, carry- Post-Augustan poetry. ing on its unrippled surface to the gulf of oblivion Memnonids, Perseids, Heracleids, Theseids, Thebaids, Achilleids, Amazonids, Phaeacids, without number.   The river of Time has happened to throw up to us a few spars from the wreckage, a few poets not, perhaps, much better than those whom it has engulfed, — Valerius Flaccus, Silius Italicus, Claudian, all of whom, together with Statius and even Lucan, Scaliger said that he would gladly give for a complete Ennius : "Utinam haberemus Ennium integrum et amisissemus Lucanum, Statium, Silium Italicum, et tous ces gascons là."   The last word, "gasconaders," which is often quoted as *garçons*, "lads," was used by Scaliger to mark the difference between the natural simplicity of Ennius and the inflated diction of the Silver Age.   Henceforth, though every year produces, in Pliny's phrase, its crop (*proventum*) of poets, Latin poetry is successful only in satire and epigram.

[1] "In non credendos corpora versa modos." — *Trist.* II. 64.

II.

EARLY LATIN POETRY.

ROMAN poetry may be said to begin in 514, with Characteristics of very early Roman poetry. Livius Andronicus, who translated the Odyssey into Saturnian verse, — a work about which we know nothing that is interesting except that Horace probably had the same feeling towards it as most schoolboys now have towards Horace, for it was the book which he had to study at school under the *ferula* of the proverbially severe Orbilius.

In the very early poets of Rome, what most strikes us is a strange unevenness of execution. They do not seem to have caught any apprehension of that subtle quality which should distinguish even the humblest poetry from the very most ambitious prose. In our own literature instances of this insensitiveness to the essential difference between poetry and prose are very rare, and they hardly ever coexist with occasional elevation. In early Latin poetry, lapses into mere prose are common, and yet we often meet real poetry side by side with them. Brilliant gifts of expression and true elevation of sentiment are found coexisting with abject humbleness of style, or even insensibility to the very existence of such a thing as style.

Macaulay quotes from Blackmore a so-called poem which is certainly marked by a "plentiful lack" of inspiration : —

> "Fancy six hundred gentlemen at least,
> And each one mounted on his capering beast;
> Into the Danube they were pushed by shoals."

But this attempt at description, bald as it is, almost soars in comparison with some specimens of early Latin poetry which have come down to us ; for instance, this passage from the epic of Naevius on the Punic War : —

> "The Romans cross to Malta, harry the place
> With fire and sword, settle the enemies' business; "[1]

or : —

> "Marcus Valerius consul leads a brigade
> On a campaign; "[2]

or this couplet from Ennius : —

> "Years seven hundred, more or less, have passed
> Since Rome with auguries august arose ; "[3]

a passage which, though it rises a little in the expression "auguries august," certainly creeps in the cautious accuracy of "more or less," and reminds us of a Dublin story, how a certain solicitor, in challenging to a duel another member of his own profession, invited him to meet him in the Phoenix

[1] "Transit Melitam Romanus insulam integram omnem
Urit populatur vastat, rem hostium concinnat."
[2] "Marcus Valerius consul partem exerciti
In expeditionem ducit."
[3] "Septingenti sunt paulo plus aut minus anni
Augusto augurio postquam inclita condita Roma est."

Park "in the Fifteen Acres, be the same more or less."

Again, Ennius, after a really fine verse invoking the Muses, goes on to explain that "Muses" is a Greek word corresponding to the Latin *Casmenae*. This is what strikes us in early Latin poetry, — real distinction and utter poverty of style side by side and hand in hand. Place beside the bald and uncouth verses quoted just now from Naevius those fine Saturnians of his : —

> " They fain would perish there upon the spot,
>   And not come back to meet their comrades' scorn ; " [1]

and beside the Ennian passage put that grand utterance which has been compared to the voice of an oracle, and which kindled the enthusiasm of the inspired Virgil : —

> " Broad-based upon her men and principles
>   Standeth the state of Rome ; " [2]

and we shall then see clearly this strange quality which distinguishes the early Latin poets from those of Greece, and other nations too, — that they were content to creep, though they knew what it was to fly, and that they seem hardly to be aware when they are on the ground and when in the clouds.

Quintilian [3] relates an anecdote which shows in what honor the epic of Ennius was held. One

---

[1] " Seseque ei perire mavolunt ibidem
        Quam cum stupro rebitere ad suos populares."

[2] " Moribus antiquis stat res Romana virisque."

[3] VI. 3. 86.

Sextus Annalis brought some charge against a client of Cicero's, and in the course of the trial proudly demanded, "Have you anything to say about Sextus Annalis?" That is, "Have you any charge to bring against *my* character?" But the words *num quid potes de sexto Annali* are susceptible of a quite different meaning. Cicero pretended to understand him to mean, "Can you repeat anything out of the sixth book of the Annals?" "To be sure I can," at once replied the consular wag,[1] and he thundered forth the sonorous line,

> " Quis potis ingentes oras evolvere belli?"

to the enthusiastic delight of his audience and the whole court. Opinion about Ennius underwent a steady change in successive ages. Lucretius calls him "immortal," *aeternus ;* in Propertius he begins to be "rough," *hirsutus ;* Ovid characterizes him as

> " In genius, mighty, but in art unskilled; "[2]

Martial complains that people are so tasteless that they will read Ennius though they have Virgil ; in the time of Silius Italicus, Ennius is so completely portion and parcel of the past that Silius introduces him as a character into his poem.

But Ennius, interesting though he is as the founder of the Roman epic and of satire, must no longer engage our attention, except in so far as he affected the early Latin drama, which is the chief

Marginal note: Anecdote illustrating the popularity of the Ennian epic

---

[1] *Scurra consularis* was a favorite sobriquet for Cicero.

[2] " Ingenio maximus arte rudis."

subject of this lecture.   As the real founder of
Roman poetry Quintilian finely says of him, in
a well-known passage,[1] that we should reverence
him as some sacred grove of venerable antiquity
whose grand old trees have more majesty than
beauty.

A generation ago, historians of Latin literature
Roman   usually discussed the question, Why had
tragedy.   Rome no tragedy?   Such critics could
find no Roman tragedy because they looked for it
only in the declamations of Seneca, which probably
were never put on the stage.   They did not go so
far back even as the "Medea" of Ovid and the
"Thyestes" of Varius, which Quintilian put on a
par with the Attic drama, or the tragedies of
Pollio, which Virgil and Horace thought worthy
of the Sophoclean buskin.   Still less did they
think of turning their eyes to the stage of Ennius, Pacuvius, and Attius.   It is indeed only comparatively recently that the efforts of Continental
scholarship have presented to us the fragments in
which these dramatists have come down to us in
such a shape as to render any literary appreciation
possible.   In a foregoing lecture we have adverted
to certain evidences that tragedy was held in estimation in the Rome of the Ciceronian epoch.
These evidences were broadly the testimony of
Cicero and of Horace.   Latin tragedy took the

[1] "Ennium sicut sacros vetustate lucos adoremus, in quibus
grandia et antiqua robora jam non tantam habent speciem
quantam religionem." — *Inst. Orat.* X. i. 88.

Greek models in inverse order, and adapted Euripides first. The Ennian version is literal, and, like Roman comedy, postulates in the audience a knowledge of Greek. Sometimes, where we have an opportunity of comparing the Latin translation with the Greek original, we find the Latin awkward and clumsy. A fine passage in the " Iphigenia in Aulis " runs : —

> " Oh, what a blessing hath the peasant's lot,
>   The happy privilege of uncheck'd tears." [1]

It is hard to give in English the Ennian version of it without exaggerating its homeliness, but it may perhaps be rendered : —

> " In this the peasant holdeth o'er the king,
>   The one may weep, the other may not well ; " [2]

The Greek and Latin passages agree in being both perfectly plain and simple ; but the Ennian is almost vulgar, and its simplicity is that of " Rejected Addresses :" —

> " Jack 's in a pet, and this it is:
>   He thinks mine came to more than his ; "

while the simplicity of the Greek is that which so deeply affects us in a great line in Webster's " Duchess of Malfi :" —

> " Cover her face: my eyes dazzle : she died young."

Perhaps we might venture to say that the vulgarity in the Latin lies in the word *honeste ;* to weep is

---

[1] ἡ δυσγένεια δ' ὡς ἔχει τι χρήσιμον
   καὶ γὰρ δακρῦσαι ῥαδίως αὐτοῖς ἔχει.

[2] " Plebes in hoc regi antistat loco : licet
   Lacrimare plebi, regi honeste non licet."

not consistent with a king's position at the head of society.

It is interesting to detect in these very ancient Passages in Ennius anticipating sentiments in modern literature. and somewhat rude efforts of a nation just emerging from absolute illiteracy something parallel to our own literature; something to remind us that there are touches of nature which make generations kin, however widely sundered in space and time.

> "What in the captain's but a choleric word,
>   That in the soldier is flat blasphemy,"

is a very true reflection of Shakespeare's; and a similar thought must have presented itself to the mind of Ennius when he wrote: —

> "To ope his lips is crime in a plain burgher." [1]

The whole spirit of the fine poem,

> "How happy is he born and taught
>   Who serveth not another's will!"

resides in the Ennian verse,

> "Most free is he whose heart is strong and clean." [2]

The fierce question of Shylock,

> "Hates any man the thing he would not kill?"

is anticipated in

> "Fear begets hate, hate the desire to kill;" [3]

and "A friend in need is a friend indeed" finds a literal counterpart in

> "Amicus certus in re incerta cernitur."

[1] "Palam muttire plebeio est piaculum."

[2] "Ea libertas est qui pectus purum et firmum gestitat."

[3] "Quem metuunt oderunt quem quisque odit periisse expetit."

It is strange to meet as early as in Ennius a maxim
which modern novelists would do well to lay to
heart : —

> " A little moralizing 's good, — a little :
> I like a taste, but not a bath of it." [1]

Pacuvius was the rival and nephew of Ennius.
Like Euripides, he was a painter as well
as a poet, and " Pictor," the surname of
Pacuvius.
the Fabii, shows that this art was then held in
high esteem.   He learned the bitterness of being
eclipsed by a younger rival, Attius, and retired to
Tarentum (the ideal retreat of Horace), there to
spend the closing years of a long and distinguished
life. Aulus Gellius tells us that there he was visited
by Attius, who read to him his " Atreus."   The
old poet found in it elevation and brilliancy, but
detected a certain harshness and unripeness.   " So
much the better," said Attius.   " The mind is like
a fruit, harsh while it is growing, but mellow when
it attains maturity.   If it be soft too soon, it is
spoiled before it ripens thoroughly.   I would fain
have something to grow out of."   This is a very
just remark.   The young man whose essay shows
nothing turgid, no ungraceful ornament or flashy
rhetoric, will never do much as a writer.   Dr. Johnson's advice to his young friend, to cut out all the
fine passages, illustrates his ticklish temper rather
than his sound judgment.   On the whole, one would

---

[1] " Philosophari mihi necesse, at paucis nam omnino haud
  placet,
  Degustandum ex ea, non in ea ingurgitandum censeo."

prefer to see a very young writer rather a dandy in his manner. The affectations are annoying, but he will probably grow out of them, if he happens not to be a prig. It is well that he should feel it necessary to dress his thoughts before he brings them into company. Ribbeck calls Pacuvius the freedman of Euripides, because, though mainly dependent on Euripides, he modifies the art of the Greek poet with far greater boldness than Ennius or Attius.

The less agreeable features in Pacuvius are his audacity in coining monstrous compounds, like *repandirostrum* and *incurvicervicum*, and his poverty of invention. The latter failing is revealed by the fact that we find in his fragments traces of three different and separate storms. No doubt he excelled in this kind of description, and so he recurs to it whenever he wants an effect.

His defects.

We have abundant proof of his popularity. Plautus parodies him more than once; Lucretius [1] borrows his expression, *hoc circum supraque*, "the spacious firmament on high;" and it was during the performance of a play of his that the actor who was playing the part of the sleeping Ilione fell into a slumber which was not feigned, while twelve hundred spectators joined in the appeal of Catienus on the stage, — the appeal to Ilione to awake. The way in which Horace [2] relates the anecdote shows that the plays of Pacuvius must have been very popular, and very famil-

His popularity.

[1] V. 319. [2] *Satires*, II. 3, 60.

iar to the audiences of the time. A fine passage
in the " Medus " (son of Medea by Aegeus[1]) proves
that Pacuvius is not merely one who can produce
ingenious philosophical reflections and vigorous
descriptions. The portrait of the unhappy de-
throned Aeëtes, a kind of ancient Lear,

> " With sunken eyes, and wasted frame, and furrows
> Worn by the tears adown his pallid cheeks,"[2]

is the work of a poet who can raise pity and terror,
and worthily describe human passion and suffering. His last triumph was at the funeral of the
murdered Caesar in the year of the city 710.
Among other songs sung in honor of the dead
was one from his " Armorum Judicium." There
was a sad appropriateness to the occasion in the
cry of Ajax,

> " To think I saved them but to murder me ! "[3]

Velleius gives Attius the palm among the tragic
poets. He took Aeschylus for his model,
not Sophocles or Euripides, as did his   Attius.
predecessors, but seems to have largely adopted
the practice called *contaminatio*, and to have fused
together different dramas, and even different au-

---

[1] If Pacuvius remembered *Eur. Med.* 722, he must have
given to φροῦδος in that verse the improbable and unexampled
sense ascribed to the word by Elmsley.

[2] " Refugere oculi, corpus macie extabuit,
   Lacrumae peredere humore exsangues genas."

But it is not absolutely certain that these verses, quoted by
Cicero (*Tusc.* III. 26), are to be referred to Pacuvius.

[3] " Men' servasse ut essent qui me perderent ! "

thors. Thus we find in his " Armorum Judicium," which he borrowed from Aeschylus, the well-known verse, taken by him from the " Ajax " of Sophocles, and afterwards adapted from him by Virgil : —

> " Be thine thy father's might, but not his fate." [1]

He also draws upon Homer, and even Apollonius Rhodius, whose very spirited description of the astonishment of the Colchian shepherds at the first sight of a ship seems to be reproduced in a passage cited by Cicero (" De Nat. Deor." II. 89).[2]

Like Ennius and Pacuvius, Attius was of humble birth, the son or grandson of a freedman. But the obscurity of his birth was to him no "invidious bar ;" to quote a verse of his own : —

> " A man may dignify his rank; no rank
> Can dignify a man." [3]

We have already heard his confident answer to the aged Pacuvius, and we are told by Valerius Maximus [4] that when Caesar entered the Collegium Poetarum, of which we have already spoken as being a kind of ancient analogue of the French Academy, Attius did not rise. He acknowledged the superior birth and rank of Caesar, but added,

[1] " Virtuti sis par, dispar fortunis patris."

[2]   " Tanta moles labitur
    Fremebunda ex alto ingenti sonitu et spiritu,"

and the following verses to

> " Vagant timore, pecuda in tumulis deserunt."

Ribbeck, p. 158, 391–410.

[3] " Homo locum ornat, non hominem locus."

[4] III. 7. 1.

"Here the question is, not who has most ancestors, but who has most works to point to."

Ennius excelled in sententious gravity, pathos,
and naturalness; Pacuvius, in elaboration

Latin tragic poets compared.

of style, which earned him the name of
doctus, and which sometimes, as in his
monstrous compounds, degenerated into pedantry
and affectation. The strength of Attius lay in his
spirit and elevation of style, for which Horace
called him *altus*, and Ovid *animosus*. His *Oderint
dum metuant*, "Let them hate me, so they fear me
too," is a thunder-word, and has ever been a favorite
quotation with tyrants from Tiberius to Bismarck.

The elevation of Attius is very marked. The
"Atreus," which he read to Pacuvius,

Elevation of Attius.

begins with a stately passage much admired by Cicero, Quintilian, and Seneca: —

> "I 'm Lord of Argos, heir of Pelops' crown,
>   As far as Helle's sea and Ion's main
>   Beat on the Isthmus," [1]

a passage which strikes us by the weight of names
great in myth-land and hero-land, and produces a
vague impression of majesty, like Milton's

> "Jousted in Aspromont or Montalban,
>   Damasco or Morocco or Trebizond,
>   Or whom Biserta sent from Afric's shore,
>   When Charlemagne with all his peerage fell
>   By Fontarabia."

---

[1] "En impero Argis sceptra mihi liquit Pelops
    Qua ponto ab Helles atque ab Ionio mari
    Urgetur Isthmos."

We are told by Plutarch that when the great tragic actor Aesopus uttered these words he entered so keenly into the spirit of the passage that he struck dead at his feet a slave who approached too near to the majesty of royal Argos.

Again, do not the following lines strongly recall the wise and sober but lofty dignity of Tennyson's " King Arthur " ?

> " Foul shame I hold it that the blood of queens
>   Should foully mix itself and make the breed
>   Of royal stock a question." [1]

And we meet now and then a sentiment quite in the vein of the " Idylls :" —

> " For him is pity, to whose low estate
>   A noble mind lends lustre." [2]

In some places the boldness of the Attian diction touches the borders of bombast, as when he says :—

> " From the reverberating cliffs around
>   Starts Echo musical with clangorous peal
>   Of startled laughter ; " [3]

or when Thyestes is described as

> " Tomb of his brood devour'd." [4]

The sound common sense which underlies this

[1] " Re in summa summum esse arbitro
    Periclum matres conquinari regias,
    Contaminari stirpem ac misceri genus."
[2] " Hujus demum miseret cujus nobilitas miserias
    Nobilitat."
[3] " Simul et circum magna sonantibus
    Excita saxis suavisona Echo
    Crepitu clangente cachinnat."
[4] " Natis sepulcrum ipse est parens."

excitability of spirit has already been illustrated by
his interview with Pacuvius. A further
instance of it is given us by Quintilian.[1] Common sense of Attius.
So great an admiration, he tells us, was
felt for the forensic powers shown in the Attian
tragedies that his friends asked him why he did
not become an advocate. "Because," he replied,
"in my plays the speakers say what I please, and
so the other characters can perfectly demolish
their arguments; but in the courts, on the contrary, I find that my adversaries invariably say
the very things I would rather they had left
unsaid."

But in Attius, as in all the Latin tragic poets,
we have to deplore a certain want of con-
trol. The easy, delicate grace of the Defects in Latin tragedy.
Greek style was unattainable by the
Latin dramatists, and they tried to supply its place
by a vigor and amplitude which are excessive and
out of place. You will remember the opening
verses of Euripides' "Phoenissae," which may be
rendered: —

> " O sun, that thro' the fires of the firmament
> Cleavest thy way, and in thy golden car
> Launchest the flames from thy swift coursers' feet,
> Ill-starr'd the ray thou sheddest once on Thebes."

How does this appear in Attius? —

> " O sun, that in thy glistening chariot borne,
> With coursers swiftly galloping, dost unfold
> A sheet of gleaming flame and burning heat,

[1] IV. 13, 43.

Why with such baleful auguries and omens
Adverse giv'st thou to Thebes thy radiant light?"[1]

The grace is lost; the attributes of the sun, which are merely glanced at (but in most stately phrase) in the Greek, are detailed and catalogued in the Latin. This is the main characteristic of early Latin tragedy. It is too much "in King Cambyses' vein." It substitutes strength for sweetness, heat for light. Our own literature supplies an analogous phenomenon and in a still more exaggerated degree. The cry "he abhorreth not evil" in the Psalms is grand in its simplicity; it becomes in the New Version by Nathaniel Brady and Nahum Tate (who, I regret to say, was a scholar of Trinity College, Dublin, and afterwards Poet Laureate in the reign of Charles II.),

"His obstinate, ungenerous spite
No execrable means declines; "

and "Why do the heathen rage, and the people imagine a vain thing?" swells (yet shrinks) into

"With restless and ungovern'd rage
Why do the heathen storm,
And in such vain attempts engage
As they can ne'er perform? "

Like Latin tragedy, the version of Tate and Brady tried to make repetition and exaggeration compensate for the absence of grace and taste.

[1] "Sol qui micantem candido curru atque equis
Flammam citatis fervido ardore explicas,
Quianam tam adverso augurio et inimico omine
Thebis radiatum lumen ostentas tuum?"

The first glimpse we obtain of a national comedy in Italy is in those charming sketches Latin comedy. which Horace and Virgil give us of rustic merry-makings at harvests and vintage festivals, in which not only rude dances found a place, but a kind of rough banter in Saturnian verse was exchanged between peasants wearing masks of bark rudely improvised for the occasion. But this "Fescennine license," even when developed into the "medley" which Livy describes at the beginning of the seventh book of his history, still wanted an essential quality of a play, namely, unity of plot, until it began to draw on the resources of the Greek drama. Thus, in the words of Livy a mere masque or revel gradually had become a work of art,[1] and a regular class of actors, *histriones*, arose. From improvised chants without dialogue or plot to a regular comedy such as those of Plautus and Terence is a very long step. Hampered as it was by police regulations, and laboring under the ban of public opinion, the histrionic impulse of Italy would never have taken this step by itself. It was forced to take its comedy straight from Athens, and to infuse into it a spirit distinctly antagonistic to the national mind of Rome. Perhaps it is in this quality in Roman comedy that we are to find a justification for the puzzling observation of Quintilian that "comedy is the weak point of Latin literature."[2] Probably, however, it is safer to attrib-

---

[1] "Ludus in artem paulatim verterat."
[2] "In Comoedia maxime claudicamus."

ute Quintilian's criticism to some revulsion of taste
against comedy strictly so called which seems to
have occurred under the Empire.[1]   It is hard, of
course, for us to institute a comparison between
Latin comedy and tragedy, because while we have
between twenty and thirty Latin comedies and not
one complete Greek exemplar with which to compare them, in tragedy, on the other hand, we have
an abundant supply of the Greek models, but not
one single perfect, or even nearly perfect, Latin
copy.

The most remarkable feature in Latin comedy
is the fact that the scene was invariably laid out of Rome, usually at Athens, and the *dramatis personae* were Greeks, not Romans ; so are the costumes and the coinage.   In all the plays of Plautus and Terence we do not find mention of a single Roman coin ; when Romans are mentioned they are called *barbari,* and Italy is

Characteris-
tic features
of Latin
comedy.

[1] We recall how strangely Horace depreciates both the
metrical skill and the humor of Plautus, and perhaps we
can infer a preference on the part of Horace for the mime,
which superseded the comic muse, when we remember that
the mime had for its butt the oddities of provincial life, and
that these moved the mirth of Horace and his friends on the
journey to Brundisium, when they laughed at the decoration
of the ex-clerk who was praetor of Fundi, and who was so
proud of his purple robe, his broad stripes, and his pan of
coals.   Indeed, other writers under the Empire show their
appreciation of this rather low form of humor.   Persius (I.
129) and Juvenal (X. 101) laugh at the provincial magistrates,
who are so proud of the office which gives them the right to
break half pints if they are not of the statutable capacity.

barbaria. Whether this was a police regulation
which insisted that the scene should be laid abroad,
lest Romans or Roman institutions should seem to
be satirized, or whether it resulted from the incapacity of the Roman playwrights to rise from mere
translation to adaptation, it is certain, at all events,
that the Roman poets themselves accepted the
situation and boasted of it. In the prologue to the
" Menaechmi " Plautus declares : —

> "We lay the scene of all the play at Athens,
> To make the drama seem more Greek to you." [1]

But still they aimed at presenting Roman society
as it unfolded itself to their eyes. Plautus makes
the Grex at the end of the "Bacchides" protest
that he would not have dreamed of making a son
rival to his father in a disgraceful intrigue, were it
not that such a case had come under his own personal observation ; and Cicero [2] declares, " I hold
the aim of the drama to be to hold up a mirror
to our manners, and to give us the express image
of our daily life." This attempt at the same time
to give the piece a foreign character, and yet to
bring the scenes home to the Roman audience, has
introduced certain confusions which give *Consequent*
a very odd semblance to Latin comedy. *confusions.*
Roman gods and ritual, Roman legal and military terms, find their way into this Greek world ;
aediles and *tresviri* jostle *agoranomi* and *demarchi ;*

---

[1] " Omnis res gestas esse Athenis autumant
    Quo illud vobis Graecum videatur magis."
[2] *Rosc. Am.* XVI.

a speaker in a play in which the scene is laid in
Aetolia, Ephesus, or Epidamnus will remark that
he has just come from the Velabrum or the Capito-
lium. We remember how, in " Hamlet," the grave-
digger sends his fellow workman from Denmark to
an English village to fetch him a stoup of liquor;
and how Shakespeare introduces English names and
characters into Athens in the "Midsummer Night's
Dream." But these lapses of memory, exceptional
in Shakespeare, are the rule in Latin comedy, which
addressed an audience by no means familiar with
the foreign world which was its scene, though we
must presume them to have had considerable familiarity with the Greek tongue; else surely Plautus
would not have made puns unintelligible without
a knowledge of Greek, or introduced three new
words [1] coined from the Greek into one verse in the

Horace's
criticism
on Plautus.
"Miles Gloriosus." Horace not only denies to Plautus humor and metrical skill,
but he charges him with a desire to make
money as quickly as possible, an indifference to
the requirements of true art, and a consequent
tendency to hurry with undue haste to the *dénouement* of his plays, a fault which he says he has in
common with the Sicilian Epicharmus. It is true
that the play is often wound up very suddenly.
Indeed, in the "Casina" the epilogue naïvely informs us that the *dénouement* will take place in-
side.[2] But, on the other hand, the "Curculio"

[1] II. 2. 58: *Euscheme, dulice, comoedice.*
[2] The mention of the *Casina* suggests to me to bespeak

is excellently constructed, and so are the "Epidicus," which he tells us he loved better than his own life, and the "Pseudolus" and "Truculentus," which Cicero informs us were the work and the favorites of his old age. It is curious that these are plays which turn on an attempt to Motifs of cheat or overreach (*frustratio*), not on his plays. the more familiar theme of love or gallantry (*amatio*). These two *motifs*, or a fusion of both, as when a man is deprived of his mistress by some clever stratagem, are by far the commonest in Plautus. Two plays, the "Trinummus" and the "Captivi," strike out a new line, and depict, one, the noble love of friend for friend, the other the fidelity of slave to master. The "Rudens" turns on a shipwreck, and the right of asylum. The "Captivi" and "Bacchides" are perhaps the best constructed of the plays, and Plautus regrets that he cannot find more models for a play like the former, where the moral tendency is so excellent.

attention to a passage in that play where the Ambrosian palimpsest has restored to us a text which probably conjecture would never have hit on, but which seems absolutely certain. The pretended bride, who was really a stout young slave in a woman's attire, is described as having put down her foot on the toe of one of her escort, *institit plantam;* but how does the verse go on?

"Institit plantam quasi jocabor."

The words *quasi jocabor* could not be explained. The Ambrosian codex gives us *quasi Luca bos,* "like an elephant," the very word which we want, and the very word which Lucretius uses for "an elephant."

The "Miles" is spoiled by the introduction of the
Defects
in con-
struction. speech of Palaestrio, explaining the plot
in the manner of a prologue, after the
action has begun.   So in the "Cistellaria" the play opens with an admirable dialogue
between the girls Silenium and Gymnasium and
an old procuress, and it is only in the third scene
that the goddess Auxilium speaks the prologue.
Another great blot on the construction of the
"Miles" is the very long though very clever diatribe of Periplecomenus on the blessings of celibacy
and the hollowness of society, which for one hundred and seventy verses completely stops the action
of the piece.   We must, however, remember that
these defects in construction would not be at all so
noticeable in plays which really rather resemble
our *opéra bouffe* than a modern comedy, — plays
in which by far the most of the scenes were sung
to the accompaniment of an instrument of music,
and in which there was no division into acts and
scenes save where the exigencies of the plot required that an actor should leave the stage at the
end of one scene, and appear again at the beginning of the next, on which occasions a flute-player
entertained the audience while the stage was
empty.

In some respects the "Amphitruo" is the most
Amphitruo. original of the plays of Plautus.   Whether
it is to be classed as a *fabula Rhintonica*
or as a ἱλαροτραγῳδία (both have been suggested), it
seems to demand some classification which will dis-

tinguish it from the other plays. "A Roman tone pervades it," as Professor Palmer remarks. " In reading the account given by Sosia of the campaign against the Teleboae, we feel as if Plautus had versified a page of some old Latin Annalist. The ultimatum of Amphitruo, with its demand for resti. tution and threat in case of refusal, the pitched battle and crushing defeat of the enemy, the slay- ing of the commander-in-chief by Amphitruo's own hand, — all these are in real Livian style." Alcmena is a high type of a Roman wife, and a *risqué* subject is treated with a delicacy which contrasts most favorably with the work of the modern imitators, Molière and Dryden.

It would be, of course, quite impossible, in the space at our disposal, to analyze, or even charac- terize, all the Latin comedies which have come down to us. We may, however, inquirè in a gen- eral manner how, on the whole, they deal with the different factors of society which were presented to them, how they deal, that is, with political, civil, and domestic life.

Political life is, owing to the circumstances which surrounded the composition and production of ancient comedy, but lightly touched. We find references to the un- fairness of the aediles in awarding the literary prizes, and to the summary proceedings of the *tresviri*, or police of Rome. These, however, are chiefly in prologues, and we cannot be sure that all the prologues of Plautus are not quite post-

Political life in Latin comedy.

Plautine ; some of them demonstrably are. They are subservient to the explanation of the plot, like those of Euripides, but generally are disfigured by cumbrous bantering of the audience. The pro- logues of Terence, on the other hand, which are undoubtedly genuine, under- take the defense of the poet's own lit- erary views, and rebut the strictures of adverse critics, thus resembling rather the *parabasis* of Greek comedy than the prologues of Euripides. But much more indicative of the political views of Plautus than his gibes at *aediles* and *triumviri* is the bitter and sustained attack on the vices of the governing classes pervading his plays, in which we so often hear that the aged reprobate, who is as ridiculous as he is vicious, is a pillar of the state, a column of the senate, a protector of the poor. It is strange that such assaults on a class should have been permitted in a city where personal allu- sion of any kind was punishable by law.

Prologues of Plautus and Terence.

To pass, then, to the civil and domestic spheres, we have very little description of profes- sional or mercantile life as such. The *mercator* might just as well be anything else as a merchant ; we hear only of his amatory intrigues. We have, however, in the "Rudens" a description of the hardships of a fisherman's life which re- minds us of an idyll of Theocritus, and in the "Menaechmi" we have a physician. Here and elsewhere we find that physicians, then as now, were prone to use terms derived from the Greek.

Civil and domestic life.

In the "Curculio" [1] even the slave Palinurus has enough knowledge of the medical art to tell Cappadox, who complains of an acute pain in his liver, that he is suffering from a *morbus hepatarius*. The letters of Cicero show us that in his time physicians wrote their prescriptions in Greek, as they now do in Latin, and that it was customary to speak of ailments and their cures by their Greek names. There is in the "Poenulus" a strange profession, that of the professional perjurer. The most common callings are those of the banker and money-lender, the parasite and the pimp, around whom cluster the professional beauties, who are by no means as good as they are beautiful. Ladies, on the other hand, *ingenuae*, whether matron or maid, are always virtuous, though often very disagreeable, as Artemona in the "Asinaria." The picture of the girls who are in the train of the pander is very strange. Philematium in the "Mostellaria," though belonging to this class, is almost charming, with her girlish love for dress and her sincere affection for Philolaches. Philocomasium in the "Miles" has enough grace to prefer Pleusicles to the wealthy captain, and to be faithful under strong temptation. Melaenis in the "Cistellaria," Philenium in the "Asinaria," and Lemniselene in the "Persa" are all capable of a disinterested love. But other Plautine girls are redeemed only by their cleverness, and the candor (if that is a redeeming point) with which they avow their

[1] II. I. 24.

depravity.   Plautus himself, both in the " Miles " [1]

Plautine drama not adverse to morality. and in the "Cistellaria," [2] dwells on the heartlessness of such women, and he constantly moralizes on the wretched end to which a life of wicked indulgence leads, with a moral fervor which probably suggested to Lucretius his terribly powerful treatment of the same theme in the fourth book (verses 1120 ff.). Even in the case of abandoned girls whom we might almost regard as attractive, Plautus never lets us forget what they are.   The atmosphere is not adverse to morality, as is that of the French novel.   Such women are not intended to attract one, like the Dame aux Camellias or Ninon de l'Enclos.   There are slaves of all kinds, but, with the exception of Tyndarus in the "Captivi" and Stasimus in the "Trinummus," they are the vilest of the vile, and seek a revenge in the abasement of their masters for the ill-treatment and oppression which is their lot.

Plautus is as ready as Cicero to apply to Rome Essentially urban. the Frenchman's aphorism about Paris: "On ne vit qu'à Paris, et l'on végète ailleurs."   He speaks in a tone of contempt of the Italian towns, and especially makes the Praenestines his butt for their habit of docking the first syllable of a word, and thus turning *ciconia*, "a stork," into *conia*.   "Do you think you are in the country?" asks one slave of another, in the "Mostellaria," when the latter is making an unseemly uproar in the street.

[1] III. 1. 190.   [2] I. 1. 66.

The late Professor Sellar remarks that Plautus could not describe a gentleman. "Nothing can be meaner than the conduct of the second Menaechmus, who is intended to interest us, in his relations with Erotion; and this failure is equally conspicuous in another of his favorite characters, Periplecomenus " in the "Miles," whose indecorous geniality is to us somewhat repulsive. In this respect, as in the gusto with which he dwells on the pleasures of good living, Plautus reminds us of Dickens more than of any other humorist. We cannot but think of the very thick strokes and glaring colors of Dickens's character-painting, of his Quilps and Pecksniffs, when we find Euclio the miser, in the "Aulularia," carefully preserving the parings of his nails, and regretting his tears on account of the waste of water which they entail.

Compared with Dickens.

All these types which we have been examining are considerably different in Terence. The braggart captain is only vain, not a fool, and is more like the Falstaff of "Henry IV." than the Falstaff of the "Merry Wives of Windsor." The parasite is simply a flatterer. The slave is not an oppressed creature at war with society, but a well-treated domestic who puts his shrewdness at his master's service, and often shows devotion and honesty. There is no longer a sharp distinction between *meretrix* and *ingenua*, except in the unfortunate condition of the former. She is as refined in her manners as her

Compared with Terence.

more reputable sister, and generally an unexpected disclosure at the end reveals that she is really a lady, and had been changed at birth. The husbands of Terence are far better husbands, and the wives — for instance, Sostrata in the "Hecyra" — are more amiable than those of Plautus. His young men are rather lovers than libertines, and his old men show them a better example. Terence, it may be said, painted men as they ought to be, Plautus as they are.

It is strange that Sedigitus places Terence only sixth in his list of comic poets, which he heads with Caecilius, Plautus, and Naevius. Cicero [1] refers to Terence as the true model of Latinity, and allows that in this matter the authority of Caecilius is small. The ancients made Caecilius first in the choice of plot, Plautus in dialogue, Terence in delineation of character. But so high was the estimate of the elegance of the Terentian style that a theory resembling that of certain ingenious American writers, concerning Shakespeare and Bacon, was actually broached in the ancient world about Terence, who was said to have been chosen by Laelius, or even Scipio himself, as the vehicle through which their clever comments on society should be presented to the world. The refinement of Terence is certainly very marked. Naevius, for instance, makes a son frankly and brutally pray for the death of his parents : —

> " I wish the gods would take my parents both." [2]

Terence. (margin note)

His refinement. (margin note)

[1] *Att.* VII. 3.

[2] " Deos quaeso ut adimant et patrem et matrem meos."

How different is the tone of Ctesipho in the
" Adelphi ! " [1] —

> "Would that my sire would so fatigue himself —
> So as to do his health, of course, no harm —
> As for the next three days to keep his bed."

Even the modern world has something to learn
from the cultured African.   Molière, in his " Ecole
des Maris," restores the Naevian brutality of the
passage to which I have referred ; and Jonas Chuz-
zlewit complains that his father, in living so long,
is flying in the face of the Scriptures.   The very
refinement of Terence has, in the minds of some
writers, been prejudicial to his fame.   An ingenious critic, M. Meyer, thinks that Ter-   Meyer's
ence was spoiled by the patronage of   view of
Scipio and Laelius.   His life was too   Terence.
easy and luxurious.   The pampered freedman lost
his powers of observation, and described a society
such as existed only in his own enervated imagination.   The *atrium* is transported into Arcadia, and
one might suppose it was the reign of Numa or
Evander.   It is, however, very doubtful whether
an observer of society does not see better from
above than from below, and it is a barren kind of
criticism which, instead of asking what were the
powers of the dramatist as revealed in his work,
pursues rather the inquiry what his circumstances
ought to have made them.

We are told that the aediles had the right of
refusing or accepting plays.   There seems to have

[1] IV. 1. 3.

always been some one to whom they referred the
Literary referees under the Republic. matter, and who did the part of the Lord
Chamberlain in England. Tarpa was the
referee in Cicero's time, as we learn from
a letter of Cicero to Marius.[1] Luscius of Lanuvium
seems to have discharged a somewhat similar function in the time of Terence, and to have regarded
his young rival with jealousy, and accused him of
plagiarism. The answer of the Latin dramatist is
characteristic. He declares he has not used the
works of his Latin predecessors. He does not
even know them. He claims for himself the merit
of complete originality, because he has taken his
plays solely (and wholly) from the Greek.

A well-known story records what a generous
Caecilius. critic of his "Andria" Terence found in
Caecilius, who certainly had not much
in common with Terence, and rather exaggerated
than modified the coarseness of Plautus. Caecilius
introduces a son declaring that it gives piquancy
to an intrigue if one's father is a bear and a miser;
it is no fun if he is generous and kind; and he
makes a husband say of his wife, —

"She ne'er was really charming till she died."[2]

Other coarse and disgusting fragments express
brutally that indifference to his wife which the
Plautine husband thought it humorous to dwell
on. But we can forgive Caecilius much when we

[1] *Fam.* VII. 1.
[2] "Placere occepit graviter postquam est mortua."

meet our old familiar gallery claptrap sentiment that —

"Many a good heart beats under a threadbare coat." [1]

Afranius, the chief of the writers of the so-called *togatae*, is the poet most frequently quoted, next after Plautus and Terence. Afranius. Unlike Terence, he confesses that he draws on the Latin as well as the Greek drama, and of Terence he declares that he has no second,[2] and that every word of his is genuine wit.[3] Cicero ascribes to Afranius that thorough knowledge of human life [4] which was so completely the appanage of Menander that a well-known verse declared it was hard to say whether Menander copied life, or life Menander. This is, perhaps, the meaning of the Horatian remark that the *toga* of Afranius fitted Menander. It is in his refined and tender view of the relation of father and son that Afranius most resembles Terence. A father, in the "Adelphi," [5] welcomes the faintest sign of grace in his son, and exclaims, —

"He blushes! All will be well."

So, in Afranius, when a son cries, "Miserable wretch that I am!" the father comforts himself with the reflection that if his son expresses regret his shortcomings are more than half atoned for.

---

[1] "Saepe est etiam sub palliolo sordido sapientia."
[2] "Non similem dices quempiam."
[3] "Quidquid loquitur sal merum est."
[4] "Illud a vita ductum ab Afranio." — *Tusc.* IV. 45.
[5] IV. 5. 10.

And he, like Terence, condemns those fathers who seek "to inspire their sons with fear rather than respect." [1]

After Afranius, Latin comedy merged into the *tabernaria*, then the mime, then the revived Atellane play, which ultimately itself gave way to the mime again under the Empire. The remark of the judicious Quintilian, already quoted, makes it hard for us to feel sure that fortune, which has given us only fragments of tragedy, has done the best for us in sparing to us so many comedies; but of one source of congratulation, at least, we may feel pretty certain, — the portion of comedy which has survived is surely the fittest.

[1] "Ubi malunt metui quam vereri se ab suis."

III.

LUCRETIUS AND EPICUREANISM.

EPICUREANISM is now no longer a hypothesis or a doctrine. It is a name given to a man's character, not to his beliefs. It is an elegant malady of the soul; a laziness and self-indulgence glorified by culture and refinement; a term devised to mitigate the word "selfish" when applied to the well-to-do; a euphemism for incapacity when it is not too ungraceful, just as "kleptomania" is a euphemism for dishonesty when dishonesty has plainly no motive. Epicureanism now awakens no enthusiasm, and seeks to make no proselytes.

Epicureanism as a doctrine dead.

But, though Epicureanism is dead, it by no means follows that the poem of Lucretius is only a baseless fabric of errors, possessing an interest merely as an example of a certain brilliant and highly interesting vagary of a very finely touched spirit. The part of the book that is dead is the system. The inner impulse which "rends the veil of the old husk," and comes forth as a living flash of light, is the enthusiasm of the poet, with his genuine pride in the "train of flowery clauses" in which he sets forth —

Sources of vitality in the poem of Lucretius.

> " The sober majesties
> Of settled, sweet, Epicurean life,"

and his abiding awe for the unchangeable laws of Nature. But, above all things else, that which keeps the work instinct with life is the fine frenzy which clothes every argument, however dry or abstruse, with all the hues of fancy, and which makes the poem like nothing else in all literature, if we except our own Tennyson's " Two Voices," which, though on a very minute scale compared with the six books "On the Constitution of Nature," yet shows as great and rare an aptitude for —

> "shutting reasons up in rhyme,
> Or Heliconian honey in living words,
> To make a truth less harsh."

Lucretius has exercised a powerful attraction, on the one hand, on students of language, who find in his poem Latin at a most interesting epoch, before it has lost the *insouciance* of childhood, but after it has outgrown the helplessness of infancy. On the other hand, free-thinkers have congratulated themselves that they have found in Lucretius an ally, and have eagerly welcomed him into their camp. The philologists, lost in admiration of the vase, have hardly tasted the strong wine which it holds. The philosophers have clutched the fruit because they thought it was forbidden, and have not paused to admire the stately branches or the lustrous leaves of the tree on which it grows. But, beside these, there is room for a greater interest, both literary and psychological, in this High Priest of Atheism, this Apostle of Irreligion, who thunders

Varied attractions of the poem.

against inspiration like one inspired, and who shows all the rapt devotion of a Stephen in his denial of immortality, — all the fervor of a Bossuet while he scatters to the winds the last perished leaves of human hope. We must, therefore, on the very threshold of our inquiry into the mind of Lucretius, investigate his relation towards God and Religion. I have called Lucretius an atheist. I am aware that technically this is a misnomer, for Lucretius provided in his system for the existence of the gods. But why did he recognize gods? What were his gods? And what was the religion which he so bitterly assailed?

Epicureanism, which explained the origin of our ideas by the theory that material images of things (*simulacra*), disengaged from external objects, struck our senses and thus became cognizable by us, was forced to rise from the idea of God which we find within us to the existence of gods themselves. Thus Lucretius was compelled, by his physical theories adopted from Democritus and Leucippus, to recognize gods. But nothing is more formidable to the mind than the conception of a Power which is outside and beyond ourselves, which is malevolent to us, and which we cannot resist. Such a power were the ancient gods to Lucretius; and the eagerness with which he goes out of his way to rail against their conventional attributes, and to protest against their supposed Providence, suggests to us, not so much a philosophic inquirer into the truth of a

Relation of Lucretius towards God and Religion.

dogma, or even a fervid preacher demolishing a heresy, as some mediaeval enthusiast who believes himself to be possessed by a devil, or to be in perpetual struggle with a devil for the life of his soul, whose reason is convinced that he is saved, but whose whole spirit shudders at the thought of damnation, — a St. Simeon Stylites who strives and wrestles till he dies, or one of those whose curse it is to suffer

> " Half the Devil's lot,
> Trembling, but believing not."

For Lucretius is ever and anon haunted by "the fear that we may haply find the power of the gods to be unlimited, able to wheel the bright stars in their varied motion." [1]

The Roman religion, which was originally, as Roman religion. in other Aryan nations, worship of the powers of Nature, never assumed the rich mantle of poetry and legend with which the Greek mythology early adorned itself. It took the stamp of the national character, and lay chiefly in rigorous observances showing much fear, little respect, and no love for the gods. The Roman legends are prosaic and monotonous, nearly always taking the form of a hero or benefactor who shows his super-

---

[1] " Nequae forte deum nobis immensa potestas
Sit, vario motu quae candida sidera verset."
V. 1209.

In the absence of any really worthy metrical version of the poem, I have used nearly always the vigorous and literal prose translation of Munro.

human quality by a fire which plays innocuously
about his head, as in the case of Ascanius in the
Aenëid, and who finally vanishes, as Romulus disappeared (*non comparuit*) in the narrative of Livy.
The sole discovery of Rome in religion is represented by the *Indigitamenta*, or lists of gods attending every moment of man's life from the cradle
to the grave. Vaticanus presides over the infant's
first cry, and Fabulanus over his earliest attempt
at articulate speech. Educa teaches him to eat,
Potina to drink, and Cuba to sleep. His goings
out and his comings in are the special care of
Abeona and Adeona. The gods of the Roman
Pantheon are inconveniently numerous. Petronius
makes the witty, wicked Quartilla remark that
"the place is so densely populated with gods that
there is hardly room for the men."[1] Some of the
deities are mere abstractions, like Salus Populi,
Securitas Saeculi. *Religio* comes from the same
root as *diligentia*, and means "regularity." There
is no Greek for it. Certainly not δεισιδαιμονία nor
εὐσέβεια. The people would stone the gods if they
offended them, like those savages who thrash their
idols when they come home after an unsuccessful
day's hunting. At the death of the beloved Germanicus, the people rose in fury and threw volleys
of stones at the temples of the gods. Ovid tells
us how Numa bargained so shrewdly with Jove

---

[1] "Utique nostra regio tam praesentibus plena est numini-
bus ut facilius possis deum quam hominem invenire." — *Satyricon*, ch. xvii.

that the god at last smiled and gave him his way.
Cicero relegates religion to the province of his
wife, and Caesar the Pontifex Maximus denies before the Senate the immortality of the soul.   The
"Senatus Consultum de Bacchanalibus" gives us
a glimpse of the shocking immorality which sometimes polluted the Roman ritual, and we even
read [1] of human sacrifices after Cannae.   Hence,
perhaps, the terrible earnestness with which Lucretius reflects on the sacrifice of Iphigenia, "a
fair maiden foully murdered by a parent, — a
maiden more meet for the marriage-bed than the
bier, — that the fleet might have good hap.   Such
crimes could religion prompt." [2]

Against this shallow, barren, and sometimes
horrible faith, what wonder that Lucretius should seize the first weapon that
came to hand, — *furor arma ministrat,*
— against a theory of divine government which
according to him had its rise, not in reason, logic,
or instinct, but in disgraceful, groveling fear.   This
was the "foul Religion" under which human life
lay crushed, "a horrid monster lowering over mankind from the sky," against which "the Greek first
dared to raise his head," and which now lies tram-
pled under the feet of the Elect, — "a victory,"
cries Lucretius, "that lifts man to the sky."   What
wonder that he should feel indignant that beings
like the ancient gods should have assigned to

Attitude of Lucretius towards it.

[1] Livy, XXII. 57.

[2] "Tantum Religio potuit suadere malorum." — I. 101.

them such a stately home as the firmament, in which revolve —

> "The Moon, and the Light of the Day, and the Night with
> its solemn fires?"[1]

Bound therefore, as we have seen, by his physical theory, to find a place for the gods in his system, he gave them a lotus-land in the —

> "Lucid interspace of world and world."

He treated them, observes M. Constant Martha, as we treat the Nawabs and Nizams of India, whom we surround with all the means of luxurious self-indulgence, in the well-grounded confidence that they will accept that condition in lieu of real power. Lucretius is mistaken in praising Epicurus for his originality. Every one knows that Epicurus borrowed his physics from Democritus and his ethics from Aristippus. His originality lay only in subordinating in his system physics to ethics, and abolishing Providence in the interests of humanity. Lucretius, following him, established a court of gods who reign but do not govern, to whom, when he addresses them in prayer, he whispers, as Voltaire said that Spinosa did, —

> "Je soupçonne entre nous que vous n'existez pas."

[1] This sublime verse (V. 1190), —

> "Luna Dies et Nox et Noctis signa severá,"

one of the finest in Latin poetry, reminds us how in another philosopher, Kant, the Sage of Königsberg, "the starry heavens above" shared with "the moral law within" the power to excite never-failing sentiments of awe and veneration.

These *fainéant* gods are no gods, and it is but technically inaccurate to speak of Lucretius as an atheist. We shall see afterwards how some idea of Providence forces its way, in spite of his system, into his naturally religious mind. For the present we will leave this part of the subject, first quoting the splendid verses in which he gives to these gods lip-service in exchange for the ill-used powers which he has taken away from them : —

"The nature of the gods must ever in itself of necessity enjoy immortality, together with supreme repose, far removed and withdrawn from our concerns ; for exempt from every pain, exempt from all dangers, strong in its own resources, not wanting aught of us, it is neither gained by favors nor moved by anger." [1]   The spirit of this sublime renunciation of Providence in the affairs of the world, which I have given in the dignified prose of the great scholar Munro, is finely caught and blended

[1] " Omnis enim per se divom natura necessest
    Immortali aevo summa cum pace fruatur
    Semota ab nostris rebus sejunctaque longe ;
    Nam privata dolore omni, privata periclis,
    Ipsa suis pollens opibus, nil indiga nostri,
    Nec bene promeritis capitur neque tangitur ira."
        II. 646–651.

This grand passage was quoted some few years ago with great effect by Mr. Gladstone in the House of Commons. It will probably stand as the last specimen of that faculty for happy quotation from Latin poetry which once adorned the debates of that assembly, but which has of late become more and more rare in its manifestation, and now seems to have completely disappeared.

with a Homeric strain in Tennyson's "Lucretius :" —

> " The gods who haunt
> The lucid interspace of world and world,
> Where never creeps a cloud, or moves a wind,
> Nor ever falls the least white star of snow,
> Nor sound of human sorrow mounts to mar
> Their sacred, everlasting calm."

Ancient Epicureanism arose at a time when Poetry, Art, Eloquence, and all free institutions languished under the Macedonian Protectorate of Greece. It lent itself to the enervated mind of that nation by the easiness of its acquisition and the simplicity of its tenets. Epicureanism actually discouraged learning, both literary and scientific, and took no trouble even to defend its own doctrines. Its *voluptas* led merely to apathy. Its physical system excited no interest among its adherents, and was adopted only to facilitate the denial of an overruling Providence and of a future life. Towards the end of the Republic, Epicureanism prevailed mainly among the upper classes. That thoughtless and voluptuous aristocracy which then was stepping so gaily to its destruction grasped the system as a relief from the fear of death, but found that the philosophy which only promised annihilation instead had no power to give real comfort. Even Lucretius turns but a haggard eye on his heaven bare of real gods and peopled by indifferent voluptuaries. That is a despairing cry of his, that "there is nothing immortal but Death. "[1] When Lucretius took up this

[1] " Mortalem vitam mors immortalis ademit." — III. 869.

dead-alive system, his eager spirit made the dry bones live. He breathed upon the system of Epicurus, and created a soul under the ribs of death.

Enthusiasm, even when it takes the form of despair, is the key-note of the poem. Epicurus discouraged the passion of love as tending to introduce an element of disquietude into that calm existence which is his ideal. Lucretius throws himself upon the passion with the fury of a wild beast, and seems to rend the limbs of some material victim. Nearly as fierce is his hatred of Ambition, and still more intense his loathing for Superstition. The feeling of conviction with which the early Christians heaped contempt on all foregoing systems seems cold and lymphatic beside the ardor of Lucretius in proclaiming his faith, and contemning all other wisdom as filthy rags. "He was a god, a very god!" (*Deus ille fuit Deus*) he exclaims of Epicurus in the beginning of the fifth book. The fabled inventions of Ceres and Bacchus, the labors of Hercules, are as nothing. Man cannot live by bread alone, but by every word that proceedeth out of the mouth of Epicurus. *He* discovered what is more sustaining than bread and wine. And what monster slain by Hercules was so foul and ugly as Religion? The poet boasts that like a bee he sucks the honeyed words of Epicurus ; that it is his delight "to watch through calm nights"[1]

Illustrated by his attitude towards the passions.

His worship of Epicurus.

[1] I. 142.

over his master's scrolls, and in sleep to dream of them.[1] Even the poverty of his native tongue (*patrii sermonis egestas*) but seldom gives him pause. The rudest instrument is good enough for the miner who has just struck a vein of gold. Like a true enthusiast, he exults most in the dullest part of his work.

His delight and belief in his work.

When he treats of the atoms, their colors and movements, he is ecstatic over his discoveries "made by labor, oh, so sweet!"[2] He dismisses objections with disdainful curtness. "This is folly" (*desipere est*) is a common retort.[3] And he claims for the doctrines which he preaches a certitude greater than that of the oracles of Apollo.[4] The Apostle speaks of the "beauty of holiness," and the Christian hymn cries, "The veil that hides thy glory rend." But Lucretius goes beyond them. He even fears lest the dazzling radiance of Epicurean truth might blind those to whom it should be too suddenly revealed. He hesitates to rend the veil that hides its glory. He regards with trembling awe and half-averted face the transfiguration of Epicurus through the medium of words.[5]

When one reads the rapturous verses in which he describes his task of making a harsh truth less bitter, likening himself to one who smears with honey the rim of the cup of medicine which the child must drink, one

His "towering passion."

---

[1] IV. 965.

[2] II. 730; III. 419.

[3] III. 802; V. 165, 1043.

[4] V. 112.

[5] II. 1033.

cannot but be astonished at the energy of his conviction. The language of Epicurus is as gentle as
the life which it inculcates. Epicurus, as well as
his successors, breathes the calm of Omar Khayyám, the apathy of the East: " It is better to lie
than to sit, it is better to sit than to stand, it is
better to be idle than to stretch forth the hands to
work." But Lucretius is like a physician who, in
recommending his patient perfect rest, should rush
at him, shake him, fling him on a bed, and shriek
at him, " Don't stir ! " Lucretius puts himself into
a violent heat with his exhortation to us to keep
ourselves perfectly cool. Well did Statius [1] speak
of the " towering passion of Lucretius " (*furor ar-
duus Lucreti*). His book is indeed " a passionate
scroll written over with lamentation and woe."

The third book of the poem stalks through the
valley of the shadow of death. Its theme
is the blackness of death (*mortis nigror*),
from the fear of which he longs to emancipate man. Like the hapless author of " The City
of Dreadful Night " he tells his fellow-men that,
though the Garden of Life be wholly waste, the
sweet flowers withered, and the fruit-trees barren,
over its wall hang ever the rich dark clusters of
the Vine of Death, within easy reach of the hand,
which may pluck of them when it will. He prof-
fers them

> " One anodyne for torture and despair,
>   The certitude of Death, which no reprieve

The valley of the shadow of death.

[1] *Silvae*, II. 7.

> Can put off long; and which, divinely tender,
> But waits the outstretch'd hand to promptly render
> That draught whose slumber nothing can bereave."

The good tidings of great joy, that there is no life beyond the grave, he announces in a spirit of exultation. "The walls of the world part asunder. I see all the inmost *The gospel according to Lucretius.* springs of nature," [1] cries Lucretius, in the rapt ecstasy of Rossetti's Blessed Damozel, who leaned out over the gold bar of Heaven and saw

> " Time, like a pulse, beat fierce
> Thro' all the worlds."

The poet looks back in awe on what he has already proved, — a world composed by the fortuitous concourse of atoms, and utterly dissociated from the gods, who luxuriate in an idle beatitude. He revels in the thought of death and the grave, but he treats with all the scorn of a Hebrew prophet the *carpe diem* philosophy which Horace has taught us to regard as the natural expression of Epicureanism. Other Epicureans pass over the topic of death lightly, and bid us not to think of it, or to think of it as little as we may. Lucretius is enamored of it. There are who have, like the sad singer of the saddest and sweetest of odes, been

> " Half in love with easeful Death,
> Call'd him soft names in many a mused rhyme."

But only one modern poet is the rival of Lucretius as a passionate lover of " lovely, soothing, delicate

[1] " Moenia mundi
Discedunt, totum video per inane geri res." — III. 16.

Death." Walt Whitman alone rises to the rapture of Lucretius when he cries,

> "Praise, praise, praise,
> For the sure-enwinding arms of cool-enfolding Death!"

and again,

> "I joyously sing the dead
> Lost in the loving floating ocean,
> Laved in the flood of thy bliss, O Death."

But it is not always by singing the praises of Death that he seeks to emancipate his fellow-men from the fear of it. The following verses, in which the similarity of the theme suggested the use of the metre of Tennyson's "Two Voices," show Lucretius in a less exultant mood, not crying, "O death, where is thy sting? O grave, where is thy victory?" not "putting under his feet," as Virgil sang,[1]

Lucretius on death.

> "All forms of fear, inexorable doom,
> And all the din that rises from Hell's maw,"

but rather whispering, "Comfort ye, comfort ye, my people," owning its terrors, but gently consoling his fellow-sufferers, and proffering them quiet counsel:—

> "'No more shall look upon thy face
> Sweet spouse, no more with emulous race
> Sweet children court their sire's embrace.

> "'To their soft touch right soon no more
> Thy pulse shall thrill; e'en now is o'er
> Thy stewardship, Death is at the door.

[1] *Georg.* II. 491.

" ' One dark day wresteth every prize
  From hapless man in hapless wise,
  Yea, e'en the pleasure of his eyes.'

" Thus men bewail their piteous lot;
  Yet should they add, ' 'T is all forgot,
  These things the dead man recketh not.'

" Yea, could they knit for them this chain
  Of words and reasons, men might gain
  Some dull narcotic for their pain,

" Saying, 'The dead are dead indeed;
  The dead, from all heart-sickness freed,
  Sleep and shall sleep and take no heed.'

" Lo, if dumb Nature found a voice,
  Would she bemoan, and not make choice
  To bid poor mortals to rejoice,

" Saying, 'Why weep thy wane, O man?
  Wert joyous e'en when life began,
  When thy youth's sprightly freshets ran?

" ' Nay, all the joys thy life e'er knew
  As poured into a sieve fell through,
  And left thee but to rail and rue.'

" Go, fool, as doth a well-filled guest
  Sated of life: with tranquil breast
  Take thine inheritance of rest.

" Why seekest joys that soon must pale
  Their feeble fires, and swell the tale
  Of things of nought and no avail?

> " Die, sleep! For all things are the same ;
> Tho' spring now stir thy crescent frame,
> 'T will wither : all things are the same."

This minor chord of *ennui*, " all things are the same," and the sad, sad word, " in vain " (*nequiquam*), which so often recur in the midst of his fervid and glad evangel, ever and anon intrude as uninvited guests at the poet's feast of reason, and cast ashes on the train of flowery clauses in which he enshrined his honeyed precepts.

It was his fierce attack on the belief in a future life which drew down on Lucretius the implacable enmity of the Christian writers, and which whelmed him under a conspiracy of silence on the part of his Roman contemporaries and successors. Virgil and Horace make allusions to him which show that they deeply admired him, but they never mention his name. Ovid only says that his work will not be forgotten (to give the sense of the Ovidian passage in the words of Tennyson) till

> " this cosmic order everywhere,
> Shatter'd into one earthquake in one day,
> Cracks all to pieces."

Cicero, indeed, wrote of him [1] that his work was marked by brilliant flashes of genius, and yet (a rare combination) by excellent art, — a passage which shows Cicero's perfect literary judgment, but which his editors have for

[1] *Q. Fr.* II. 9 (11), 3.

the most part perverted by inserting a *non*, and making Cicero thus deny either artistic finish or brilliancy of genius to his illustrious contemporary. The other writers and thinkers of Rome have regarded the poem (to use the image of Constant Martha) as some *triste bidental,* — some spot blasted with lightning. As the ancient Romans fenced off the place which Jove had smitten with his thunderbolt, lest some unwary footstep should trespass on a region accursed of God, so they kept aloof and closed their ears to the sombre strain which breathed the stern note of defiance of death. The statement of Jerome that Lucretius was maddened by a love-philter Tales about his life. and perished by his own hand, and the other record that he died on the day when Virgil assumed the *toga* of manhood, are myths of the kind so frequent in the ancient world, and have no weight save in so far as they suggest the wrath of the gods which ought to have pursued the author of the poem on the "Constitution of Nature," and mark the fact that Lucretius was, as it were, the literary godfather of the poet who wrote the "Georgics."

We must call to mind certain points of view which greatly mitigate the audacity of the Lucretian assault on the doctrine of a future life. This belief was not firmly held Doctrine of a future life in the ancient world. even by the most orthodox thinkers of his time. Cicero acknowledges that the letter [1] which Sulpicius sent him on the occasion of his

[1] *Fam.* IV. 5.

daughter Tullia's death embraced every source of
consolation which the case admitted ; yet there is
no allusion in that letter to the comfort which would
have been afforded by the belief in the happiness
of Tullia in another state.   " If," writes Sulpicius
— a sad " if " — " if the dead have any consciousness, the girl will be grieved to think that you
persevere in obstinate grief."   In a letter written
a few months after to Torquatus,[1] Cicero speaks
of death, if it should befall him in that troublous
time, as being after all only annihilation (*sine ullo
sensu*).   Even Seneca, long after the time of Lucretius, calls the immortality of the soul a beautiful dream (*bellum somnium*), and describes its adherents as asserting rather than proving a most
acceptable doctrine.[2]   The traditional pictures of
the future abodes of the blest and the damned
were universally discredited.   Future life, even
when regarded as possible, was the object, not of
hope, but of fear.   At best it was a sphere of *ennui*
and inaction.   The open rebels against Zeus had
at least the dignity of suffering, but the rank and
file of the dead languished in a world which was
but a pale shadow of this, — a world without hope
or aim, a "land of darkness as darkness itself, and
of the shadow of death, without any order, and
where the light is as darkness."   Even the heroic
Achilles[3] sees nothing comfortable in a future
life : " Rather would I live upon the soil as the
hireling of another, with a landless man that had

[1] *Fam.* VI. 4.   [2] *Ep.* 102.   [3] *Odyssey* XI. 488.

no great livelihood, than bear sway among all the
dead that are gone." Such was the pale realm
whose walls Lucretius battered with such fierce
exultation, — walls to which no trembling hopes
looked up as to an abiding city, or a treasure house
where rust and moth corrupt not, and where thieves
cannot break through and steal.

A brilliant French critic, M. Patin, has used a
striking phrase about the poet of Epi-   The "anti-
cureanism. He says there is in Lucre-   Lucretius"
tius an anti-Lucretius which is forever   in Lucretius.
pulling him back from the extreme consequences
of his theory, and forcing him into conclusions
more in accordance with his ardent and enthusiastic temperament. It will be opportune here to
glance at some of the manifestations of the anti-
Lucretius in Lucretius. As Lucretius deprives the
gods of all influence over Nature, he is obliged to
account for the existence of Nature by the postulate of a fortuitous concourse of atoms. But here
we are surprised to meet with expressions quite
inconsistent with this cold materialism. What have
principles, conditions, laws (rationes, foedera, leges),
to do with the freaks of blind Chance? How can
Nature be called *creatrix* or *gubernans*, "creative"
or "regulative,"[1] if she is bound fast in the fetters
of Fate? We have even *Fortuna gubernans* in I.
108. What is this but a *Deus* (or *Dea*) *ex machina*
who brings about the *dénouement* of a drama which
else would have had a lame and impotent conclusion indeed?

[1] I. 680, v. 78.

In VI. 640 he ascribes to Nature those volcanic convulsions which he elsewhere expressly dissociates from divine influence. And what but divine influence is the hidden power (*vis abdita*) of which he says [1] that it "constantly tramples on human grandeur, and is seen to tread under its heel the insignia of human power, and make sport for itself of them"?

Nature, presented by Lucretius as a mother in II. 990, again appears as a cruel stepmother in V. 778, where she is described as casting the newly born infant, naked and weeping, on the inhospitable shore of life, more helpless than the brutes, and more able to feel and deplore its helplessness; then fostering the growth of tares and all noxious weeds, and trying to wrest from wretched man the scanty portion of the earth which she has granted him wherefrom to extract a meagre sustenance with the sweat of his brow. Everywhere Nature has the attributes of will and personality. Again, he subtilizes the soul, the soul of the soul, up to the very verge of spirituality. It is from his vivid and beautiful illustrations of the interdependence of body and soul that Virgil has taken two fine passages, — that in which Dido "sought the light of heaven and groaned when she found it," [2] and that in which the fingers of the dying man twitch with the longing to grasp the hilt of the sword again. [3]

Above all, in the *clinamen* of the atoms, or the

[1] V. 1230.   [2] IV. 688.   [3] X. 396.

causeless deviation of the atom-stream from the right line, we have an active, intelligent principle thrusting itself in spite of his materialism into his system. In the words of De Musset, —

"Despite ourselves to Heaven we raise our eyes."
("Malgré nous vers le ciel il faut lever les yeux.")

He is not a fatalist. He recognizes a nameless force (*vis nominis expers*) which he finely calls " an influence torn from the grasp of Necessity " (*fatis avolsa potestas*), and which is not unlike Matthew Arnold's postulate of a " tendency that makes for righteousness."

The very language of Lucretius is tinged with a deep religious fervor which reminds us of Milton. We recall the " hideous hum " of the oracles when we read of " the awful state " in which the image of the divine mother of the gods is carried through the lands, and how she "mutely enriches mortals with a blessing not expressed in words."[1] Indeed, if the philosophy of Lucretius can be described as a poisonous plant at all, it is at least one of those venomous flowers which supply healing influences, too. There is nothing in his system of morality which can shock us except some of his theories with regard to the passion of love, and in extenuation of them we must remember how coarsely the spirit of the time regarded womanhood. Moreover, we can hardly be wrong in seeing in the poet himself evidences of

Language of Lucretius religious.

[1] II. 610, 624.

some physical defect or mental craze animating him
with a furious hatred of the passion itself.   His
master Epicurus looked on it but as a disturbing
influence.   Lucretius assailed it as a bane and a
curse.   Not his the "tears that love can die;" his
rather to heap "shards, flints, and pebbles" on the
grave of love.   He has a delight like
Lucretius
compared
with Swift.
that of Dean Swift in showing the seamy
side of the passion, and indeed in this
respect strongly reminds us of the great Irishman
whose bones moulder in St. Patrick's Cathedral in
Dublin, whose heart, in the desperate words of his
epitaph, "cruel indignation now no longer rends." [1]
"What a vulture," writes Thackeray, "it was that
tore the heart of that giant!" [2]

[1] "Ubi saeva indignatio ulterius cor lacerare nequit."

[2] The following passages from Thackeray's admirable
Lectures on the English Humorists of the Eighteenth Century
will suggest to readers of Lucretius that the comparison with
Swift is not merely fanciful: "As is the case with madmen,
certain subjects provoke him, and awaken his fits of wrath.
Marriage is one of these; in a hundred passages in his writings he rages against it, — rages against children."

Again: "And it was not merely by the sarcastic method
that Swift exposed the unreasonableness of loving and having children. . . . In fact our great satirist was of opinion
that conjugal love was unadvisable, and illustrated the
theory by his own practice and example, — God help him! —
which made him about the most wretched being in God's
world.   'My health is somewhat mended,' he writes in
May, 1719, 'but at best I have an ill head and an aching
heart.'"

In another trait Swift resembled the Latin poet: "Swift

The true charge against Epicureanism is not that it debases morality, or

> "makes divine Philosophy
> Procuress to the lords of Hell,"

but that it tends to extinguish energy by enfeebling the springs of action. According to it, passion and action are alike folly; there is no virtue but egotism; the true wisdom is apathy. Originality of Lucretius. The extraordinary originality of Lucretius is shown in the strenuous spirit which he breathes into this flaccid and lymphatic creed. We seem to see a St. Anthony fiercely fighting the passions that fiercely tear him, — a St. Simeon Stylites who has not succeeded in quenching his ambition, but only in giving it another object, passionate in the vaunting of his victory over himself, and leaping with all the ardor of a young lover into the arms of his "passionless bride, divine Tranquillity."

It may seem strange that Lucretius should have chosen verse as the vehicle of his teaching, especially as Epicurus wrote in prose Vehicle of his teaching. and condemned poetry on principle. However, he had the precedent of Xenophanes and Empedocles, and among his own countrymen that of Ennius, who

was a reverent, was a pious spirit. . . . Through the storms and tempests of his furious mind the stars of religion and love break out in the blue, shining serenely, though hidden by the driving clouds and the maddened hurricane of his life."

translated Epicharmus. He tells us that his design
was "to make a harsh truth less bitter." Do we
not find in our own time the novel forced into
the service of some particular school of religious
thought; and do we not meet even certain purists
who condemn novel-reading as a practice, but make
an exception in favor of such works of fiction as
embellish and promote those particular church principles which they themselves affect?

In the poem of Lucretius, beside certain amusingly *naïf* and (one might almost say)
puerile speculations, we find real contributions to knowledge, which science now
accepts, and which were truly remarkable discoveries in the time of Lucretius. Among the most
crude is his theory of the causes of sleep, in the
fourth book (910 *sqq.*), to which he carefully be-
speaks the attention of his readers in some very
fine verses. According to him, "sleep mainly takes
place when the force of the soul has been scattered about through the frame, and in part has been
forced abroad and taken its departure, in part also
has been thrust back and has withdrawn into the
depths of the body; after that the limbs are re-
laxed and droop. For there is no doubt that this
sense exists in us by the agency of the soul; and
when sleep obstructs the action of this sense, then
we must assume that our soul has been disordered
and forced abroad: not indeed all, for then the
body would be steeped in the everlasting chill of
death. If no part of the soul remained behind

concealed in the limbs, as fire remains concealed
when buried under much ash, whence could sense
be suddenly rekindled through the limbs, as flame
can spring up from hidden fire?"

Another passage of amusing *naïveté* is his way
of accounting for the terror manifested by the
lion in the presence of the cock.[1]   "Moreover,
ravenous lions cannot bear to face and gaze upon a
cock with flapping wings putting night to rout, and
summoning the morn with shrill voice.   In such
wise the lions at once bethink them of flight,
because sure enough in the body of cocks are certain seeds, and these, when they have been discharged into the eyes of lions, bore into the pupils
and cause such sharp pain that, fierce though they
be, they cannot continue to face them."   We are
reminded of the attempts of the Royal Society
in the time of Charles II. to account for a non-
existent phenomenon.   The theories explaining
the greater weight of a dead than a living fish
were not less far-fetched and fanciful than the
hypothesis of Lucretius to account for the imaginary tremors of the king of beasts.

Epicurus is contented with any explanation, provided that it does not postulate divine or Epicurean-
spiritual agency.   In fact he often gives ism a thor-
his reader two incompatible theories, and belief.
bids him take whichever he pleases.   A good Epicurean does not hesitate in his choice between
science and his system.   Polyaenus, on his conver-

[1] IV. 706.

sion to Epicureanism, declared his conviction that there was no such thing as geometrical proof. Catholicism was once as thorough-going. I have myself seen an old edition of the "Principia," by a learned abbé, who took care to explain in his preface that, though the conclusions of Newton constituted a good discipline for the exercise of the mental faculties, and therefore might be studied with profit, yet they must not be regarded as true, inasmuch as a Bull of the Holy Father had spoken of the sun as revolving round the earth! In a similar spirit Lucretius, after setting forth[1] a theory of the antipodes with amazing scientific accuracy, rejects it as "a fond thing vainly invented" (*vanus error*). The same theory was afterwards repudiated by the Christian church. It is remarkable, as M. Constant Martha has well observed, how speculative beliefs sometimes, so to speak, change sides. Here we have Epicureanism and early Christianity ranged hand in hand against history and science. So, again, Lucretius believes in a final destruction of the world, while the religious of his time held that it would be eternal. It is now the orthodox who maintain the Lucretian view, and the free-thinkers who take the other side. These considerations should teach us that we ought not either to embrace a scientific theory because we think we recognize in it an ally to religion, or to reject it as a suspected foe. Ajax tells us in a

Relation of scientific theories to religion.

[1] I. 1053.

pathetic passage of the play of Sophocles, how a sad experience has taught him that we should look on our friends as those who may one day be our enemies, and on our enemies as those whom time may yet draw to our hearts. Such ought to be the attitude of the true friend of religion towards scientific theories. He should consider only their absolute worth. About their relation to religion he may be mistaken, or the friend of yesterday may be the foe of to-morrow.

To set against the absurd speculations which we have been considering, it will be interesting to point to places in which Lucretius or his predecessors have really anticipated modern scientific research : Anticipations of modern science in Lucretius.

Lucretius recognizes that in a vacuum every body, no matter what its weight, falls with equal swiftness;[1] that the atmosphere is material;[2] that in youth the repair of the tissues is greater than the waste, the contrary being the case in old age;[3] the circulation of the sap in the vegetable world is known to Lucretius;[4] and he describes falling stars, aerolites, etc., as the unused material of the universe.[5] But, far above and beyond these particular anticipations of modern thought, we have in the whole atomistic theory what is now the basis of the molecular hypothesis, which latter only adds the existence of chemical as well as mechanical changes among the atoms, but leaves the general

[1] II. 237.   [2] I. 27.   [3] II. 1122.
[4] I. 347.   [5] II. 547.

conception the same. Snow and fire, according to Lucretius, come from different combinations of the same atoms, just as a tragedy and comedy are made of the same letters differently disposed.[1] Finally, the Darwinian natural selection, struggle for existence, and survival of the fittest are distinctly adumbrated, in Book V. 873 : "They doubtless became the prey of others, unable to break through the bonds of fate by which they were confined until Nature caused that species to disappear."[2]

It is, indeed, food for deep reflection when we observe the intense interest and confidence which this mighty intelligence feels in the childish physical theory which he has embraced. It is to him a source of ever new and ever present delight. The pool of water in the street fills him with wonder and awe. It is but a few inches deep, yet to the eye its profundity is that of the reflected heavens. Like this is the mind of Lucretius himself. The most trivial things become invested with a sombre sublimity, an august bigness, as soon as they begin to reflect his majestic spirit.

Intense interest of Lucretius in his work.

Decidedly the most remarkable feature in the whole poem is the solemn beauty of imagery and language into which he bursts in unfolding his thorny speculations. Examples of this are abundant, and an excellent instance is the passage so exquisitely

Beauty of imagery and diction.

---

[1] I. 824.   [2] V. 875–877.

reproduced in Tennyson's " Lucretius," where he
celebrates —

> " The all-generating powers and genial heat
> Of Nature when she strikes through the thick blood
> Of cattle, and light is large, and lambs are glad
> Nosing the mother's udder, and the bird
> Makes his heart voice amid the blaze of flowers."

I know of no other poem except Tennyson's
" Two Voices" in which the same wealth of poesy
is enlisted to explain and beautify abstruse argument. Nearly every verse of the " Two Voices"
illustrates this exquisite marriage of poetry and
logic. This passage will serve as an example as
well as another : —

> " Again the voice spake unto me:
> ' Thou art so steep'd in misery,
> Surely 't were better not to be.
>
> " ' Thine anguish will not let thee sleep,
> Nor any train of reason keep :
> Thou canst not think, but thou wilt weep.'
>
> " I said : ' The years with change advance ;
> If I make dark my countenance,
> I shut my life from happier chance.
>
> " ' Some turn this sickness yet might take,
> Ev'n yet.'   But he : ' What drug can make
> A wither'd palsy cease to shake ? '
>
> " I wept : ' Tho' I should die, I know
> That all about the thorn will blow
> In tufts of many-tinted snow ;

" ' And men, through novel spheres of thought,
Still moving after truth long sought,
Will learn new things when I am not.'

" ' Yet,' said the secret voice, ' some time,
Sooner or later, will gray prime
Make thy grass hoar with early rime.

" ' Not less swift souls that yearn for light,
Rapt after heaven's starry flight,
Will sweep the tracts of day and night.

" ' Not less the bee will range her cells,
The furzy prickle fire the dells,
The foxglove cluster dappled bells.' "

We may observe a very similar faculty in the
Latin poet in many places, for instance in II. 576–
580: "With death there is ever blending the wail
of infants newly born into the light ; and no night
has ever followed day, no morn ever dawned on
night, but hath heard the mingled sounds of feeble
infant wailings and of the lamentations that follow
the dead and the black funeral train." The whole
thought is but a step in his ratiocination, but it
insensibly clothes itself in images, and brings pictures before our eyes. And we see the born word-
painter in such expressions as "the wiles and force
and craft of the faithless sea, the treacherous, allur-
ing smile of the calm ocean ; " [1] "the shells that
paint the lap of Earth ; " [2] "and now, shaking his
head [a fine touch], the aged peasant laments that
the toil of his hands has come to nought ; " [3] "then

[1] II. 555.   [2] II. 374.   [3] II. 1164.

all these vapors gather together above, and, taking shape as clouds, on high weave a canopy beneath the firmament." [1]

Lucretius has now won his place among the great poets of the world. He has survived the anathemas of pious zealots and the plaudits of the enemies of all faith and belief. We now see how religious is the irreligion of this Titan. We hear in his sombre strains not the sneers of the encyclopaedist, but the high words of Prometheus on the Caucasus. At last the world has learned that intrepid audacity combined with noble sincerity may have a beauty which is like the beauty of holiness. At last Lucretius —

Place of Lucretius among the poets of the world.

> " Lifts
> His golden feet on those empurpled stairs
> That climb into the windy halls of heaven."

We see in him a sage who dwells on the lofty vantage-ground of science, and from his philosophic observatory looks down with disdain on the petty interests of the world. But he looks down on the world with a godly joy (*divina voluptas*) and a holy awe (*horror*). And we see in him an eager student of Nature, who has been raised by a naturally religious cast of mind, through cold and intangible abstractions to which he tried in vain to cling, — raised out of Nature and up to Nature's God.

[1] V. 466.

IV.

CATULLUS AND THE TRANSITION TO THE AUGUS-TAN AGE.

PASSING from the ghosts that haunt the early prime of Latin literature and, in fragments which often the merest chance has preserved for us, "come like shadows, so depart," we have reached a firm land, with living and breathing poets, a land that echoes to the cries of two great spirits, Lucretius and Catullus, the one tormented by the painful riddle of the earth, the other by the pangs of disprized love. We have seen Lucretius in his austere, almost religious, seclusion, hardly glancing at any passing event, looking down with the pity and disdain of an anchorite on the struggles of fashion and ambition, and scowling with the fierce indignation of a Swift on the joys and pangs of love. In him the man was nothing, the philosopher was everything. In Catullus we meet one for whom philosophy was nothing, and the keynote of whose song is man and man's heart. Catullus had studied Greek sympathetically and well, but it was only for literary purposes. The Greek philosophy which was so attractive to his contemporaries, especially Cicero, was to him only words "and the chatter of solemn graybeards."[1] A lecture on Lucretius pursues the

Lucretius and Catullus contrasted.

[1] "Rumoresque senum severiorum." — V. 2.

history of the poet's mind ; a lecture on Catullus pursues the history of his heart.

It is, perhaps, easy to exaggerate the importance, as an influence on a man's life, of that The poem of Catullus the history of his heart. train of emotional experiences which we call love ; but in the case of Catullus it was all-powerful, — his love was his life... Since this is so, and since) the history of the poet's heart has been set forth by himself in that marvelous series of poems tracing his infatuation for Lesbia from its rapturous beginning to its early estrangement ; thence to that reconciliation which shows something of the sweetness of lovers' quarrels composed, but more of the bitterness of remembering happier things ; and finally to the furious scorn with which the lover " tears his passion from his bosom, though his heart be at the root," — is it not marvelous that not a single editor, down to Mr. Postgate, whose recent and scholarly edition has done so much for the text of Catullus, should have given us the poems in the order in which they must have been written ? Yet such is the case. Editors continue to present us in the eleventh ode with the final repudiation of Lesbia, while we have in the fifty-first the rapture of reciprocated love, in the sixty-eighth the first beginnings of suspicion, in the seventy-sixth settled despair, in the eighth the vain effort to forget and passionate longing for the past which can never come again, and in the eighty-third hopeful auguries drawn from the unfriendly demeanor of Lesbia

toward her lover in the presence of her husband.
The principle on which the poems are arranged in
their present order is so utterly illogical and un-
chronological that it has been surmised — and, we
could well believe, with justice — that the juxtaposi-
tion of poems written at widely different times, and
under widely different influences, may have arisen
from a merely mechanical principle of arrange-
ment which bade the first copyists choose in each
case such poems as would just fill up the page on
which they were engaged, and not run over into
the next. I will endeavor to rectify this error, and
place beside each other in their right order a few
of the poems in which Catullus has struck those
terrible chords which have given us the very vibra-
tions of his heart, — chords as true as those of
Burns or Shakespeare, and as artistic as those
of Keats or Shelley.

Catullus was a contemporary of Cicero, Lucretius,
and C. Julius Caesar, and died most
probably in 54 B. C. at the age of thirty.
All his poetry was written in the last six
years of his short life, between his twenty-fourth
and his thirtieth year. He had Celtic blood in his
veins, coming from Verona in Cisalpine Gaul,
which was then indeed meet nurse of poetic children, and was about to give to Rome Virgil and
Cornelius Gallus, as well as the writer of what is
perhaps the most perfect prose style ever achieved,
the historian Livy. His intimates were all the
most distinguished men whom the time and the

Position and circum- stances of Catullus.

town produced, — the Metelli, Hortensius, Manlius Torquatus, Memmius, the two Ciceros. The great orator, whom he salutes as —

> " Most eloquent of all the line
> From Romulus who claim," [1]

never actually mentions the name of Catullus, but the orator has undoubtedly borrowed from the poet two happy expressions which we meet in his correspondence : once when he says that a public man should be " more sensitive than the tip of the ear ; " [2] and again, when he echoes in " ocellos Italiae villulas " [3] the charming apostrophe to Sirmio in the thirty-first ode : —

> " Thou of all isles and all peninsulas
> The very eye."

The family of Catullus was old and high, though no member of it had attained that official rank which was the condition of nobility technically so called. Though he often sportively alludes to his

[1] *Carm.* XLIX. Here and in some other places I use the often excellent but somewhat unequal translation of Sir Theodore Martin, sometimes venturing to remodel his version a little with the view of bringing out some point on which one may wish specially to dwell, but which naturally is not so prominent in his rendering. In some places where I could not take quite his view of the tone of the poem, as in VIII, beginning " Miser Catulle desinas ineptire," and in a few other shorter pieces, I have essayed a translation of my own.

[2] " Auricula infima molliorem " (*Q. Fr.* II. 13, 4) ; cp. " mollior imula auricilla " (Catull. XXV. 2).

[3] *Att.* XVI. 6, 2.

want of money, as when he tells one friend that his "purse is full of cobwebs," [1] and another that his house is exposed to the worst draught he knows, namely, a draft of fifteen thousand two hundred sesterces' morgage on it, [2] yet he cannot have been what we should call poorly provided for. We know that he had two country-houses, one near Tivoli and another on the Lago di Garda, to which he often retired, and which he describes as delightful retreats ; moreover, he could afford to keep a private yacht large enough to carry him from Bithynia to Italy. His intimates and associates in Rome were the highest in rank, birth, and distinction.

The woman to whose fascinations and falseness we owe much of what is best in the poetry of Catullus, the *belle dame sans merci* who first made him a poet and then a corpse, was, as is now generally admitted, Clodia, the sister of Cicero's enemy, wife of the great noble the Consul Metellus, and consequently about the grandest lady in the world. Rich, highly cultivated, witty, very beautiful, and conscious of the "aspiring blood" of the Claudii in her veins, the Palatine Medea, as she was called, seems to have had for the Roman youth of her time an absolutely irresistible attraction. When she turned the head of Catullus, a brilliant youth of two-and-twenty, she was herself past thirty years of age, with her ruinous charms in the full luxuri-

Clodia, the Lesbia of Catullus.

---

[1] "Plenus sacculus est aranearum." — XIII. 8.
[2] *Carm.* XXVI.

ance of their poisonous bloom. For her beauty was of that Junoesque type which even in Southern Italy requires time to enable it to expand to its full flower. Known to us as she is only from the railings of her bitter enemies, perhaps the three greatest masters of the art of invective that ever wrote, — Cicero, Caelius, and Catullus, — she appears, indeed, as a monster of almost incredible profligacy, but also as a great and well-marked personality in her generation. We must of course make allowance for the manners of a time when no limits whatever were set to the license of abuse, — a time when no one thought it indecorous in Cicero to apply such terms as " swine," " ordure," " carrion," to his political opponents in the Senate, and when such was the standard of manners in that " assembly of kings " that Cicero, in a letter to his brother,[1] relates as an every-day incident how rival orators spat in each other's faces ; a time when, if a magistrate wanted to address the people, he was obliged to carry the Rostra by assault, and to maintain his occupancy at the risk of his life. It is true that in the period of Catullus we begin to see the rise of something which we should now call society, the dawn of the *beau monde*. But the society of which we catch glimpses in the poems of Catullus and the letters of Cicero is still very rudimentary. Catullus thinks it a good joke to accuse a guest of stealing the napkins ; and the comparatively refined Cicero banters Atticus about the poorness of the fare

[1] *Q. Fr.* II. 3, 2.

which he serves up on such expensive plate of the fern-pattern, and wonders what it would be if the service were earthenware.[1] In such an age it is not surprising that the license of personal invective should be really unlimited. Furious and now un-utterable charges were publicly made against every public man by his opponents, and against private enemies by the man who could win the ear of the public. The assertions of Cicero and Catullus, that Clodia reached the last and most public stage in the career of infamy, we need not believe, any more than we believe that Caesar was addicted to every unspeakable vice. To impute such crimes was the fashion of the time. Different ages do not understand each other.[2] But we have good grounds for looking on Clodia as being a woman of daemonic fascination and cruelty, and a great social force in Rome at a time when society was beginning to form itself in a city to which for centuries the home-keeping aristocracy had failed to give the semblance of a social centre and seat of fashion and gaiety. When we think of Clodia with her large, burning eyes, now overflowing

[1] "Sed heus tu! Quid cogitas? in felicatis lancibus et splendidissimis canistris, olusculis nos soles pascere : quid te in vasis fictilibus appositurum putem ? " — *Att.* VI. 1, 13.

[2] Expressions in constant use by the Puritans and Cove-nanters would now afford a presumption of imbecility, or at least gross insincerity. Therefore the Puritans are often spoken of as hypocrites and fools. But they were nothing of the kind, only subsequent ages did not understand their modes of expressing themselves.

with tears over the death of her sparrow, now flashing with malicious joy as she and her boy lover, in
fulfilment of a sportive vow, commit to the flames,
with expressions certainly not too weak, the feeble
work of a rival literary aspirant, the Annals of
Tanusius, whom Catullus after his fashion pillories
under the metrically equivalent name of Volusius,[1]
we feel that we are in the presence of a very woman, who had also many of the qualities which in
Bohemian life knit man to man. Her sensuous
exuberance of form is conveyed to us by many a
dexterous touch : —

> " Therein my lustrous goddess with soft step
> Enter'd, and 'neath her glistering foot the sandal
> Creak'd as she trod." [2]

Here is no "airy, fairy Lilian," no Titania, no
poet's unsubstantial dream, but a ripe and real woman of warm flesh and blood, such as Rubens
painted. Though Clodia was woman enough to
weep over her dead sparrow till her lovely eyes
were red and swollen, she had enough of the man
in her to take a deep interest in politics. It is
surely more than a coincidence that the *liaison*

[1] " Annales Volusi, cacata charta,
    Votum solvite pro mea puella . . .
    At vos interea venite in ignem,
    Pleni ruris et inficetiarum,
    Annales Volusi cacata charta." — *Carm.* XXXVI.
[2] " Quo mea se molli candida diva pede
    Intulit, et trito fulgentem in limine plantam
    Innixa, arguta constitit in solea." — LXVIII. 70-72.

between her and Catullus was uninterrupted until the conservatives — to whom belonged Catullus, like Cicero, Hortensius, Lucretius, Nepos, Varro, and others highly distinguished in literature and oratory — felt forced to break with Caesar and the democratic party. In the year 62, when Catullus came to Rome from his native Verona, Cicero was still on friendly terms with Clodius. That feeling was soon turned to one of bitter hostility ; but for a considerable time after this Cicero endeavored to maintain amicable relations with the revolutionists, and he succeeded in doing so until the establishment of the first Triumvirate.

This was just the time when Clodia began to cast off Catullus. Her husband the Consul was now dead, poisoned (said common report) by the hand of his wife, and the latest victim of her deadly

M. Caelius Rufus.

kisses was M. Caelius Rufus, the friend and correspondent of Cicero. He was a brilliant young man, especially famed for the witty and satirical character of his oratory. Cicero writes to him : "In the whole course of my life I have never found any one more *au fait* in politics," [1] and he was on the democratic side. He was tall and handsome, with a keen wit, and one of the best dancers of the day, an accomplishment which gave him a start in the race for the favor of Clodia, who was herself passionately fond of dancing. This was the Rufus whom Catullus calls —

[1] "Πολιτικώτερον te adhuc neminem cognovi." — *Fam.* II. 8, 1.

> "The heart in which my friendship found repose,
> The viper that has crept into my life,"

and whom he apostrophizes as

> "Trusted by me not wisely, but too well.
> Not wisely! Nay, to my own dire defeat." [1]

Caelius was Clodia's lover for two years. Per-·
haps his sharp tongue cost him her favor. Quintilian tells us that he gave her a very coarse nick-
name which clung to her, [2] but this was probably
after he had received his dismissal. Luckily for
him, he had not the deep sensibilities of Catullus,
and he seems to have met his private and public
vicissitudes with the same airy banter and *bonhomie*
which makes his correspondence with Cicero so
fresh and piquant. But the Palatine Medea could
not be flouted with impunity. A boy of seven-
teen, no doubt another victim of Clodia's, was put
up to bring against Caelius serious and groundless
charges of battery, poisoning, attempted murder,
and what not. This brought forth the celebrated
speech of Cicero for Caelius, in which he paints
the whole life of Clodia as one of unexampled profligacy, and represents Caelius as an industrious
student who for a moment fell under her perni-

[1] "Rufe, mihi frustra ac nequiquam credite amico
    (Frustra! immo magno cum pretio atque malo),
  Sicine subrepsti mi, atque intestina perurens
    Ei misero abripuisti omnia nostra bona?
  Eripuisti eheu nostrae crudele venenum
    Vitae, eheu nostrae pectus amicitiae." — **LXXVII.**

[2] *Quadrantaria*, VIII. 6, 53.

cious influence, and in which he calls up the great censor Appius Claudius Caecus from the dead to bear witness against his degenerate descendant. "He is blind," cries the orator with scathing invective, "so he will not have the pain of looking on such a creature." "Did I make the Appian Way, he will ask you, that you might career along it with the husbands whom you have seduced from their wives?" Then follows much in this tone which would be impossible now in any court; then it was quite parliamentary, and it procured the acquittal of Caelius.

But we have nothing to do with Caelius except as the successor and supplanter of Catullus, nor even with Clodia except in so far as she affected the destiny of Catullus,

"Making a poet out of a man,"

like the great god Pan in Mrs. Browning's poem. Let us take a few characteristic utterances of the young lover-poet, illustrating his feelings at each stage of his ruinous passion.

It is ushered in with notes of joy as rapturous as a skylark's, and of love as tender as the cooing of a dove. Words cannot say nor figures count the number of kisses that would be enough, and when countless kisses have been given, the telltale record must be rubbed out. With what? With as many more kisses to cover the first.[1] Surely this is,

Poems illustrating the growth of the passion of Catullus.

[1] *Carm.* V

in the words of Polonius, "the very ecstasy of
love;" and we have beside it the utter tenderness of the poems on the dead sparrow, and the
transport of love which inspires the imitation of
Sappho.[1] The glow of his passion dazzles us until
a relation which must even then have been regarded as vicious assumes the guise of innocence.
The white heat imparts a look of purity. We
do not feel as much shocked as we ought to
be when he compares his Lesbia to so pure and
noble a heroine as Laodamia. And when he glorifies his friend Allius for a service so base as
that of providing at his house a place where the
guilty lovers may meet, we can only wonder at his
unlimited powers of self-acquittal, — a trait which
cannot but recall to us another poet with many
points of similarity to Catullus, the bright spirit of
Shelley, that " beautiful and ineffectual angel, ever
beating in the void his luminous wings in vain."
The unconcealed and unaffected joy and pride of
Catullus, when he tells in a passage already quoted
how Lesbia came to him to the house of Allius
from the very arms of her husband, the proud patrician consul Metellus, stand without a parallel
for *naïf* unconsciousness of the existence of a
moral law, until we read the letter in which
Shelley sends a polite invitation to the wife whom
he has just abandoned to come and share with him
and her rival the delights of a tour in Switzerland.
And Shelley thought himself an enthusiastic lover

[1] *Carm.* LI.

of the Good, and took much trouble to show his
friends how beautiful Virtue was. With the same
apparently unconscious innocence Catullus tells us
how he exulted as he heard the threshold creak
under the sandal of his lustrous goddess. But
soon a dark and menacing cloud falls over the
surface of this well of love, so deep and apparently
so clear. Catullus hears from his friend that while
absent in Verona he has rivals in Rome. Hence
bickerings and reconciliations on his return to the
city. Lesbia is held lower in his esteem, but he
owns that he cannot love her the less. He is content "to dote yet doubt, suspect yet strongly
love." At last he hates her, but he loves her too,
and he writes, in words to which Fénelon points
as the perfection of passionate simplicity,

"I hate, yet love: you ask how this is so.
　Who knows? But I'm in torment: that I know."[1]

The next phase is when he prays only for insensibility, for deliverance from his passion, as from a
desperate disease. He apostrophizes himself and
cries : —

"Why longer keep thy heart upon the rack?
　Give to thy soul a higher, nobler aim.
And tho' thou tear thy heart out, look not back
　In tears upon a love that was thy shame.

"'T is hard at once to fling a love away
　That has been cherish'd with the faith of years.
'T is hard: but shrink not, flinch not. Come what may,
　Crush every record of its joys and fears.

[1] "Odi et amo, quare id faciam fortasse requiris.
　Nescio, sed fieri sentio et excrucior." — *Carm.* LXXXV.

" O ye great gods, if ye can pity feel,
　　If e'er to dying wretch your aid was given,
　See me in agony before you kneel,
　　To beg this plague from out my core be driven,

" Which creeps in drowsy horror thro' each vein,
　　Leaves me no thought from bitter anguish free;
　I do not ask she may be kind again,
　　Nor pure: for that can never, never be.

" I only crave the health that once was mine,
　　Some little respite from this sore disease.
　If e'er I earn'd your mercy, powers divine,
　　Grant me — O grant to a sick heart some ease." [1]

But the most characteristic and the most heart-rending of all this series of poems is the one in which he pours forth in burning scazons, which ring like handfuls of earth thrown on a coffin, his agony in remembering happier things; in which he tries to brace himself up to endure, and breaks down in a wild burst of rage against his tormentress. The poem might have for its heading those divine words in " Christabel : "

　　　" And to be wroth with one we love
　　　　Doth work like madness in the brain."

The scazontic metre, which the Greeks call " limping " and " broken-hipped," is one of which it is

---

[1] LXXVI.: " Siqua recordanti benefacta priora voluptas," from 10, " Quare jam te cur amplius excrucies ? " to end, " O Di, reddite mi hoc pro pietate mea." The version is that of Sir Theodore Martin somewhat modified, especially in the last verse.

very difficult to reproduce the effect in English.
Here is an attempt to do so : —

"Ah, poor Catullus, learn to put away
        Thy childish things.
    The lost is lost, be sure: the task essay
        That manhood brings.

"Fair shone the skies on thee when thou to fare
        Wast ever fain
    Where the girl beckon'd, lov'd as girl shall ne'er
        Be lov'd again.

"Yes, fain thou wast for merry mirth ; and she —
        She ne'er said nay.
    Ah, gayly then the morning smil'd on thee
        Each happy day.

"Now she saith nay: but thou be strong to bear,
        Harden thy heart;
    Nor nurse thy grief, nor cling to her so fair,
        So fixt to part.

"Farewell !   I 've learn'd my lesson: I 'll endure,
        Nor try to find
    Words that might wake thy ruth, or even cure
        Thy poison'd mind.

"Yet will the time come when thy heart shall bleed,
        Accursèd one,
    When thou shalt come to eld with none to heed,
        Unwooed, unwon.

"Who then will seek thee?   Who will call thee fair?
        Call thee his own?
    Whose kisses and whose dalliance wilt thou share?
        Be stone, my heart, be stone ! "[1]

[1] "Miser Catulle, desinas ineptire. . . . At tu, Catulle, des-
tinatus obdura" (VIII.).   I read *impotens ne sis* in verse 9

At last he sends her his final farewell. It is by
the mouth of Furius and Aurelius, no very dear
friends of his, and thus perhaps he desires to add
a sting to his repudiation of his cruel mistress.
His love is dead: "Ruin's ploughshare" has
driven "elate full on its bloom:" it is as utterly
destroyed past all retrieval as the wild flower at
the meadow's edge which the passing plough has
shorn from its stalk.[1] The poem is in Sapphics,
and probably that metre was chosen in direct reference to his rendering from Sappho in the fifty-first

of the Latin, and in verse 23 of the Latin I accept Mr. Bury's
Scelesta, anenti quae tibi manet vita? It is strange that Mr.
Postgate has not at least mentioned this brilliant conjecture.
Anere, "to grow an old woman," is paralleled by *senet* =
senescit in IV. 26, and the verb is actually found in Plautus,
Mercator, IV. 4, 15: "Satis scitum filum mulieris: verum
hercle anet" ("a fine figure of a woman, but i' faith she
grows old"). In the verse before, *cum rogaberis nulla*
means "when you will never be asked for." The expression
is quite characteristic of the Catullian age. *Nullus venit*,
"not a bit of him came," and similar phrases, are common
in the letters of Cicero.

> [1] "Pauca nuntiate meae puellae
>   Non bona dicta,
>   Cum suis vivat valeatque moechis,
>   Quos simul complexa tenet trecentos,
>   Nullum amans vere, sed identidem omnium
>   Ilia rumpens:
>   Nec meum respectet ut ante amorem,
>   Qui illius culpa cecidit velut prati
>   Ultimi flos, praetereunte postquam
>   Tactus aratro est." — XI. 15–24.

ode, the only other Sapphic poem in the collection. "In this metre," he would say, "I breathed the exultation of my love's spring; and in this I will couch the bitter disillusion of its premature decay and my deliverance from a long anguish." His life did not long survive his love. Probably about this time were written those touching lines to Cornificius from his sick-bed, in which he tells his friend and brother poet that it goes ill with him and is like to go worse, asks him for a line, just a few words, and pathetically begs him to let the words be suitable to his sorry plight, and sadder than the tearful dirges in which Simonides was wont to weep those that died poets and died young.[1] Macaulay says of this little poem, and of the other two which I have just quoted: "They affect me more than I can explain : they always move me to tears."

But though the history of Catullus is mainly the history of his heart, and though his poems of the sensibilities are as exquisite as any ever written, — more exquisite than any other ever written, in the opinion of that great scholar and critic, the late H. A. J. Munro, — we must remember that the hand which here struck

Other poems of Catullus.

[1] "Male est, Cornifici, tuo Catullo,
Male est mehercule et ei ! laboriose,
Et magis magis in dies et horas.
Quem tu, quod minimum facillimumque est,
Qua solatus es adlocutione?
Irascor tibi.   Sic meos amores?
Paulum quid lubet adlocutionis
Maestius lacrimis Simonideis." — XXXVIII.

so true a note did not fail in other keys. Of all
the poems which he has written, those which appeal to us at all (for a few of them are utterly
alien from modern sympathies) are addressed to
feelings which are independent of time and circumstances, and move us now as strongly as they
moved the Romans who first heard them. His
deep affection for his brother, who died young in
the Troad, and whose grave he visited when on a
tour through "the famous cities of Asia," shows
that his excesses had not exercised that baneful
influence on his character which Burns deplores
in the exclamation,

> "But, oh! it deadens a' within
> And petrifies the feelin'."

It is remarkable that he does not seem to antici-
pate a future conscious existence in which he and
his brother might meet, though he suggests such a
source of comfort to his friend Calvus in his grief
for his beloved Quintilia. How favorably do the
buoyant hendecasyllables in which he sings of
the loves of Acme and Septimius compare with the
artificial prettinesses of Horace on similar themes,
even in the celebrated amoebaean ode beginning,

> " Donec gratus eram tibi,"

of which a great scholar of the Renaissance said
that he would rather have written it than be King
of Spain! It would be interesting to compare the
two in detail if our space permitted it. However,

the question between Catullus and Horace, who has spoken so slightingly of his truly inspired predecessor in lyric poetry, has been well debated between Munro and Conington, the professors of Latin at the time respectively in Cambridge and Oxford. The chief heads of the discussion will be found at the end of that charming book, Munro's "Criticisms and Elucidations of Catullus." I may be permitted to say that I agree with Munro in assigning the palm to Catullus as a lyrist, for reasons which will be evident to any one who may read the lecture on Horace.

The other shorter poems display a friendliness and manliness of tone reminding us of Burns and of Byron, never of Moore, though Byron in his "English Bards and Scotch Reviewers" calls Moore the young Catullus of his day. Indeed, this fancied resemblance to the Irish lyric poet, who in his polish of diction and shallowness of feeling far more closely resembles Horace, has had a very unfavorable influence on the work of translators of Catullus. Even Sir Theodore Martin, by far the best of them, is sometimes led into the rollicking vein of the Irish melodist, occasionally even when the Latin is laden with the deepest feeling. To illustrate this we have only to point to the seventy-fifth poem, beginning with the words,

Mistaken comparison of Catullus with Moore.

" Nulla potest mulier tantum se dicere amatam,"

and ending with the bitter confession that the poet's

heart is so perverted by his enslaver that, though nothing now could make him esteem her, yet nothing could make him cease to love her. Surely, though the versification is ingenious, the tone is missed in the version : [1] —

> " O Lesbia, surely no mortal was ever
>   So fond of a woman as I am of you :
>   A youth more devoted, more constant was never :
>   For me there 's enchantment in all that you do.

> " Yes, love has so wholly confused my ideas
>   Of right and of wrong, that I 'll dote on you still
>   As fondly, as blindly, although you may be as
>   Demure or as naughty as ever you will ! "

Again, in the seventieth poem [2] there is a certain dignity and seriousness which has quite disappeared in the jaunty light-heartedness of —

> " My mistress says there 's not a man
>   Of all the many swains she knows,
>   She 'd rather wed than me, not one,
>   Though Jove himself were to propose.

> " She says so ; but what woman says
>   To him who fancies he has caught her,
>   'T is only fit it should be writ
>   In air or in the running water."

[1] In the latest edition, 1875, this poem has been retrans-lated. Sir T. Martin himself condemns the above version.
[2] " Nulli se dicit mulier mea nubere malle
>   Quam mihi, non si se Jupiter ipse petat.
>   Dicit : sed mulier cupido quod dicit amanti
>   In vento et rapida scribere oportet aqua."

Moore himself disclosed what a great gulf lay between his literary tone and that of Catullus when he rendered the celebrated couplet already quoted, beginning *Odi et amo*, into this frigid quatrain :

" I love thee and hate thee, bùt if I can tell
   The cause of my love and my hate may I die!
 I feel it, alas ! I can feel it too well,
   That I love thee and hate thee, but cannot tell why.'

The inimitable ode to his villa at Sirmio has been attempted over and over again, but never, as I think, with anything like success. I would only observe that I think the last three lines have not been fully explained. I would render the lines : —

Ode to his villa at Sirmio.

" Rejoice, bright Sirmio, in thy master's joy,
   And you, ye wavelets, merrymen of the mere,
   Smile all the smiles ye have to greet me home." [1]

Ludius is a " merryman," or " tumbler," and Scaliger saw that under *lidie* of the MSS. there lurked this original and natural comparison of the tumbling wavelets to " merrymen." Certain waterfalls in England are still called merrymen by the local peasantry ; and one of R. L. Stevenson's clever tales is called " The Merry Men," taking its name from " those big breakers that dance together." In Plautus,[2] when the lover prays the bars of his

---

[1] " Salve, O venusta Sirmio, atque hero gaude
      Gaudente, vosque, O ludiae lacus undae,
      Ridete quidquid est domi cachinnorum."

XXXI. 12–14.

[2] " Pessuli, heus pessuli . . . fite causa mea ludii."

Curc. I. 2, 36.

mistress's door to leap up out of their sockets and let him in, he cries, " Be merryandrews for my sake." *Domi habere* is "to have at one's command," " to keep a stock of." Sir Theodore Martin, recognizing the meaning as being "laugh all the laughs you have," suggests the pretty rendering, —

" Let all your wealth of smiles be wreathed for me."

A version published in London in 1707 gave the meaning accurately, but too elaborately, in

" Laugh till your stock of laughter 's wholly spent,
    And all your magazine of merriment."

Broadly one would point to the shorter poems of Catullus as showing a power of relating an incident, or describing a scene, in terse idiomatic Latin, which is approached only by Terence in his plays and Cicero in his letters, and which is perhaps best exemplified in the tenth poem, where Catullus gives a sketch of the requests to which he was subjected on his return from Bithynia. The other most prominent feature is his extraordinary power of dealing with metre, as displayed in his nuptial ode (LXI.) on the marriage of Manlius and Vinia, and in his Hymn to Diana (XXXIV.),[1] which has been beautifully translated by Professor Jebb in "Translations:" —

The shorter poems.

[1] "Dianae sumus in fide
    Puellae et pueri integri,
    Dianam pueri integri
        Puellaeque canamus."

" Diana guardeth our estate,
  Girls and boys immaculate ;
  Boys and maidens pure of stain,
  Be Diana our refrain.

" O Latonia, pledge of love
  Glorious to most glorious Jove,
  Near the Delian olive-tree
  Latona gave thy life to thee,

" That thou shouldst be forever queen
  Of mountains and of forests green ;
  Of every deep glen's mystery ;
  Of all streams and their melody :

" Women in travail ask their peace
  From thee, our Lady of Release :
  Thou art the Watcher of the Ways :
  Thou art the Moon with borrow'd rays :

" And as thy full or waning tide
  Marks how the monthly seasons glide,
  Thou, Goddess, sendest wealth of store
  To bless the farmer's thrifty floor,

" Whatever name delights thine ear,
  By that name be thou hallow'd here ;
  And, as of old, be good to us,
  The lineage of Romulus."

But nowhere is his astonishing mastery of metre
more triumphantly shown than in that unique literary *tour de force*, the " Attis."

Of this poem Sellar justly says that, regarded as
a work of pure imagination, it is the
most remarkable poetical creation in the
Latin language.   It tells how Attis, a beautiful

The " Attis."

youth, the adored of the society in which he lived, whom his admirers escorted to the Palaestra crowned with garlands, finds it suddenly borne in upon him in a kind of awakening or conversion that he must leave the whole world and cling to Cybele; how he sails with a troop of like-minded devotees to the Phrygian Ida, where with tambours and cymbals, with trumpets also and with shawms, they worship the great turret-crowned Mother till sleep overcomes them on the top of the mountain; how, when the sun rises in the morning, it repents Attis of the service of the Goddess; and how Cybele unyokes from her car a lion, which pursues him back into the forest and terrifies him into obedience. Catullus does not seem to have followed any of the legends which have come down to us, but to have taken a mere empty mould of a story, and to have poured into it a hot flood of strange Oriental fanatic passion, quite alien from Roman sentiment and experience. The very conception of the beautiful and much-courted youth is un-Roman, yet there is nothing extant which even hints at a like poem in Greek, and the "Attis" certainly forces on our minds the impression of an original creation. The poem is utterly untranslatable into English. The sudden change of gender which intimates that the votary of Cybele has become her votaress, the tumultuous rush of the metre in which most of the lines end in five short syllables, the numerous diminutives and strange compound words, all render it inimitable.

Tennyson's experiment in this metre is no doubt familiar to most readers, and perhaps George Meredith's. They and Professor Ellis have at least caught the salient feature of the rhythm, that agglomeration of short syllables at the end of the verse, which suggested to Tennyson — by far the best of the imitators — the employment of polysyllables in that place with the accent thrown back as far as possible, words like "legionaries," "charioted," "confederacy." The last attempt made is by Mr. Grant Allen, who in a little book forming the sixth volume of the Carabas Library has endeavored with some ingenuity to connect the Attis myth with tree-worship. But his rhythm does not seem to me even remotely to suggest that of Catullus. His first lines are —

"Across the roaring ocean, with eye and with heart of
    flame,
To the Phrygian forest Attis in an eager frenzy came," —

a tame and tranquil movement to my ear, suggesting the metre of the well-known missionary hymn,

"From Greenland's icy mountains, from India's coral
    strand,"

rather than the torrent rush of the Catullian strain. I regard the metre as antispastic, to use a technical term, each line showing an iambic succeeded by a trochaic movement. The device by which Catullus imparted to his metre such an irresistible rush and impetus was the frequent resolution of the long syllable of the final dactyl, — an effect im possible to reproduce in English, in which we cannot pronounce together five short (that is, unaccented) syllables, like "sonipedibus," "hederigera," "columinibus," "nemorivagus."

It is interesting to observe how Tennyson's fine classical instinct — fortified no doubt by careful study, probably of some exhaustive commentary like that of Professor Ellis, where the point to which I am about to refer is duly noted — kept him right in a splendid line which he borrowed from the "Attis" for his "Tithonus." I refer to the noble passage where the horses of the Sun

Figure borrowed by Tennyson from the "Attis."

> " Shake the darkness from their loosen'd manes,
>   And *beat the twilight into flakes of fire.*"

Surely Tennyson had in his mind the passage in the "Attis" where Catullus says of the rising Sun,

"And he smote on the dim dawn's path with the hoofs of his fiery chariot-steeds." [1]

A less learned and accomplished scholar than Tennyson might have supposed that Catullus had present to his fancy the much less striking figure of the Sun "driving away the darkness of night;" but the Latin is fortunately decisive and inexo-

[1] "Pepulitque noctis umbras vegetis sonipedibus."—LXIII. 41.

The magnificent phrase, "the dim dawn's path," for "the morning sky," reminds us of Milton's

> " Thither came Uriel flying through the even,"

where Bentley, with such strange lack of poetic feeling, wished to correct "even" to "heaven."

rable : *pellere* in Catullus never means " to drive away," always " to smite," " to strike." An ignorance of the usage of the poet would rob him of a most magnificent piece of imagery. This delicate touch has been missed by Mr. Grant Allen, who thus renders the sunrise passage : —

" But when golden-visaged Phoebus with radiant eyes again
   Surveyed the fleecy ether, solid land, and roaring main,
   And with mettlesome chargers scattered the murky shades
      of night,
   Then Attis swift awakened, and Sleep fled fast from his
      sight."

Though some of the poems of Catullus dance like those waves of the Lago di Garda which he calls "merrymen," yet we have in him, as in all the great Latin poets, a prevailing chord of sadness, a mournful minor key. Even his gay dedication of his yacht, which "declares no pinnace could outstrip her," ends with the sad reflection, "portion and parcel of the past." [1] As Dante in his "Vita Nuova" tells us with what agony the thought came to him that Beatrice could die, so Catullus even in his wildest rapture cannot put aside the thought of the darkness of death,

Sadness of Catullus.

     " Into whose maw goes all that's prettiest," [2]

and the certainty that

       " Suns will rise and set again :
          But for us, when once doth wane

---

   [1] " Sed haec prius fuere."— IV. 25.
   [2] " At vobis male sit, malae tenebrae
      Orci, quae omnia bella devoratis." — III. 13, 14.

> This poor pageant's little light,
> We must sleep in endless night." [1]

Lucretius and Catullus we have already found coupled together by Cornelius Nepos as representing the culminating point of Republican poetry. And Nepos was right. "When we find," writes Momm-sen,[2] "not merely his contemporaries electrified by these fugitive songs, but the art critics of the Augustan age also characterizing him along with Lucretius as the most important poet of this epoch, his contemporaries as well as his successors were completely right. The Latin nation has produced no second poet in whom the artistic substance and the artistic form appear in so symmetrical perfection as in Catullus. And in this sense the collection of the poems of Catullus is certainly the most perfect which Latin poetry as a whole can show." Catullus is, moreover, the connecting link between the Republican and the Augustan school. The "Marriage of Peleus and Thetis," his longest piece by far, has been shown by Munro to be the work of his last year of life, and it displays unmistakable signs of a perusal of the poem of Lucretius. It is elaborately, one might almost say awkwardly, constructed on the Alexandrine model. But we cannot help feeling that the word

(side note: Catullus the connecting link with Augustan poetry.)

---

[1] "Soles occidere et redire possunt:
Nobis cum semel occidit brevis lux
Nox est perpetua una dormienda." — V. 4-6.
[2] *Roman History*, iv. 591, Eng. Trans.

"awkward" is ill-associated with such a poem, even though the laws of art cry out against the long episode which in a not very long poem tells so beautifully the sad tale of the desertion of Ariadne. To take the least enthusiastic view of it, it is interesting as the earliest specimen in Latin of a careful effort to construct a really epic poem in hexameters. It is the first example of that thoroughly diligent elaboration which Horace enjoins on his contemporaries, and of which Virgil and Ovid had conceived so high an ideal. It is from this point of view that Catullus has been well called by M. Patin " La Préface du siècle d'Auguste."

The successive stages in the elegiac poetry of

Elegiac poetry of the Augustan age. the Augustan age are marked by Propertius, Tibullus, and Ovid. The early Greek elegy was as opposite as possible in its spirit to the elegy of the Augustan age. Callinus and Tyrtaeus employed it to rouse their countrymen to patriotism and heroism; Solon made politics its theme; and Theognis and Phocylides enshrined in it their proverbial philosophy and shrewd moralizings on life. Mimnermus is the only early Greek elegiac poet whose muse is associated with love. It is the Alexandrine poets, Philetas, Callimachus, and Euphorion, to whom Cicero refers as the models of "the new school" (οἱ νεωτερίζοντες), and who really gave its tone and scope to the Latin elegy. With Propertius love is still ardent passion, but the characteristic reverence and seriousness, the *gravitas* of the

Roman character, has deepened into gloom ; in
Tibullus love is tender affection mixed with melancholy, and there is still strong sympathy with the
grandeur of the Roman character and state ; in
Ovid love is mere pleasure, intrigue, gallantry,
and all *gravitas* has completely disappeared. Love
is with him merely physical desire, and the lover
aspires to nothing better than *bonne fortune.*
The poet has forgotten how to suffer like Catullus,
and has learned how picturesque it is to *souffrir*
like Alfred de Musset. Ovid prepares us for the
state of morals which called forth the sarcasms of
Tacitus and the execrations of Juvenal.

The late Professor Sellar, in his valuable volume
on Horace and the elegiac poets, which
appeared after his lamented death, has Propertius.
happily remarked that readers of Propertius in the
present day will be disposed, according to their
temperament, to apostrophize him in one or other
of two verses from his own poems. Those who
feel neither his own personality nor that which he
has imparted to his Cynthia to be very congenial,
and who think that it is possible to have too much
of lovers' quarrels and reconciliations, — that love
is, after all, only the flower of life, not its root or
even its fruit, — will shut up the book of his poems,
exclaiming in his own words, —

" Maxima de nilo nascitur historia."

The more sympathetic readers will say with a
sigh, —

" Ardoris nostri magne poeta jaces."

To the one the four books of elegies will be " much
ado about nothing ; " to the others Propertius will
ever be "the bard that lent love's passion words."
I belong to the latter class, and that is the reason
why I have put him before Tibullus, to whom
chronologically he is somewhat posterior.   When
we leave Propertius, we abandon really ardent sincerity in the expression of the passion of love,
never again to meet it in Latin poetry.

The poetry of Tibullus is to his —

 " As moonlight unto sunlight and as water unto wine."

The characteristic of Tibullus is not ardor, but
tenderness and self-abnegation.   He writes to
Delia with apparent sincerity : —

  " I am not worth a single tear of hers ; " [1]

and after she has proved faithless to him, he can
express a grateful and affectionate re-
membrance of her mother.[2]   He depre-
cates the life of a soldier because he prefers the
peaceful joys of the country, not for the reason of
Propertius, that time is wasted which is not spent
in love.   Tibullus might have written sincerely : —

  " I could not love thee, dear, so much,
   Loved I not honor more."

[1] " Non ego sum tanti ploret ut illa semel."
[2] " Vive diu mihi dulcis anus : proprios ego tecum,
  Sit modo fas, annos contribuisse velim :
 Te semper natamque tuam te propter amabo :
  Quidquid agit sanguis est tamen illa tuus."
        I. 6. 63.

Tibullus.

To Propertius such a sentiment would have been a blasphemy against love, on whose shrine everything, even honor, ought to be sacrificed.

Propertius does not seem to have been congenial to his contemporaries. Horace sneers at him more than once, and it has been suggested that Propertius was the bore whom he met on the Sacred Way.[1] But, whatever were the personal characteristics of Propertius, he was undoubtedly a great poet. If one had to select the finest poems written in Latin elegiacs, perhaps one would not err in choosing that poem in which Propertius describes the ghost of Cynthia appearing to him immediately after burial,[2]

Propertius and Ovid compared.

> "Sunt aliquid Manes: letum non omnia finit,"

and the address [3] of Cornelia to her husband beginning,

> " Desine, Paulle, meum lacrimis urgere sepulcrum."

Aeacus, in an admirable passage in the "Ranae" of Aristophanes, suggests that the question of superiority between Aeschylus and Euripides might be decided by placing verses of each poet in a bal-

---

[1] Mr. Bury, in his masterly history of the Roman Empire to the death of M. Aurelius, pointedly writes of him: " He seems to have been a man of weak will, and this is reflected in his poetry. It has been noticed by those who have studied his language that he prefers to express feelings as possible rather than as real; his thoughts naturally run in the potential mood."

[2] IV. 7.   [3] IV. 11.

ance and weighing them by butcher's weight.[1]
Tried by this test, his pentameters would make
those of Ovid kick the beam. In Ovid the pentameter always "falleth in melody back." In Propertius it often soars above the "silvery column"
of the hexameter, and dominates the couplet.
Ovid would probably have thrown into the scale
the fine pentameter which is engraved over the
cemetery in Richmond by the banks of the James
River, — the cemetery which contains all that is
mortal of the Southern victims of the American
civil war : —

> " Qui bene pro patria cum patriaque jacent."

But Propertius would have been able to choose one
of half a dozen pentameters laden with weighty
meaning to set against it ; perhaps the pentameter
admired so much by Dean Merivale, —

> " Jura dare et statuas inter et arma Mari ; "

or the proud boast of Cornelia when she pointed to
the blameless life of Paullus and herself from their
marriage to her death, —

> " Víximus insignes inter utramque facem ; "

or the verse wherein the poet, thinking of the
"vast and wandering grave" which whelmed the
young life of his friend Paetus, exclaims in that
elegiac ode which Sellar aptly compares to the
"Lycidas," —

> "Nunc tibi pro tumulo Carpathium omne mare est."

---

[1] τί δέ ; μειαγωγήσουσι τὴν τραγῳδίαν. — *Ran.* 798.

Ovid never even attempts to deal seriously with
love except when he describes the passion of a woman for a man, as in his Ovid.
"Heroides," and there we meet a quality in his
style which at once marks him out as the herald of
the Silver Age, — the rhetorical tinge with which
the letters from the heroines are imbued and which
recalls to our minds the *suasoriae* of the schools of
rhetoric. This defect is less seen in the poems in
which Ovid was more sincere, as in the "Art of
Love," which was justly regarded by Macaulay as
the greatest of Ovid's works, and which reminds
Sellar of Byron's "Don Juan," as a poem in which
a true vein of real poetry occasionally mingles with
cynical worldliness and warm sensuousness. But
the rhetorical strain is very present in the "Metamorphoses," for which the poet himself claims the
palm, and to which he trusts for his immortality.
The attractiveness of this work lies in its descriptions, — another mark, as we shall see, of the Silver
Age; but the attempt to divest it of the character of a Dictionary of Mythology by interweav-
ing the stories after the fashion of the "Arabian
Nights" is only partially successful. Sellar points
out how his gods are emptied of all dignity and
grandeur, adding the just and acute remark,
"Though in no ancient poem do the gods play a
larger part, no work is more irreligious." If any
one desires to see how a dainty conceit may be
made not only gross but grotesque by a foul imagination, let him compare the fifteenth poem in

the second book of the " Amores " with the " fool-
ish song" in " The Miller's Daughter," beginning, —

> " It is the miller's daughter,
>   And she is grown so dear, so dear,
> That I would be the jewel
>   That trembles at her ear;
> For hid in ringlets day and night
>   I'd touch her neck so warm and white."

In the "Tristia" and " Ex Ponto " we have an attempt to misapply the elegiac muse, and to force
her whose song should be of

> " The hope, the fear, the jealous care,
>   The exalted portion of the pain
> And power of love,"

to record the petty troubles of *une âme désorientée*,
a soul ill at ease amid its surroundings.   We
could have well spared the " Fasti,"— a mechanical
effort to produce the effect of a patriotism which
the writer did not feel, and to efface the inefface-
able impression of lightness and insincerity which
his poetry leaves. We should have been fortunate
if we had preserved in its place his tragedy, the
" Medea," which ancient critics pronounced to be
his masterpiece.   In the "Remedia Amoris" and
the "Medicamina Facie" we have an example of
the most impossible of all feats which a writer can
essay — the attempt to imitate his past self.   Many
writers have achieved amazing imitations of others,
but those who have tried to reproduce the pecul-
iarities of their former selves have always failed

pathetically. Nevertheless, no other classical poet has furnished more ideas than Ovid to the Italian poets and painters of the Renaissance, and to our own early poetry from Chaucer to Pope, who, like Ovid,

" Lisped in numbers, for the numbers came."

V.

VIRGIL.

No poet or writer of antiquity, we may safely affirm, no uninspired writer except perhaps Aristotle,

Influence of Virgil on subsequent thought and letters.

has had a greater influence on the world of thought and letters than Virgil. Aristotle, of course, in the hands of the schoolmen was for centuries the only study of Europe; his philosophy has thus usurped a very undue share of the attention of civilization, and has through the Latin impressed its mark on all the languages which have a Latin basis. To it, and to it alone, we owe such common words as "actually," "habit," "predicament," "energy," "motive," "maxim," "principle," and many others. The peddler who recommends the "quality" of his wares, and offers a reduction on taking a "quantity," little thinks that he is using words which, but for the philosophy of Aristotle, would never have found their way into his language. But the influence of Virgil on posterity, though not so direct, is perhaps quite as marked, and is the more wonderful as exercised, not by a teacher, but by a singer.

The impression produced by him was as immediate as it was intense. Horace said of him that nature never produced a fairer soul, and Propertius prophesied that his coming epic would surpass the

"Iliad." When he entered the theatre, an awkward, slovenly youth with toga all awry, His success
the house rose to do him honor. The immediate
and
"Aenëid" furnished the text-book which enduring.
taught Seneca, Petronius, and Juvenal what perfection was possible for their native tongue. Tacitus conned it till the Virgilian diction so colored
his style that a Virgilian parallel often dispels the
obscurity of a corrupt passage in the "Annals" or
"Histories," and still oftener decides the question
between two rival emendations. St. Augustine
often refers to Virgil as the highest bloom of pagan
art. A legend of the Middle Ages relates how St.
Paul, coming on the tomb of Virgil, exclaimed,
"What a man I should have made of you if I had
met you in your life!"[1] From the mists of the
Middle Ages he peers out at us as the mightiest of
magicians who have —

> "Learned the art that none may name
> In Padua far beyond the sea;"

and in a mediaeval romance, "Reynard the Fox,"
Virgil and Aristotle are coupled together as en-
chanters. Dante took him by the hand to lead
him from the ancient to the modern world. "Or
se' tu quel Virgilio," — these are the words of awe
and veneration with which Dante in the "Divina
Commedia" greets his immortal predecessor in Ital-

---

[1] "Quem te, inquit, reddidissem
Si te vivum invenissem,
Poetarum maxime!"

ian poetry. The modern world at once welcomes him through the mouth of Bacon, who calls him " the chastest poet and royalest that to the memory of man is known." The very stones cry out. Scratched on the baths of Titus have been found the words *tantae molis erat*, and on a wall in Pompeii is scribbled *conticuere omnes*. From his own time to the present century, Virgil has been recognized as the type of perfection in poetry. Before the year 1500, ninety editions of his work had been published, and so many since the revival of letters that there are said to be as many editions as the years that have passed since his death.

The reaction against Virgil which the present
Reaction against Virgil in the present century.
century has witnessed may be said to date from the epoch-making lectures of Niebuhr; and since that time the question whether Virgil deserves a place among the great poets of the world has been a duel between France and Germany, in which all the cunning of fence has been on the side of France. His ascendency in France was early and complete. Scaliger ranked him above Homer and Theocritus; and Voltaire said, " If Homer is the creator of Virgil, Virgil is certainly the finest of his works." Voltaire, according to M. Renan, understood neither the Bible, nor Homer, nor Greek art, nor the ancient religions, nor Christianity, nor the Middle Ages, yet is a most instructive writer, for he had the courage of his convictions and always spoke out. " Virgil," writes Sainte-Beuve, " the

moment when he appeared, became at once *the poet* of all the Latin races." On the other hand, Germany has followed the lead of Niebuhr : Bernhardy and Teuffel deny him all creative power ; and Mommsen classes the " Aenëid " with epics like the " Henriad " and the " Messiad." The English school has been nearly as enthusiastic as the French, and has recently made a splendid contribution to the fame of Virgil in the magnificent ode of Tennyson, to which I shall have further occasion to refer.

Undoubtedly Virgil has suffered most from a comparison with Homer, and especially Comparison since the quite recent awakening of im- with Homer. aginative interest in periods of nascent and immature civilization. The critics of the last century felt an interest in past ages only in so far as they presented points of similarity to their own ; hence they delighted in the subjectivity and the conscious power of the Latin epic, and failed to find any attraction in the *insouciance, naïveté*, and child-like simplicity of the Greek. Time, it may safely be anticipated, will still more completely confirm the primacy of the Greek epic ; but in the mean while it may be interesting to point to certain features in the Latin poem which present a strong contrast to the Greek.

It has been denied that the " Aenëid " is an epic poem at all. This question is not very important. The " Aenëid," like the rose, " by any other name will smell as sweet." Undoubtedly it endeavors, and with but moderate success, to reconcile two

The Aenëid
as an epic
poem. conflicting elements — a traditional epic framework, and the feelings and manners of Virgil's own highly artificial age. No one can fail to observe at once the prevailing effort to reproduce Homer externally. His characters are borrowed, his similes, his incidents, even some of the most trifling, as when Nisus in the " Aenëid "[1] loses the race in consequence of precisely the same misadventure which befell Ajax in the " Iliad." [2]   But when we look for internal resemblance, when we view the poems as it were from within, and ask how each poet looked at the world, the *contrast* is what strikes us. Wherein ought two epic poets to agree more closely than in their way of regarding war? Here we find the difference between Homer and Virgil

Contrast
with the
Greek. most marked. No sooner is the Greek poet in the *mêlée* of the combatants than he is drunk with the joy of battle; it is his delight to chronicle the most ghastly wounds, and to tell how the victor jeers at his prostrate foe. The Latin poet, in the tenth book of the " Aenëid," forces himself to sustain for a while this uncongenial strain. But his heart is not in it. He gives us, as in duty bound, the arm hanging from the shoulder by the sinews, the thick blood vomited from the dying mouth, and tells how the slayer,

[1] V. 333.   [2] XXIII. 774.

> " Tugging hard with labor wrenches back
> The weapon striking deep amid the bones." [1]

But he turns even more gladly than the reader from the sickening scene, and takes refuge in a mere list of killed and killers : [2] —

> "Caedicus Alcathoum obtruncat, Sacrator Hydaspen ;
> Partheniumque Rapo et praedurum viribus Orsen ;
> Messapus Cloniumque Lycaoniumque Ericeten."

In VII. 481, he speaks of "the cursed lust insane of war and blood." [3] Even in the very thick of the fight, instead of luxuriating in the carnage like his Greek master, his mood is so gentle that when he relates the painful incident of the death of the twin sons of Daucus by the hands of Pallas, his first thought is what a joy the twins must have been to their parents, who, —

Gentleness of mood.

> " Sore perplext, each for the other took,
> Nor wished the sweet uncertainty resolved." [4]

When Aeneas [5] thrusts his spear through the tunic of Lausus, we read how it

> "rent the vest
> His mother's hand had broidered o'er with gold."

[1] X. 383. This is the version of Canon Thornhill, which, with other recent versions, is further considered in an Appendix on recent translations of Virgil. Meantime I will give his, Conington's, or Morris's renderings of passages from Books VII.–XII., and Sir C. Bowen's for Books I.–VI.

[2] X. 747–749.   [3] " Scelerata insania belli."
[4] X. 302.   [5] X. 818.

His heart is not in the battle ; he is really on the
Contrast side of the mothers who curse it.[1] He
with Homer's
enjoyment of tells us, not how the braves reveled in
battle. the delight of the approaching conflict,
but how the mothers felt its horrors, —

"And trembling caught their children to their breasts." [2]

Homer's Zeus can afford to neglect the murmurs
of the other Olympians, so long as he can feed his
eyes on the sight that he loved : —

"Apart from the rest he sate, and to fill his eyes was fain
With the gleam of the brass and the fate of the slayers and
them that were slain." [3]

We sometimes meet a passage in the "Iliad"
which makes us feel uncertain whether we are in
presence of the childhood of the world, or of something more like its modern barbarism, — in myth-
land or in Zululand. When Iphidamas falls under
the sword of Agamemnon,[4] the poet commiserates
his fate in perishing,

"Or e'er he had joy of his bride and the gifts that he gat
her withal,"

and then goes on to detail the valuable consideration, one hundred beeves, one thousand goats, and
so forth, which he had given for a bride he was
never to possess : the pity of it was that he had had
no return for his expenditure. If this way of look-

---

[1] "Bellaque matribus detestata." — Hor. *Od.* I. i. 25.

[2] "Et trepidae matres pressere ad pectora natos."

[3] *Il.* XI. 75.   [4] *Il.* XI. 240.

ing at wedded love is essential to the true epic vein, we have something to console us for the absence of the epic spirit in the *anima cortese Mantovana.*

It is probably to this reluctance to deal with scenes of carnage that we owe a very charming feature in the "Aenëid." It is because he feels constrained to look for other means of interesting his read-

Virgilian catalogues compared with Homeric.

ers in the war that he gives his picturesque and elaborate descriptions of the gatherings of the leaguered clans, with their arms and accoutrements, which, in the magic use made of historic names, remind us of like qualities in Scott and Milton, and which transcend in affluent detail and poetic coloring the meagre catalogues of the "Iliad," as much as the Homeric battle-pieces surpass the Virgilian. In Homer the different Greek peoples are all exactly the same, and differ very little from the Trojans ; in Virgil some dozen tribes are minutely differentiated. Moreover, those same catalogues have enabled him to give detailed expression to his enthusiastic invocation in the "Georgics" of his native land : [1] —

> " Hail, clime of Saturn ! mighty mother of tilth,
> Mighty mother of heroes ! "

[1] *G.* II. 173. On the subject of Virgil's catalogues, Mr. Gladstone observes : "Virgil, in his imitation of the Homeric catalogues, . . . with vast and indeed rather painful effort, carries us through his long list at a laboriously sustained elevation." Nettleship has admirably shown that the cata-

All this is, of course, conscious art, and brings be-
Conscious fore us an age which looks behind and
art of Virgil. around itself like a man, not straight in
front like a child. Thersites is as hideous as the
spiteful sister, or the wicked uncle, or the bad giant
must be perforce in the child's fairy tale, which can
see no goodness in things evil, and does not care to
make any appeal to experience to correct the exuberance of fancy. Here, as a contrast, is the tem-
perately drawn picture of Drances, the Thersites
of the "Aenëid" :[1] —

> "True to his wont, unfailing Drances rose,
> His spiteful soul by Turnus' glory vexed,
> And thwart-eyed envy's bitter-rankling stings, —
> Rich, nor withal a niggard of his wealth
> For party needs; ready and shrewd of tongue,

logue is an essential and integral part in the design of the
Aenëid, which puts before its readers an Italy infested by
savages, and even monsters, but finally, through the agency of
Aeneas, subdued and civilized. In addition to this, the catalogue is highly interesting as an instance of the first attempt
to enlist archaeology in the service of imagination, — an effort
which has, "with, indeed, rather painful effort," been made
by M. Flaubert in *Salammbo*. Other statements of Mr.
Gladstone concerning Virgil, in his *Homeric Studies*, show a
curious inaccuracy, combined with a definiteness of language
which experience has since taught him to avoid. When he
wrote (vol. iii. p. 532) that Virgil "has nowhere placed on
his canvas the figure of the bard among the abodes of
men," it is strange that he should have forgotten not only
Cretheus (IX. 774), but even the bard Iopas, who occupies
such a prominent place at Dido's feast, fully described at the
close of the first book of the *Aenëid*.

[1] XI. 336.

> But cold and spiritless of hand for war;
> No mean adviser deem'd at council board;
> A deep intriguer, versed in all the arts
> Of faction and cabal."

Exaggeration Virgil is studious to avoid; yet he will actually reverse the truth in the interests of art. What could be more charming than the picture which he draws of the fleet of Aeneas gliding up the Tiber: —

> " So grateful now with shouts auspicious raised
> They speed their way begun, the well-pitched keels
> All slipping lightly through the shoaly flood,
> While woods and waves with utter wonder see
> The shields of warriors flashing far ahead,
> And painted hulls afloat upon the stream;
> With beat of oars they wear out day and night,
> And, mounting, leave full many a bend behind
> And lengthy reach, with varied foliage fringed,
> And, pictured in the river's stilly depths,
> Cleave the green forests 'neath the grassy plain." [1]

His learning told him that, at the time of Aeneas' supposed arrival in Italy, and long after, the banks which bordered the river near its mouth were a waste of sandy flats.[2] But no frowning scene should meet the eyes of the fated author of the Roman race. He describes the Ostia of his own day, with its charming environs, with the banks of the river dotted with villas and gardens to the very city,

[1] VIII. 91.

[2] Servius tells us that the historian, Fabius Maximus, describes the region bordering the mouth of the Tiber as " agrum macerrimum litorosissimumque."

while its surface is gay with a flotilla of pleasure-boats.

But we must remember that we are not reading in the "Aenëid" a modern romance. The character of Aeneas has been condemned as imperfectly realized, and as cold and unfeeling; even his good qualities, such as his filial piety, have been ridiculed [1] as un-epic. But one charge has been brought against the treatment of his character which rests on a completely modern conception. It is alleged that the real hero of the poem is Turnus, who is ready to die for the woman whom he loves; and Mr. Gladstone especially dwells on "the superior character and attractions of Turnus." On this point I would quote the acute and decisive comment of the late Professor Nettleship : —

Aenëid not to be treated as a romance.

"When Aeneas lands in Latium to seek the alliance of Latinus and to found his city, divine oracles, widely known throughout the Italian cities, had spoken of a stranger who was to wed Latinus' daughter, and to lay the foundation of a world-wide empire. Aeneas, through his ambassador, announces his landing, and asks for a simple alliance with Latinus; Latinus offers this and the

---

[1] Among the pictures found at Pompeii is one which caricatures the flight of Aeneas from Troy. It represents an ape in armor carrying an aged ape on its shoulders, and leading a young one by the hand. Compare also Ovid, *Trist.* II. 533, 534, where he cannot resist a jest at the expense of the immaculate Aeneas.

hand of his daughter besides. The king can in any case bestow his daughter as he chooses ; and in reading Virgil it must be remembered always that Lavinia is never really betrothed to Turnus, who is only a suitor among other suitors, and differing from the rest in nothing but his ancestry and his beauty, and in having the favor of the queen-mother Amata on his side. To stir up a war for the sake of mere personal inclination against a cause manifestly favored by the will of the gods would, from the point of view of the ancient religions, as surely have been thought impious and perverse as, from a modern point of view, it appears natural to centre our interest on the adventurous warrior who is ready to sacrifice his life for his love. But Virgil is not to be read as if he were a modern writer of romance, but to be interpreted according to the ideas of his time. We find in the 'Aenëid' no genuine trace of sympathy either for Turnus or for the cause which he represents. Such sympathy is a feeling induced by the spirit and associations of modern literature. When the treaty between Aeneas and Latinus is apparently concluded, it is the element of obstinate female passion, represented among the gods by Juno, and among men by the queen Amata, joined to the headstrong violence of Turnus, which confounds the peace and embroils all in a long series of discord. The queen of heaven, unable to bend the gods above, stoops to move the powers of hell."

We must not expect in Aeneas a character with

whom we can sympathize from a romantic point
of view.   He is the Man of Destiny,
and must go where the Fates lead him.
But he has all the high qualities which
may belong to the Man of Destiny.   His manners
are always princely; even in the scenes where he
is forced to cast off Dido, impelled as he is by a
higher will than his own, he preserves the grand
air, a mien worthy of Aristotle's Megalopsyche.
The episode of the death of Lausus strikes the
note of mediaeval chivalry; the noble words addressed by Aeneas to the dying boy might have
been spoken by Sir Launcelot, or shall we say Sir
Percivale or Sir Galahad?   For the character of
Aeneas, as has been observed by Sellar, "is more
like that of the milder among the spiritual rulers
of mediaeval Rome than that either of the Homeric
heroes or of the actual consuls and imperators who
commanded the Roman armies and administered
the affairs of the Roman state.   It has been said
of him that he was more fitted to be the founder of
an order of monks than of an empire."

But the mission of Aeneas was no quest of the
Holy Grail, but to carry out the divine decree by
which Rome was to rule the world for the world's
good.

Virgil showed great judgment in his choice of
Aeneas as his hero.   He was determined to abandon the mythological epic handled so skillfully by
the Alexandrine school of poetry.   Varro Atacinus,
Cornelius Gallus, Calvus, and Catullus — the last

with distinguished success — had worked this vein ;
and Statius and Valerius Flaccus were
destined afterwards to achieve with it a
success which we now find it difficult
to understand.   In the beginning of the third
Georgic, however, Virgil declares his belief that
that vein is exhausted, *omnia jam vulgata*, and he
resolves not to adopt it.   On the other hand, the
historical epic had been successful in the hands
of Ennius and Naevius, and was destined again to
win laurels for Silius Italicus and Lucan.   Even
in his own time, poems were constructed on the
defeat of Vercingetorix and the death of Caesar.
Neither of those two schools of poetry did Virgil
propose to join.   He wished to take a middle
course, and to write an epic which should resemble one school in taking for its plot the fortunes of Rome, and the other in linking itself with
the cycle of Greek mythology.   ·In the " Eclogues "
and "Georgics" he had begun by seeking his inspiration from Alexandria ; and in the "Aenëid"
we often find him walking in the steps of the Alexandrine poets, especially Apollonius Rhodius.   Yet
in the same poem so close a follower is he of the
old singer of his country's weal and woe that Seneca
calls him an Ennianist, — no term of praise in his
mouth.   Indeed, as a poem which, while professedly
relating the adventures of an individual, really has
for its hero the poet's own nation, the "Aenëid"
resembles no work of imagination so closely as it
resembles the series of Shakespeare's historical
plays.

Choice of Aeneas as a hero.

Virgil found the required link between the two
kinds of epic in the person of Aeneas, and he had
in him a hero in every way fitted for his purpose.
Aeneas is invariably put by Homer in a most dignified light.   He is coupled with Hector as one
of the two great champions of Troy; it is to him
that appeal is made in time of trouble, and he
never fails to answer it.   His first appearance in
the " Iliad " [1] has little to suggest to us the reserved and somewhat stilted hero of the " Aenëid."
He comes out "like a lion," and rushes on Diomede with a terrible roar.   Diomede smites him
on the hip with a huge stone which he hurls at
him.   But here, as elsewhere, Aeneas is under
the special care of the gods, and escapes the hu-
miliation of defeat.   His appearances are few and
short, and invariably excite the interest of the
gods.   If Virgil had chosen a hero more prominent in the " Iliad," he would have exposed himself to a dangerous comparison with Homer; a
less dignified hero would not have been a worthy
ancestor of the Roman race.

The " Aenëid " is addressed to patricians, — to
the Trojugenae of Rome.   Its most striking characteristic is the prevailing distinction of
its tone.   The poet seems always to
have before his mind's eye the homes,
the lives, the habits of the great and noble.   A
curious instance of this is afforded by VII. 579 ff.,
where the frenzy of Amata's wanderings is illus·

Distinction
of tone in
the Aenëid.

----

[1] V. 299.

trated by the gyrations of a top whipped by boys "round great empty courts." The simile — one of the few of which Virgil seems to have been the creator, not the borrower — is far from happy, indeed is almost grotesque; but it suggests that the scene of the boys' play is some great noble's palace. The same remark applies to another of his similes, — one which perhaps comes next to this in its far-fetched oddity, and which the poet borrowed from Apollonius Rhodius. A ray of light reflected from a tub of water is by the Greek compared to the fluttering heart of Medea, by the Latin to the fluctuating mind of Aeneas. The allusion to the princely mansion is quite peculiar to the Latin poet; there is not even a hint of it in the Greek : [1] —

> "And turns to every side his shifting thought:
> E'en as in brazen water-vats the beam
> Of trembling light reflected from the sun,
> Or radiant image of the silvery moon,
> Keeps ever flitting every place around,
> From wall to wall, and upward darting now
> Plays on the fretwork of the paneled roof."

Here the poetry of the simile in the Greek poem has evaporated in the Virgilian reproduction of it. But conversely in the fine verses : [2] —

> "Through shadow the chieftain soon
> Dimly discerned her face, as a man, when the month is but young,
> Sees, or believes he has seen, amid cloudlets shining, the moon," —

[1] VIII. 21–25.   [2] VI. 453.

the whole poetical power of the passage consists
in the application of the image to the sudden
recognition by Aeneas of the pale and shadowy
form of his forsaken love, dimly discerned through
the gloom of the lower world.   In the Greek [1]
nothing is denoted but the indistinctness with
which Lynceus discerns the distant Heracles. So,
too, in a fine passage [2] in the sixth book, Virgil
breathes pure poetry into the verses of Apollonius Rhodius, which merely compare a concourse
of people, " thick as leaves in Vallombrosa,"
to the forest foliage scattered by the breath of
Autumn ; in Virgil, the withered leaves are the
pale ghosts, and the frost is the chill touch of
Death : —

" Down to the bank of the river the streaming shadows re-
        pair,
  Mothers, and men, and the lifeless bodies of those who were
  Generous heroes, boys that are beardless, maidens unwed,
  Youths to the death-pile carried before their fathers were
        dead.
  Many as forest leaves that in autumn's earliest frost
  Flutter and fall, or as birds that in bevies flock to the coast
  Over the sea's deep hollows, when winter chilly and frore
  Drives them across far waters to land on a sunnier shore."

Conington has on this passage a note of characteristic fineness of perception : " The well-known
reversal of the comparison in Shelley's 'Ode to the
West Wind,' where the 'leaves dead' are compared
to 'ghosts from the enchanter fleeing,' and desig-
nated as

            [1] **Ap. R. IV. 1479.**   [2] **VI. 309.**

> ' Yellow and black and pale and hectic red
>   Pestilence-stricken multitudes,'

will illustrate what was in Virgil's mind."

Was it this passage which suggested to Dante Gabriel Rossetti these lines of Shakespearean bigness of conception and Tennysonian perfection of execution ? —

> " How then should sound upon life's darkening slope
>   The ground-whirl of the perish'd leaves of Hope,
>   The wind of Death's imperishable wing ? "

But I have already, perhaps, said more than enough on the general characteristics of a poem which, more than any other great work of imagination in any language, really depends for its interest rather on its episodes, and on the brilliancy of verses taken here and there apart from their context, than on our grasp of the poem as a whole. It is this feeling which has dictated the barren-seeming yet withal fascinating discussion as to the relative merits of the first six books of the " Aenëid " and the last six. It is at once apparent that the " Aenëid " falls into two halves, and that in the first we have an " Odyssey," and in the second an " Iliad." The one contains the adventures and wanderings of Aeneas till he reaches the mouth of the Tiber ; the other his struggles to win his way by the sword in the promised land. The first half has generally been greatly preferred. It has been held that, having gained the dizzy altitude of his

First six books of the Aenëid compared with last six.

midflight, it was inevitable that he should "stoop from his aëry tour." The terrors of the siege of Troy, the adventures of the voyage which finally led him to Carthage, the passionate love-tale of which Carthage was the scene, the descent into Hell, — all this had beggared the resources of imagination. Voltaire made himself the champion of this view, while Chateaubriand espoused the other side. The latter maintained that the most tender and impressive utterances of the poet are to be found in the last six books. Even if this were true, it would hardly prove his case; but it seems to me that by far the larger number are to be found in the earlier books, which, moreover, are much more impressive and picturesque. There is no other female character in the poem which can compare with Dido in delicacy and vigor of portraiture; and the second and third books hang like a gorgeous drop-scene before the tragedy enacted in the fourth. Yet, on the other hand, one can see that the poet's task was far harder when he left the scenes glorified by all the prismatic hues of Greek imagination, and turned to the yet unsung shores of Italy. Was he conscious of an inferiority in the execution of the latter portion of his work? I think not. At the beginning of the seventh book, in invoking the Muse, he exclaims,—

> "A grander scene is opening on my view,
> A loftier chord I strike;"[1]

[1] " Major rerum mihi nascitur ordo;
Majus opus moveo."

and it is in a passage in the ninth book that he
contemplates for Nisus and Euryalus an immortality to be conferred by his poem : —

> "Blest pair ! if aught my verse avail,
>   No day shall make your memory fail
>   From off the heart of time,
>   While Capitol abides in place
>   The mansion of the Aenëid race,
>   And throned upon that moveless base
>   Rome's father sits sublime."

Juvenal selects the description of Allecto in the
seventh book as the highest specimen of Virgil's
inspiration ; and Dante seems to have been most
deeply moved by the closing scenes of the work
when he speaks of Italy as the land —

> " Per cui morío la Vergine Cammilla
>   Eurialo et Turno et Niso di ferute."

The discussion to which I have referred suggests
to me that it would be interesting here to advert to
a few places in Virgil's poems which de-
rive a peculiar interest either from their   *Famous passages in Virgil.*
own perfect beauty or from some pleas-
ing historical association.   I do not desire to point
to whole passages of sustained beauty or grandeur,
but merely to put before your eyes a few of the
jewels of Virgil which can best shine with little or
no setting in the way of context.   The poetry of
Virgil lends itself to this kind of treatment.   From
the earliest times the literary merit of isolated passages was a theme of discussion.   Seneca[1] thought

[1] *Ep.* 79, 5.

that no human skill could surpass the description of Aetna in the third book,[1] while Aulus Gellius[2] considered it too elaborate. ·Tennyson gave a crowning instance of his marvelous insight into the character and genius of Latin poetry when in the poem to Virgil he sang of

" All the chosen coin of fancy flashing out from many a
golden phrase,"

and again of

" All the charm of all the Muses often flowering in a lonely
word."

Let us here consider a few of those golden phrases.[3] Macaulay thought the finest passage in Virgil was that where a boy's love at first sight is told in the "Eclogues," VIII. 37–41 ; I give Sir C. Bowen's version of it, though it is hardly adequate : —

" 'T was in our crofts I saw thee, a girl thy mother beside,
Plucking the apples dewy, myself thy pilot and guide :
Years I had numbered eleven, the twelfth was beginning to
run :
Scarce was I able to reach from the ground to the branches
that snapp'd.
Ah, when I saw how I perish'd! to fatal folly was rapt ! "

In this exquisite passage the most exquisite touch,

" Scarce was I able to reach from the ground to the branches
that snapp'd,"

---

[1] III. 571.   [2] XVII. 10.

[3] Many of these passages are brought together in a very eloquent and appreciative paper on Virgil by Mr. F. Myers, first published in the *Fortnightly Review* several years ago, and now included among his collected essays.

is quite the poet's own. The rest is from Theocritus. We often see how Virgil can turn dross
into gold, but here — greater marvel still — we
find him gilding the refined gold of the Greek
poem, and in the process making it more lovely and
precious. In a future lecture I shall put before
you a certain verse from Statius, which I think is
the worst verse in Latin poetry. Many would be
disposed to quote as the *best* verse in Latin poetry
Virgil's

" Sunt lacrimae rerum et mentem mortalia tangunt."

It does, indeed, strike one with a sense of wondrous
beauty and pathetic dignity. But I am not sure
that all its meaning has yet been fully unfolded.
Sir C. Bowen translates it,—

" Tears are to human sorrow given, hearts feel for mankind."

And such is the accepted view of the meaning of
words which have always seemed to me to come
bitter from that wellspring of sadness which made
the poet marvel why the dead should desire to live
again. It was this minor key in Virgil's poetry
that was ringing in Tennyson's ears when he apos-
trophized him so beautifully as

" Thou majestic in thy sadness at the doubtful doom of
humankind."

Surely, in this famous verse, *sunt lacrimae rerum*,
Virgil meant more than Wordsworth in the " Laodamia " when he wrote

" But tears to human suffering are due."

Surely these words, which seem full of a natural
magic, come to us with a diviner air and a grander
message than this.   Dr. Henry, one of the very
greatest of modern Virgilian scholars, has greatly
added to the impressiveness of the verse by a refined and scholarly interpretation of the word *rerum*
as meaning "in the world," just as in the phrase
dulcissime rerum.   The meaning would then be,
"There are such things as tears in the world,"
"tears are universal, belong to the constitution of
nature, and the evils of mortality touch the heart."
This is a great improvement on the ordinary explanation of this celebrated and oft-quoted verse.   But
may not the words, which cannot but strike one as
fraught with some new and exquisite fancy, bear a
meaning far more definite, weighty, and distinguished?   Aeneas is gazing at the picture of the
Trojan war in the temple of Juno in Carthage.   As
he looks he weeps, and cries, "E'en things inani-
mate (*res*, the material picture) can weep for us,
and the works of man's hands (*mortalia*) have
their own pathetic power."   That is, "Here in a
strange land, where men knew me not till but yesterday, I find a painted picture to accord me sympathy and call forth my tears."   The verse which
follows falls in with this view : —

"Then on the lifeless painting he feeds his heart to his fill." [1]

Inani, as Conington observes, is not a mere gen
eral epithet, but has a pathetic sense, implying

[1] " Sic ait atque animum pictura pascit inani."

that the subjects of the picture are numbered with the lost and past. *Rerum* is the lonely word in which flowers all the charm of all the muses. I should add that, in another passage in the " Aenëid," [1] *mortalis* means " the work of man's hands."

There is one verse in the fourth book in which all the pathos of Dido's abandonment may be said to be concentrated. It is when she addresses Aeneas as *hospes*, " guest," and adds, —

> " Since Fate but that cold name allows
> To one whom once I call'd my spouse." [2]

Servius tells us that when Virgil was reading aloud the " Aenëid " to the emperor and his court, the poet's voice faltered as he pronounced those pathetic words.

A natural magic touches another passage in the same book, which depicts the sense of utter loneliness which haunts the dreams of the deserted queen. This is Sir C. Bowen's rendering of it : —

> " In all her visions the fierce Aeneas appears,
> Hounding her ever to madness, and she seems left evermore
> Desolate, traveling always a long, lone journey with tears,
> Seeking her people of Tyre on a silent wilderness shore."

Her lover is gone, and with him everything, — even her subjects, whom she has offended by giving herself to a stranger. In her waking hours she never contemplates such a thing as abandon-

[1] XII. 740.
[2] " Hoc solum nomen quoniam de conjuge restat."

ment by her subjects. Only her hopeless dreams
present her to herself as deserted by him who was
to her all the world, and therefore utterly alone.
If Ilia's dream in Ennius at all suggested this
exquisite passage, then Ennius has done at least
one great thing.

Perhaps the oftenest quoted passage **in Virgil**
is —

> " Varium et mutabile semper
> Femina."

It is curious that the translation of these very
familiar words in Conington's prose version far
surpasses in poetical color not only his own metrical rendering, but also those of Sir C. Bowen
and Canon Thornhill. "A thing of moods and
fancies is a woman" admirably brings out the
characteristic use of the neuter in the Latin, and
is far more expressive than Conington's —

> " A woman's will
> Is changeful and uncertain still,"

or Bowen's —

> "Woman is ever fickle and light,"

or Thornhill's —

> " A changeful thing at best,
> From love to hate soon shifts a woman's heart."

The perfect description of the dying Dido ends
with an immortal line, —

> " Quaesivit caelo lucem, ingemuitque reperta."

Here is Sir C. Bowen's version of the scene : —

" Thrice on her couch with an effort she raised her ; pillowed her head
Thrice on the elbow beneath her, and thrice fell back on the bed.
Upwards she lifted her wandering gaze, and above and around
Sought in the heavens for the light, and groaned when light she had found."

She groaned, the sight of the light bringing back vividly to her mind the troubles she had endured in it. So rapidly does the poet pass from point to point that the reader is left to make out for himself the delicate connections. Tired and disgusted with the world as Dido is, she cannot die without taking a last look at the light in which she had once been so happy. But the sight of the light serves only to bring back with increased distinctness the recollection of her misery, and *with a deep groan* she closes her eyes again and dies. It is the dying human being who

"Upwards lifted her wandering gaze, and above and around
Sought in the heavens for the light."

It is the woman Dido, deserted and betrayed, who

"groaned when light she had found."

"There is no so touching word," writes Dr. Henry, " in the whole 'Aeneïd' as this one word *ingemuit, groaned,* placing as it does before the mind capable of such sympathies the whole heart-rending history in a single retrospective glance. Show me anything at all like it in the ' Iliad.' "

Another famous verse introduces us again to the scene when Virgil read his poem to the court. We are told that he read with "a magic fascination," *lenociniis miris.* Augustus and Octavia burst into tears when he came to the words, —

> " Child of a nation's sorrow ! If thou canst baffle the Fates'
> Bitter decrees, and break for a while their barrier gates,
> Thine to become Marcellus." [1]

I have already quoted the verse —

> " And trembling mothers caught their children to their
> breasts." [2]

It is adapted from Apollonius Rhodius, but the Greek poet takes three verses to express the idea, and then only says that the mothers *embraced* their children. In *pressere,* " caught them to their breasts," we have again the charm flowering in a single word.

Fénelon could not read or repeat without tears those high and dignified words in which Evander welcomes Æneas to his rustic palace : —

> " Dare thou as nobly too, my honor'd guest,
> To spurn at pomp, and, rivaling the God,
> Set in thy foot, nor scorn our poor estate." [3]

[1] " Heu miserande puer, si qua fata aspera rumpas,
  Tu Marcellus eris." — VI. 883.

[2] " Et trepidae matres pressere ad pectora natos."

VII. 518.

[3] " Aude hospes contemnere opes et te quoque dignum
  Finge Deo, rebusque veni non asper egenis."

Dryden writes of this passage: "For my part I am lost in the admiration of it. I contemn the world when I think of it, and myself when I translate it."

Having dwelt at some length on certain passages in the "Aenëid" which have most deeply moved mankind through the successive generations, one feels that this is perhaps the fitting time to point to some of its defects. I would say at once that the fifth book is all bad. Not only is it an excrescence on the natural body of the poem, but it contains the worst examples of Virgil's slavish adherence to the text of Homer. There is in it, too, some very un-Virgilian coarseness. Menoetes sitting on the rock, and discharging from his stomach the salt water which he has swallowed, is a disgusting picture; the prayer of Cloanthus to the sea-gods is worthy only of burlesque; indeed, the book has scarcely a redeeming feature. Next in order of demerit comes the tenth with its endless battle-scenes, which were evidently as wearying to the writer as they are to the reader. Doubtless this is the reason why we find Virgil's mechanical execution to be at its worst in this book. The task was uncongenial, and the words and numbers refused to flow. Probably the feeblest verse in Virgil is — as Mr. Myers observes —

"Sed non et Tröius heros
  Dicta parat contra, jaculum nam torquet in hostem;"[1]

[1] "But not the Trojan hero, too, essays
      A speech; for at the foe his lance he hurls."

a verse which suggests a modern exercise painfully achieved by a schoolboy and inspired by a *gradus*.

The tenth book, however, has fine passages, and, so far as it is an evil, it is a necessary evil, for battle-scenes are, we may suppose, *de rigueur* in an epic poem. But the fifth might have been omitted with great advantage, and Varius and Tucca would have consulted their friend's reputation if they had excised it. It has passages which are inconsistent with the rest of the poem. To take only one, Nisus and Euryalus appear in the fifth book, yet in the ninth they are introduced as if for the first time. The fifth book was certainly an after-thought, and was probably constructed with a view to impart a certain symmetry to the whole work. When one thinks of the very uncharacteristic instances of bad taste which it supplies, and of its inconsistency in some places with confessedly authentic parts of the poem, one is tempted to hazard a conjecture that Virgil left behind him only eleven books, and that Varius and Tucca wrote or procured another book to raise the number to twelve.

Virgil is essentially a religious poet. The fourth Eclogue has been held to derive its inspiration from the expectation of a coming Messiah. But, however that may be, the child shadowed forth as the king of the peaceful world is essentially the product of a deeply religious spirit. The motto of the Georgics might well be said to be *Ora et labora;* and the "Aenëid" is above all things

Virgil a religious poet.

a religious poem. This, indeed, largely accounts
for what is unheroic in the character of Aeneas.
Evander is perhaps the most pleasing as he is certainly the most characteristic of Virgil's creations.
He is a perfect example of a good old man of the
good old type. Virgil might be described, as Dante
has been described, as a "theologian to whom no
dogma was foreign" (*theologus nullius dogmatis
expers*). The duty of Aeneas is to bring the gods
into Italy : the glory of the victory may fall to Latinus ; his own aim is to fulfill his destiny. From
this point of view Gaston Boissier selects, as the
verse which unfolds the whole plan of the " Aenëid,"
a line in the twelfth book (192), —

> " The gods and worship I shall claim to give ;
> Let sire Latinus bear the sword of war." [1]

The real defect in the character of Aeneas, from
the point of view of art, is that it occasionally slips
into the Homeric mould. On the side of Turnus
are the bolder spirits, and the characters drawn
with a freer hand. Of these Mezentius is the
most daring. But even here the religious spirit
is present. When the body of his son is brought
in, what is the instinctive gesture of this atheist prince, this *contemptor divum* ? He raises his
hands to heaven.[2] Whenever Virgil recounts any
incident of a barbarous type, such as the murder
of Misenus by Triton through jealousy, or when

[1] " Sacra deosque dabo : socer arma Latinus habeto."
[2] *Aenëid*, X. 845.

he records a very crude tradition, like the transformation of the galleys into goddesses of the sea, he adds some such phrase as, " if we can believe it," or, " I tell an old tale as 't was told to me ; " and he cannot suppress an exclamation of astonishment at the vindictive temper of Juno, —

> " Can wrath so dire abide in heavenly minds? "[1]

The religious aspect of Virgil naturally leads us up to the strange circumstance, already mentioned, Virgil as a that the Middle Ages glorified Virgil into saint, a saint and degraded him into a wizard. He was placed among the Prophets in the Cathedral of Zamorra, and invoked as Prophet of the Gentiles in Limoges and Rheims. The rubric of Rouen directed that on Christmas Day the priest should say, —

> " Maro, Maro, Vates Gentilium
> Da Christo testimonium,"

to which Virgilius was to reply, —

> " Ecce polo demissa solo nova progenies est."

I have already referred to the mediaeval romance and as a which couples Aristotle and Virgil as magician. magicians. Gower, in his "Confessio Amantis," tells us how Virgil

> "A mirrour made of his clergie[2]
> And set it in the townes eyes
> Of marbre on a pillar without,"

[1] " Tantaene animis caelestibus irae? "
[2] Learning, skill.

that the Romans might behold if there were any
enemies within thirty miles.   But by far the most
interesting account of Virgil as a magician is to
be found in a very rare romance, of which an
English version was printed at Antwerp in 1510,
under the title: " This boke treateth of the lyfe
of Virgilius, and of his deth, and many marvayles
that he did in his lyfe tyme by whychcraft and
nygromancie thorowgh the helpe of the devylls of
hell." [1]   We read in the second chapter of this romance how " the son of Remus, that was also
named Remus, slewe his unkell Romulus, and was
made emperoure, and so reyned emperoure."   In
his reign Virgil was born.   His mother was " one
of the greatest senyatours dawghters of Rome,
and hyghest of lynage."   When Virgil was at
school in Toledo, he was initiated into the secrets
of necromancy in a way which reminds us of a
well-known tale in the " Arabian Nights."   " One
day when the schollers had lycence to go play and
sporte them in the fyldes after the usaunce of the
olde tyme, he spyed a great hole in the syde of a
great hylle."   Going into this hole, he wandered
on till he saw " a lytell bourde marked with a
word," and heard a voice calling him, which said,
" I am a devyll conjured out of the bodye of a cer-
tayne man, and banysshed till the day of judemend,
without that I be delivered by the handes of men."
Virgil agreed to release the devil if he would show

[1] Sir Walter Scott made copious extracts from this romance in the notes to the *Lay of the Last Minstrel.*

him how to get the "bokes of nygromancy" that
he possessed. The devil consented, whereupon —

"Virgilius pulled open the bourde, and there was a lytell
hole, and thereat wrange the devyll out like a yeel, and cam
and stood byfore Virgilius lyke a bygge man. Thereof Virgilius was a stoned, and merveyled greatly thereof that so
great a man myght come out at so lytell a hole. Than sayd
Virgilius, Shulde ye well passe into the hole that ye cam out
of ? Yea, I shall well, sayd the devyll. Than said Virgilius,
I hold ye the best plegge I have that ye shall not do it.
Well, sayd the devyll, thereto I consente. And than the
devyll wrange hymselfe into the lytell hole ageyn ; and as he
was there in, Virgilius kyvered the hole ageyn with the bourde
close, and so was the devyll begyled, and myght nat there
com out ageyn, but there abydeth shutte styll therin. Than
called the devyll dredfully to Virgilius, and sayd, What have
ye done ? Virgilius answered, Abyde there styll to your day
apoynted. And fro thensforth abydeth he there. And so
Virgilius becam very connynge in the practyse of the black
scyence."

When he came to be old, Virgil resolved to re-
new his youth by his magic arts. So he took with
him a trusted man to a "castell that was without
the towne," the entrance to which was guarded by
"coper men with flayles in their handes sore smy-
tinge." Then he ordered his man to slay him, and
hew him in pieces, and salt him in a barrel under
"a lampe, that nyghte and day therin may droppe
and leke, and thou shalt ix days longe fylle the
lampe and fayl not ; and whan this is all done,
than shall I be renued and made yonge ageyn."
After much persuasion the trusty servant was prevailed on to execute his master's will. When seven

days had elapsed, the emperor missed his counselor, and finally frightened the trusty man into guiding him to the place where the body of Virgil was : —

"And whan they cam afore the castell and wold enter they myght nat because the flayles smyt so faste. Than sayd the emperoure, Mak cease this flayles that we may cum in. Than answered the man, I know nat the way. Than sayd the emperoure, Then shalt thou die. And than thorowgh the fere of dethe he turned the vyce and made the flayles stande styll, and than the emperoure entered into the castell with all his folke, and sowghte about in every corner after Virgilius; and at the laste they sowghte so longe that they cam into the seller where they saw the lampe hang over the barrill where Virgilius lay in, deed. Than asked the emperoure the man, Who had made him so herdy to put his mayster Virgilius so to dethe; and the man answered no word to the emperoure. And than the emperoure with great anger drew out his swerde and slewe he than Virgilius's man. And whan all this was done than sawe the emperoure and all his folke a naked chylde iij tymes rennynge about the barrill saying the words : Cursed be the tyme that ye cam ever here. And with these words vanyshed the chylde away, and was never sene ageyn; and thus abyd Virgilius in the barril deed."

The great Latin poets are all profoundly sad. Catullus, Lucretius, and Virgil look on life as a place —

"where men sit and hear each other groan."

The Greek epic now and then strikes a chord in a minor key with that exquisite truth and fullness which it achieves without an effort, as in —

"Even as the leaves, such is the race of men;"[1]

[1] οἴη περ φύλλων γενεή, τοιήδε καὶ ἀνδρῶν.
Iliad, VI. 146.

Or —

> " The fates have given to man a patient mind ; " [1]

Or —

> " What boots the storm of wailing, for the gods
> Thus have ordain'd for mortals, that poor man
> Should live in woe, but gods know nought of grief ! " [2]

But the melancholy is but for a moment, and gives way at once to the joy of life, of triumph, even of revenge ; if there is a bitterness it arises from a fountain of mirth : but the sadness of the Latin poets is abiding. Virgil marvels why the dead should desire to live again : [3] —

Sadness of Latin poetry.

> "O my father ! and are there, and must we believe it, he said,
>
> Spirits that fly once more to the sunlight back from the dead ?
>
> Souls that anew to the body return and the fetters of clay ?
> Can there be any who long for the light thus blindly as they ? "

When Odysseus seeks to console the dead Achilles with the thought that he is a great prince among the dead, Achilles answers him and says : [4] —

> " Nay, speak not comfortably to me of death, great Odysseus. Rather would I live upon the soil as the hireling of

---

[1] τλητὸν γὰρ Μοῖραι θυμὸν θέσαν ἀνθρώποισιν.
    Iliad, XXIV. 49.

[2] οὐ γάρ τις πρῆξις πέλεται κρυεροῖο γόοιο.
    ὡς γὰρ ἐπεκλώσαντο θεοὶ δειλοῖσι βροτοῖσιν,
    ζώειν ἀχνυμένοις. αὐτοὶ δέ τ' ἀκηδέες εἰσίν.
    Iliad, XXIV. 524–6.

[3] *Aenëid*, VI. 721.

[4] *Odyssey*, XI. 488, Butcher and Lang's translation.

another, with a landless man who had no great livelihood,
than bear sway among all the dead that are no more."

All the great Latin poets died young; neither
Catullus nor Lucretius reached middle age, and
Virgil had barely passed it. He had attained the
age at which two other great poets died, who perhaps might best be linked with Virgil, at least
as regards the immediate and enduring dominion
which they acquired over the highest minds in
their own and subsequent ages, — the Athenian
Menander and our own Shakespeare. To the Englishman and the American especially, who, following a precedent already well established in the time
of Seneca, Petronius, and Juvenal, have made Virgil a text-book in every school, his poetry comes
appareled in the "celestial light" which illumines
the morning of life. Like "the smell of violets
hidden in the green," it —

> " Pours back into his empty soul and frame
> The times when he remembers to have been
> Joyful and free from blame."

A graceful eulogist of Virgil has spoken of —

> " the silent spells
> Held in those haunted syllables."

It is by the ghost of our childhood that they are
haunted, and the echoes of the old school quad-
rangle and the class-room, where we conned our
daily task. At a verse from the "Aeneïd," the
sun goes back for us on the dial; our boyhood is
recreated, and returns to us for a moment like a
visitant from a happy dreamland.

VI.

HORACE.

WHEN we come to Horace we come face to face
with that one of all the classical writers, in either

Comparative neglect of Horace in his own time.

prose or poetry, who may be said to have
endeared himself most to the modern
world, and perhaps especially to the
English-speaking portion of it. Virgil
and Horace in this respect present to us a somewhat singular contrast. We have seen that the
fame of Virgil was at once assured, even before
the appearance of his greatest poem ; that his contemporaries and his immediate successors regarded
him with the highest admiration and pride ; that no
one dared to raise his voice against the universal
acclaim till Niebuhr, in the beginning of this century, made invidious comparisons between him and
Homer ; and that since that time opinions about
his place in poetry have been to some extent divided. It is altogether otherwise with Horace.
Horace was no doubt admired by Augustus, Maecenas, and Pollio. In a subsequent age Petronius
Arbiter credited him with "a subtle happiness"
of expression (*curiosa felicitas*) ; and Persius said
of him that his satiric touch is so light that his
victims smile under his lash, while Juvenal couples
him with Virgil as being a text book in schools.

But we do not find that the critics of his own time
admitted him to that sacred Valhalla of Roman
poets of which Virgil was the acknowledged king.
Ovid calls him *numerosus*, or musical (Trist. IV.
8. 49) ; but in another passage (Art. Am. III. 333)
in which he enumerates and rapidly characterizes the great Latin poets, Virgil, Tibullus, Propertius, Gallus, Varro, we have not a word of Horace.
Velleius recognizes Catullus, Tibullus, Virgil, Ovid,
but never mentions Horace. Quintilian's estimate
of him is but moderate : " Of lyricists Horace is,
perhaps, the only one worth reading. He occasionally shows elevation (*insurgit aliquando*), has
plenty of sweetness and grace, and is most happily
daring in figures and expressions. If any dead
poet be coupled with him, it must be the late Caesius Bassus. But there are living lyricists far
greater than Bassus." If Quintilian thought it a
question whether Caesius Bassus, the friend and
editor of Persius, did not deserve to be placed beside Horace, while declaring that there were many
living lyricists far superior to Bassus, we can hardly
see how the end of the judgment can be understood except as a qualification of the beginning.
Indeed, to say of a lyric poet that he *occasionally
rises* is certainly to damn him with faint praise. I
doubt if there is a single recognition of Horace as
a Roman poet, and not merely a skillful versifier,
before the time of Fronto, who, writing to Marcus
Aurelius, calls him a *memorabilis poeta ;* and unfortunately *memorabilis* may mean " worthy of men

tion" as well as "distinguished," while there is nothing in the rest of the judgment to tell us in what
sense Fronto wished the epithet to be understood.
At all events the words are not such as would be
used of a poet who had long won securely his niche
in the temple of fame.

But to the modern world, down to this very
date, Horace is almost an idol. He has
forged a link of union between intel-
lects so diverse as those of Dante, Mon-
taigne, Bossuet, Lafontaine, and Voltaire, Hooker,
Chesterfield, Gibbon, Wordsworth, and Thackeray.
Mystic and atheist, scoffer and preacher, recluse
and leader of fashion have in Horace one subject on which they are sympathetic with each
other. Gibbon never traveled without a copy of
his poems in his pocket; Hooker fled with his
Horace to the fields from the reproaches of a railing wife; Thackeray is content if his hero, the
future man of the world, has enough Latin on leaving school " to quote Horace respectably through
life." Indeed, a certain *modicum* of Horace is
often the remnant of classic lore that the average
Englishman and Irishman care to carry with them
into the arena of active life. A fancied slight to
the memory of Horace is resented in England as a
personal insult, and a visit to Italy is nothing unless
you have done your duty to the shrine of the poet.
The letter of a correspondent in Milman's " Life of
Horace " tells us that at the present day English
travelers visit the site of the Sabine farm in such

His great
popularity
in modern
times.

numbers, and trace its features with such enthusiasm, that the resident peasantry believe Horace to
have been an Englishman, not being able to conceive any source of interest but compatriotism in
one so long dead, and nowhere to be found in the
calendar of saints. In an article which appeared
in the " Quarterly Review," some time ago, I put
forward some views about the relation of Horace to
his predecessors, and his sincerity as a love-poet,
which evoked in the London press several letters
from country gentlemen and others, who did not
even affect for the moment to discuss the truth of
the opinions propounded, but heaped abuse on the
writer of the article, who was, fortunately for himself, anonymous.

As I propose in this lecture to lay before you
some of these views, which I hold to be true, and
which I believe will be more interesting to you than a more orthodox treat- The sources
ment of the subject might be, I would of his attractiveness.
ask leave first to declare my belief that we owe
to Horace a precious store of pointed aphorisms
and shrewd comments on life, which, apart from
all controversies about his place in poetry, must
ever establish a kind of personal relation with his
reader, and must have a permanent (perhaps an
increasing) value for the world. His odes, moreover, as regards diction and metrification, are a
marvelously successful experiment. Whatever may
be thought about the meaning which underlies
them, their form is perfection itself, and they defy

imitation. No attempt to reproduce their effect
in Latin or in any other language has met with
even a moderate measure of success. Since Statius so completely failed to revive in his "Silvae"
the Horatian Sapphic and Alcaic, each new attempt to copy them has only added a new proof
that the mould in which they were made was shattered beyond all mending when it fell from the
hands of Horace.

We will now venture to approach some of those
questions which modern Horatiolatry regards as
blasphemous. I will confine myself in the main to
points on which I conceive the existing evidence
to have been to some extent overlooked or misapprehended.

"Horace," writes an excellent critic, the late Professor Sellar, in the "Encyclopaedia Bri-
tannica," "establishes a personal relation
with his reader, speaks to him as a personal
friend, tells the story of his life;" and again :—

Professor Sellar on Horace.

"From his Satires, which deal chiefly with the
manners and outward lives of men, we know him in
his relations to society and his ordinary moods; from
his Epistles, which deal more with the inner life,
we best understand his deepest convictions and
the practical side of his philosophy; while his Odes
have perpetuated the finest pleasure which he derived from art, nature, and the intercourse of life."

Are his writings really the artless and candid
expression of his personal feelings and experiences ? I think the answer to that question should

not be as unqualified as that given by Professor Sellar and the great majority of modern critics. While I recognize as just in the main the words in which the scholars of to-day broadly characterize the work of Horace, I cannot help feeling that there are some aspects of the question which have been almost entirely neglected. One of these is the relation of the poet towards his predecessors, and especially Lucilius. I think you will agree with me that the facts which I will put forward show that from this point of view the estimate of the nature of Horace's work must be considerably modified.[1]

Relation of Horace towards his predecessors.

Horace, like all the poets of his time, conceived it to be the function of his art either to reproduce in Latin the masterpieces of Greek literature, or to adapt to the taste of his own age the old poets of his own land. When he went to school at Rome, Orbilius, that ancient dominie whom the fame of his pupil has immortalized, made him learn Homer in the original Greek, and the translation of the "Odyssey" into Latin Saturnian verse by his fellow-countryman, Livius Andronicus. The course of the schoolboy's studies prefigured the two careers open to the man's literary aspirations. Horace might attempt either to reproduce for his Latin readers the poetry of Hellas, or to set in a modern and more musical key the rough notes already uttered by the Calabrian Muse.

[1] The references to Lucilius are to the edition of his fragments by L. Müller, Leipsic, 1872.

He did both, and fortunately for us he made a wise
choice in adopting his models in both cases. In
the one, instead of addressing· himself to Callimachus, Euphorion, and the Alexandrine school,
which so fascinated Catullus, Propertius, and even
Virgil, he went back in his Odes to the well-head
of Greek poetry, to Alcaeus, Alcman, and Archilochus ; in the other, he left Naevius and Livius to
be thumbed by schoolboys in their native uncouth-
ness, and turned his attention to the polishing of
the rude satire of Lucilius, in which he rightly detected an affinity to the Old Comedy which was
the crowning glory of the Attic stage. He found
in the Satires of Lucilius not only a rough-hewn
commentary on life and manners, but even literary
criticism, and easy-going descriptions of every-day
events, which only required some polishing and
refining to make them thoroughly acceptable to
the court of Augustus and the *salon* of Maecenas.

Horace com-
pared with
Pope.
In fact, Horace seems to have done for
Lucilius very much what Pope did for the
coarse tales of Chaucer, for the rough
philosophizing of Dr. Donne, and even for the Epistles of Horace himself. In the descriptive pieces
especially we recognize in the Latin satirist the
same art which enabled his English imitator to re-
commend Chaucer's tale of January and May to the
more refined susceptibilities of the court of Queen
Anne. Pope saw that some of the tales of Chaucer
were of such a character that they could be made
very pleasing and interesting to the court, but

that their almost unintelligible archaism as well as their coarseness of treatment would prevent their ever being much read in their original form. He accordingly wove out of the strong homespun of Chaucer and the frigid classicality of the eighteenth century a kind of showy stuff that suited well the

> " Teacup times of hood and hoop,
> And when the patch was worn."

Lucilius had merits and defects very similar to those found in Chaucer by Pope. He affords us instances of ruggedness and originality unique among the Roman poets. The fragments which time has spared to us certainly hardly bear the traces of that intellectual culture and moral breadth which are ascribed to him by the voice of antiquity. But we must remember that the Lucilian fragments have come down to us only to illustrate irregularities of diction and idiom, and they must have had excellent qualities : else how are we to account for the high estimate of them formed by Cicero, Juvenal, Tacitus, Quintilian, and Horace ?

Merits and defects of Lucilius.

In his moral essays Horace seems to have used Lucilius in the same way as he himself and the English satirist Donne were afterwards used by Pope ; while in his descriptive pieces Horace treated Lucilius as Pope treated Chaucer. When Pope makes George I. figure in his verses as Augustus, we feel that he is doing what no Englishman would have done, unless he

How used by Horace.

were trying to accommodate Horace to his own time. When he writes, —

"Our wives read Milton and our daughters plays,"

he is not describing his own times, but giving a modernized version of Horace, in which Augustus appears as George I. and Homer as Milton. Similarly we find that when Horace refers to the typical gladiator he uses the name of Pacideianus, the gladiator in Lucilius, whom (were he not engaged in a restoration of Lucilius) he would no more have thought of mentioning than a writer of a generation ago would have thought of naming Mendoza instead of Tom Sayers as the typical prize-fighter of his time.

Now and then we come on fragments of Lucilius showing clear traces of a narrative which ran parallel with that of Horace; and in these cases we see that the difference between the two is to be found just in the absence of those defects which Horace points out as the salient blots on the style of the old poet, — roughness of structure and diction, prolixity, and immoderate use of Greek words and phrases. Confirmation of this will be found in many of the passages which we shall compare, but it may be instructive here to adduce one clear instance of the correction, in the Horatian restoration, of each of these faults in the Lucilian original.

In a well-known passage Horace is inculcating that duty of moderating one's desires which

he so often preaches.　He ends with the remark :[1] —

> " Say you 've a million quarters on your floor:
> Your stomach is like mine : it holds no more."

(In my quotations from the Satires and Epistles I
nearly always give the excellent version of Conington.)　Quite similar is the argument as well as
the illustration in a fragment of Lucilius,[2] but the
concluding words corresponding to " you can't eat
more than I " are " aeque fruniscor ego ac tu,"
where *fruniscor* is an old form of *fruor* only to be
found in ante-classical Latin.

As a specimen of the prolixity of the old poet
we may refer to a fragment preserved by Porphyrion on Epist. I. 1. 73, where Horace refers very
briefly to a well-known apologue : —

> " I 'll give the fox's answer to the lion:
> ' I 'm frightened at those footsteps ; every track
> Leads to your home, but ne'er a one leads back.' "

In the Lucilian fragment [3] we have evidence that
the condition and looks of the lion were described,
and the perverse impulse which made the fox
approach the den, and then there was a regular
dialogue between the two beasts.

The tendency to use Greek expressions, when
Latin would have served the purpose just as well,
would receive illustration from most of the parallel passages in the two writers, but one will serve.

[1] *Sat.* I. 1. 45, 46.　　[2] XVIII. 3.　　[3] XXX. 80–87.

The familiar phrase, "sic me servavit Apollo," [1]
which concludes the episode of the bore encoun-
tered on the Sacred Way, no doubt had its origin
in the Lucilian τὸν δ' ἐξήρπαξεν Ἀπόλλων.

Before entering further into the question what
may be inferred from Lucilian echoes in
Horace, it will be necessary to remind
you of the way in which these fragments
have come down to us. They have not been preserved by the reverent hands of collectors of literary gems or pregnant aphorisms. They have been
handed down by grammarians who wished to pro-
vide their rules with examples and exceptions. The
old poets were used by them chiefly to illustrate
irregularities of expression, and it is quite possible
that this circumstance has led us to form an exaggerated conception of the roughness and uncouth-
ness of early Latin poetry. Except a few verses
quoted here and there by literary men of the world
like Cicero and Quintilian, we owe our knowledge
of Lucilius entirely to grammarians who wished
to illustrate an unusual gender, such as *palumbes*
masculine, a singular usage, as *rictus* applied to
human beings, or rare forms, like *manducari* (depo-
nent) and *comest* for *comedit*. It is to a passage
preserved by Nonius [2] to illustrate the last two
forms that we owe a fragment which
seems to show that the bore whom
Horace met on the Sacred Way, far
from being Propertius, as a French critic main-

Source of Lucilian fragments.

Probable Lucilian origin of Sat. I. 9.

---

[1] *Sat.* I. 9, *fin.*   [2] XXIII. 15.

tained, had no objective existence for Horace at
all, but was only a Lucilian bore *réchauffé*. The
fragment is,[1] —

> " Surprising his victim, in closest embrace
> He enfolds him, and browses all over his face," —

words which seem plainly to point to the importu-
nate effusiveness of one who would fain claim a far
closer intimacy than really existed; the more
clearly when we remember that the Satire begins
with words found together in Lucilius — *ibat forte*
is quoted from him by Nonius — and ends with
words which we meet in Lucilius in their Greek
dress.

By a similar chance the surviving fragments of
Lucilius present us here and there with
expressions which make it seem highly
probable that the celebrated account of
the journey to Brundisium — though no doubt the
journey was actually made by Horace in the company of Maecenas — is not a genuine record of
adventures which they actually met, but rather a
polished version of a piece in which Lucilius gave
a versified account of a journey from Rome to
Capua, and thence to the Straits of Messina. The
fragments have come to us solely from the grammarians, and nothing but the chance that they
contained some anomaly of diction or usage has

The journey to Brundi-sium.

---

[1] " Adsequitur neque opinantem, in caput insilit, ipsum
Commanducatur totum complexu' comestque."

Frag. IV. 42.

preserved them for us. They are, in my opinion,
enough to show that Horace took his idea of
writing a metrical itinerary from a similar performance on the part of the older poet, and introduced from it into his own account incidents which
are hardly likely to have occurred to two independent travelers.   Two different journeys might of
course have many features in common ; but some
coincidences are so minute that we cannot but believe that the later narrative adopted them from the
earlier.   To begin with, the same criticism on the
state of the roads is to be found in both, except
that the old poet describes their condition as *labo-
sum*,[1] and the later, characteristically avoiding the
archaism, as *factum corruptius imbre,* —

> " Made worse than ever by the recent rains."

Then, some quarrel or semi-humorous exchange
of scurrilities, like that between Sarmentus and
Messius Cicirrhus, is clearly indicated in Lucilius ;
but while Sarmentus compared his adversary to a
wild horse, the Lucilian *scurra* describes [2] his oppo-
nent more violently as a

> " Buck-tooth'd Bovillan with projecting tusk, —
> An Aethiop rhinoceros."

Of the " many retorts " of Cicirrhus lightly dis-
missed by Horace, there seem to have been some
on the part of his Lucilian prototype which would
much better have been suppressed ; but he, as well

[1] III. 10.   [2] III. 8.

as Cicirrhus, concluded with an allusion to the
meagre and puny figure of his adversary, much
more violent, however, in its expression, for "so
meagre and diminutive"[1] is the modified Horatian form of the vigorous Lucilian phrase, —

"A dead-alive sketch of an atomy."[2]

To make assurance double sure, an incident mentioned in the 85th verse of Horace's Satire (I. 5)
had its counterpart in Lucilius (III. 55), as we learn
from a note of Porphyrion on Sat. I. 6. 22, telling us that in old times skins of beasts were used
as bedclothes.   Finally, we have in the Lucilian
itinerary gritty bread, a town not to be expressed in
a hexameter verse, and *macros palumbes* corresponding to the *macros turdos* of Horace.   Surely Horace
took in hand the narrative of Lucilius, and, in describing a similar journey made by himself, introduced into it whatever incidents he found amusing
in the old poem, toning down roughness and archaism of expression, pruning redundancy, and omit-
ting the coarsest details.   Gibbon, in reference to
some of the episodes in this particular piece, asks,
not unnaturally, how could any man of taste reflect
on them the day after?   We may further feel a difficulty in the fact that, when Maecenas was going
on a mission of *haute politique,* he took no one
with him but literary men little conversant with
politics, and buffoons like Sarmentus and Cicirrhus.

[1] "Gracili tam tamque pusillo." — *Sat.* I. 5. 69.
[2] "Vix vivo homini ac monogrammo." — II. 20.

It would seem that these difficulties may fairly be met by the theory that the trivial — sometimes far from pleasing — incidents of the journey are merely survivals from the Lucilian poem, which Horace felt bound to introduce into his own with somewhat less startling realism, and that he omitted such actual circumstances of the tour and persons of the *entourage* as did not fall conveniently into the Lucilian framework.

In the dinner of Nasidienus did Horace describe an entertainment at which he was actually present, or did he merely refurbish a Lucilian account of a similar occasion?
The dinner of Nasidienus.
Horace, no doubt, may have been the guest of a rich and vulgar *parvenu*, but, if he was, so was Lucilius ; and the Lucilian host, like the Horatian, rubbed the table with a purple cloth (*gausape purpureo*), praised the fare which he had provided, claimed the honors of a discoverer in the science of gastronomy, and lectured his guests on the influence of the moon on articles of food. Moreover, as Horace and his fellow-guests found the dishes to have a strange and unfamiliar taste,[1]

> " For fish and fowl — in fact whate'er was placed
>   Before us — had, we found, a novel taste, "

so the goose served on the Lucilian table was fed on grass, not corn ; the endive was gathered from the roadside, and the cheese smelt of garlic, — the criticism on the dinner being the same, but the

[1] *Sat.* II. 8. 28.

details, as usual, fuller in the old poet. Chance
has not preserved for us any allusion to the down-
fall of the hangings ; but we have some commonplaces of consolation quite in the same vein as the
platitudes with which Nomentanus and Balatro affected to comfort Nasidienus under the disaster of
the descent of the awning on the table : " Life is but
a game of chance, let us take what we can get ; it
will be all the same in a hundred years."[1] Just
as Pope perceived that some of the tales of Chaucer might be made quite acceptable to the court
of Queen Anne, if unintelligible archaism and excessive coarseness were removed, so Horace saw
that the humor and keenness of observation which
made the Lucilian " Saturae " household words to
Cicero might still win their way pleasantly to the
molles auriculae of Augustan Rome, if modernized
and pruned of redundancy and pedantry.

It was not only in the descriptive pieces that
Horace reset and polished the uncut dia-   Horace's
monds of his rude predecessor. Some-   moral es-
times we find that the whole train of   says.
thought in one of his moralizing essays on man
is due to the elder poet. It is a singular accident — indeed, it almost amounts to a miracle
when we remember what was the vehicle of the
fragments — that chance should have sometimes
preserved for us several apparently consecutive
utterances of the old satirist, and that thus, in
some cases, beside the restored structure we can

[1] XIV. 10.

discern the traces of the original edifice. The
first Satire of Horace seems to be as clearly a modernized version of Lucilius as Pope's imitations
are modernized versions of Horace. Nonius, in
illustrating a meaning of *olim*, quotes a passage [1]
from Lucilius which shows that the latter, like
Horace, had adduced the ant as a type of fore-
sight. I have already referred to the passage in
which Horace drives home the Lucilian lesson that
enough is as good as a feast, using the same illustration, but banishing the obsolete verb *fruniscor.* The rest of the Satire deals with the insatia-
bleness of the fool,[2] the universal and excessive
pursuit of riches,[3] and the undue weight given to
property in the estimate of a man's worth.[4] All
these notes are, as we have seen, struck in the
fragments of Lucilius, and in both poets [5] the lesson is enforced by the instance of the punishment
of Tantalus.

Again, in the third Satire of the first book
there is reason to believe that the train of thought
is in the main Lucilian. Nonius, in proving the

[1] " *Sic* tu illos fructus quaeras adversa hieme olim
     Queis uti possis et delectare domi te." — XIX. 2.

[2] V. 48.

[3] " Rugosi passique senes eadem omnia quaerunt," a fragment handed down by Nonius as an example of *passus,* "dry."

[4] "Quantum habeas tantum ipse sies tantique habearis "
(V. 22), preserved by a scholiast on Juvenal III. 142, and
clearly the origin of " nil satis est, inquit, quia tanti quantum
habeas sis" (Horace, *Sat.* I. 1. 62).

[5] Hor. *Sat.* I. 1. 68; Luc. III. 59.

use of *differre* in the sense of "to be different
from," quotes a verse in which Lucilius uses
verrucae to point a moral, as Horace does in the
seventy-third verse of this Satire in recommending
mutual forbearance; and there are clear statements
in the "Saturae" of the Stoic paradox so familiar in
Horace, that the ideal wise man is master of every
art, not only beautiful, rich, and puissant, but
even the best cobbler.[1]   In touching on the same
theme of avarice in the second book of the Satires
(III. 155), we find that he has taken from Lucilius
(XXVIII. 33) the physician's warning to the
miser that he is killing himself to save the cost of
a basin of rice-gruel, and that in the fifth Satire of
the same book he has borrowed the visit of Ulysses
to Tiresias in the underworld (XXX. 113) to in-
quire how he is to amass wealth and repair the
inroads made on his fortune by the greedy suitors
of Penelope; and that the two poets agree in
making light of her fidelity to her absent spouse.
The favorite Horatian doctrine (*e. g.* Sat. II. 2. 129–
135), that we have no abiding city here, and that
the goods of fortune are but a loan to us, finds
characteristic expression in a fragment of Lucilius
(XXVII. 7) in which he says that he feels he has
only the use (*chresin*), not the possession of all that
is counted his.   And the celebrated passage in the
same Satire (II. 2. 28), the keynote of which is
"Cocto num adest honor idem?"—

[1] "Sarcinatorem esse summum, suere centonem optume."
XXVIII. 45.

> "What? Do you eat the feathers? When 't is drest
> And sent to table, does it still look best?" —

is obviously borrowed from the Lucilian

> "Cook cares not a jot for the gaudy tail, if the fowl be
> plump and fat."[1]

The Gallonius who points the moral is a Lucilian character, and we have in the fragments the fish "caught between the bridges" of Sat. II. 2. 32.[2] Even in the condemnation of undue admiration of the ancients, the Augustan satirist seems to have walked in the steps of the Republican, whom we find ridiculing a passage from the "Thyestes" of Ennius, and the monstrous compounds of Pacuvius.[3]

It is to be observed I do not dwell on mere coincidences of expression, which of course are frequent, but only on such coincidences as seem to show that certain pieces of the two poets had a common basis and frame, and proceeded from the same starting-point along the same lines to the same conclusion. Parallelism, even in the use of rare expressions, such as *cerebrosus* for "angry," and *sententia dia* for "a wise saw," do not, of course, add material support to our argument, except as showing a mind thoroughly imbued with the vocabulary of the "Saturae." But more

---

[1] "Cocu' non curat caudam insignem esse hilum dum pinguis siet." — XXVII. 12.

[2] "Pontes Tiberinu' duo inter captu' catillo."— *Incert.* 50.

[3] "Nerei repandirostrum incurvicervicum pecus."

significant is the employment by both of a far
from obvious figure. When Horace Example
writes ("De Arte Poetica," 431) that the of a figure
borrowed
wailing of a hired mourner at a funeral from Lu-
is often more expressive and affecting cilius.
than genuine grief, —

> "Hired mourners at a funeral say and do
>   A little more than they whose grief is true," —

he does not think it necessary, as a modern writer
would, to tell his readers that he did not conceive
the simile himself, but took it from the Lucilian
couplet, —

> "As hireling mourners o'er a bier with tearing of hair and
>   shrieks
>   Eclipse by art the heartfelt pain of woe that hardly
>   speaks." [1]

Nay, more : Horace in drawing upon Lucilius would
have claimed and received the praise of originality
as conceived by the Latin poets and critics, who
sincerely ascribed that quality to any writer who
selected a new model instead of merely producing
a new imitation of an already hackneyed masterpiece. Thus we find Plautus complaining that it
is hard to *find* a Greek play which enforces the
moral that honesty is the best policy, and in which
virtue triumphs in the end. The idea of construct-
ing such a plot does not seem even to have occurred to the Latin dramatist.

[1] "Ut mercede quae conductae flent alieno in funere
      Praeficae multo et capillos scindunt et clamant magis."
                                                            XXVII. 18.

It is not in the Satires only that Horace has ad-

dressed himself to the task of refurbish-
ing the work of his predecessor.   The
fourteenth Epistle of the first book is clearly a Lucilian restoration.   The Epistle professes to be addressed to his *vilicus*, or farm-bailiff, who, being
obliged to live in the country, longs for town.
Horace contrasts with this feeling his own preference for the country, and accounts for that preference by his sense of the immunity which rural
retirement enjoys from the besetting sins of envy,
hatred, and malice and all uncharitableness.   This
is not the kind of letter which we should have expected the poet to address to a common drudge
(*mediastinus*) ; nor was it ever meant to meet his
eyes : it was written to be admired by Maecenas
and his friends as a clever restoration of an an-
tique.   There is not a remarkable expression in the
letter which has not its origin in Lucilius ; and it
is very singular that the accident whereby grammarians have preserved for us several words and
phrases from the old piece should have revealed a
fact which would otherwise never have been suspected.   Horace tells his bailiff that there are
weeds of the mind as well as of the soil, and pro-
poses to try whether he or his bailiff will prove
the more successful weeder, the one in the moral
field, the other in the material : —

> " Let 's have a match in husbandry : we 'll try
> Which can do weeding better, you or I."

Now Nonius, in illustrating a strange use of the verb *stare*, quotes from Lucilius a phrase, —

"My soul 's thick-set with thorns," [1]

which strikes the dominant chord of the piece. Further, each writer [2] describes his mind as chafing against the restraints of the body, and longing to burst its barriers and be away. Lucilius [3] sighs for a sphere in which he is not "given a squint" (*strabonem fieri*) by looking askance at the blessings of his neighbors. Horace says that in the country no one looks askance at (*obliquo oculo limat*) the good things of others, and that that is the reason why he likes it better than the town. Horace declares that the "savage wilds" (*inhospita tesca*), as some people call them, are charming to him ; Lucilius says that as he roams through the "savage wilds," using the very same words, all his imaginings take on a new grace and charm. It can hardly be questioned that we have in this case a clear Lucilian basis for a Horatian piece ; and that Horace did little more than soften down the asperities of the earlier poem, and give it an imaginary connection with his own daily life. [4]

---

[1] "Stat sentibu' pectus." — V. 4.

[2] Hor. *Epist.* I. 14. 69 ; Luc. V. 2, 3.

[3] XXVII. 8.

[4] A very curious parallel in our own literature to the Horatian use of the raw material of Lucilius has lately been brought to light by a letter of Mr. Walter Skeat to the *Athenæum* of August 8, 1891, in which he shows that Shakespeare, in the famous soliloquy of Hamlet, "To be or not to

In the Epodes and Odes the models of Horace
The Epodes and Odes. were nearly altogether Greek, but we come occasionally on a figure of speech or fancy which does not suggest a Hellenic origin. Goethe once complained of the " fearful realism " of Horace, and we certainly have some examples of this in the Odes, where it would seem most out of place. Perhaps one of the most tasteless efforts of fancy in these poems is the comparison between the insatiable desire of riches and the unquenchable thirst of dropsy,[1] and it can hardly have had a Greek source. If he did not take the idea from Lucilius, it is certainly a curious coincidence that that poet, with whose works he was so familiar, should have said that a covetous person had a "spiritual dropsy." [2] Probably enough, many of the expressions of Horace which have been condemned by modern taste as unsuitable to lyric poetry would be found to be due to Lucilius and the old Latin literature, though chance has not disclosed their origin. This would account for such strange deviations from the lyric manner as Horace makes when in an Alcaic ode he calls his she-goats " wives of a foetid spouse ; " [3] sings of "long-eared oaks," [4] and " the lust that drives

be " (Act III. Sc. 1), adopted largely the train of thought of a long passage in the *Romaunt of the Rose*, and even borrowed some of the expressions.

[1] " Crescit indulgens sibi dirus hydrops." — *Carm.* II. 2. 13.
[2] "Aquam te in animo habere intercutem." — XXVIII. 27.
[3] " Olentis uxores mariti." — *Carm.* I. 17. 7.
[4] " Auritas quercus." — *Carm.* I. 12. 11.

mad the horses' dams ; "[1] or pictures Venus as
"snuffing up the incense ; "[2] and Doom, with her
paraphernalia of huge nails, wedges, clamps, and
molten lead.[8]   Probably if we had more numerous
fragments from the works of Lucilius, or if they
had come down to us in a *florilegium*, like that in
which Stobaeus preserved so many of the gems of
Euripides, we should find that the Epodes owed a
great deal to the old poet.   At present we cannot
find in them any trace of Lucilius, except a line
preserved to illustrate the meaning of *sudum* as applied to "fair weather,"[4] which recalls the clearly
insincere execrations hurled on the departing Mae-
vius in Epode X.

Many different views have been taken of the
nature of the Odes and the relation of
that portion of Horace's work to the
rest.   Diametrically opposite theories
have been propounded.   Between the *dictum* of
Gruppe, "Horace is Horace only in his Odes,"
and that of Lehrs, "the real Horace is never
found in his Odes," almost every intervening
shade of opinion has found defenders.   Dr. Ver-
rall, in his highly ingenious "Studies in the Odes
of Horace," sees in them the most pointed yet
covert allusion to obscure incidents in the private
history of the Augustan court, its supporters and

Divergent views about the Odes.

---

[1] "Quae solet matres furiare equorum." — *Carm.* I. 25. 13.
[2] *Carm.* IV. 1. 21.   [8] *Carm.* I. 35. 17.
[4] "Nec ventorum flamina flando suda secundent."
XXIX. 102.

its assailants, and the secret intrigues which threat-
ened the yet unstable throne of the Emperor.
Others, like Sir Theodore Martin, are content to
dwell on "the consummate grace and finish of the
Odes," and to regard them only as the passing expressions of varying phases of artistic feeling, but
not conveying, at least in the love-songs, the sincere sentiment of the writer.   The most recent of
the critics of Horace, whose views I will put before you anon, sees in them nothing but mere exercises in the handling of the Greek metres.   But
in one judgment all must agree : good or bad, real
or artificial, they have defied imitation.   No attempt to reproduce their effect has had even a
moderate measure of success.

A consideration which seems to me to have
been hardly sufficiently taken into account by the many critics of the Odes
is the fact that Horace looked on himself as a
restorer, — as one whose task it was to clothe
the beauties of Greek lyric poetry in a Latin
garb.   Keeping this view before us, we may doubt
the objective reality of the incident related in
the fourth Ode of the third book, how the wood-
pigeons that draw the car of Venus found the
child poet, destined to be the singer of Love,
asleep on the hillside, weary and drowsy after his
play, and covered him with leaves to protect him
from the snakes and wild beasts.   There is little doubt that both here and also in a much less
fanciful passage, when he tells how he joined in

Imaginary incidents.

the flight at Philippi, ingloriously leaving behind
him his shield, he is merely introducing, as in duty
bound, into the life of the Roman lyrist the legends connected with the masters of the Greek
lyre. If divine protection was vouchsafed to the
infancy of Pindar, Stesichorus, and Aeschylus,
surely the Muses of Calabria must have been
equally careful of the tender age of the Roman
lyrist; and if Alcaeus, Archilochus, and Ana-
creon fled weaponless from the field of battle, why
should Horace fail to make in his own case a similar confession? There was no fear that it would
be understood literally. The very Pompeius, to
whom he addressed that confession, had often
borne the brunt of battle beside him in the campaign under Brutus. He would no more take in
its literal sense the self-accusation of cowardice
than the immediately succeeding boast that Mercury carried the poet unhurt through the foe, like
the favorites of the gods in Homer, wrapped in a
dense cloud.

When Maecenas presented Horace with his Sabine farm he conferred on him the very Horace's
gift which was most suitable to the poet's Sabine farm
a welcome
requirements and desires. He tells us present.
himself how the first fig is the signal for the under-
taker's train to appear in the streets of Rome,[1] and
how the leaden breath of Auster then gives an unmistakable signal to city folk to seek the seaside or

[1] " Ficus prima calorque
Designatorem decorat lictoribus atris." — *Epist.* I. 7. 5.

the Latin or Sabine hills. Horace seems generally
to have managed to turn the head of his little mule
towards the country in the malarious months, sometimes going so far as Tibur or Tarentum, which he
tells us [1] were his favorite resorts. But it was not
until he experienced the generosity of Maecenas
that he ever left Rome, save at seasons when it
was an imperative necessity to go. It was this very
intimacy with Maecenas which made a rural retreat absolutely indispensable. Juvenal maintains
that ease of circumstances and material comfort and
luxury are essential conditions of success in the
poet's art. If Virgil had had nothing better than
water to drink, all the snakes would have fallen from
the viperous tresses of Allecto. But Horace was an
exception to his rule. He tells us that it was the
boldness inspired by stern necessity which drove
him to poetry. As long as he was the poor hack
whom poverty had driven to literature he could
call his time his own, even in Rome ; but as the
friend of Maecenas, privacy became for him impossible. We read again and again how he was
besieged by politicians, literary aspirants, even pro-

[1] " Tibur Argeo positum colono
    Sit meae sedes utinam senectae,
    Sit modus lasso maris et viarum
        Militiaeque.

" Unde si Parcae prohibent iniquae
    Dulce pellitis ovibus Galaesi
    Flumen et regnata petam Laconi
        Rura Phalantho." — *Carm.* II. 6. 5–12.

fessional newsmongers and diners-out, for information direct from the fountain-head of policy and
fashion; and how men shook their heads, and
admired his profound reserve, when he told them
that he was not the depositary of the secrets of
Augustus and Maecenas. There was no secure
leisure in Rome for the intimate of Maecenas, and
no real work could be undertaken unless there
were a refuge to which to fly. When Maecenas
conferred on him a farm in the Sabine hills, about
thirty miles, or a day's journey, from Rome, he
gave the poet what was not only a luxury but a
necessity.

But Horace was not a lover of the country for
its own sake. It is to him delightful **But Horace**
only as a retreat from the worries of **was not a lover of the**
town, and when he is most enthusiastic **country.**
in the praises of his life in the country we find that
the pleasures on which he dwells most are those
which belong more fitly to town. " O noctes ce-
naeque Deûm !"[1] is his exclamation when he
thinks, not of the entertainments of Maecenas and
Pollio, but of the dinners in his Sabine farm, where
the local notabilities sat round his plain but plentiful table and discussed, not art or scandal, but philosophy and the conduct of life, garnishing their
discourse with homely but appropriate "old saws
and modern instances." In the Odes, where especially we should expect to find genuine love of Nature if any such feeling were his, he alludes to

[1] *Sat.* II. 6. 65.

Nature, not to express his aesthetic pleasure in
her various moods, but to point his philosophic
maxims.   The changes of the weather and the
courses of the seasons are described only to introduce the reflection that our hopes, too, and our
fears, have for their objects only that which is
mutable, and our griefs as well as our joys should
be moderate and brief.   His Odes breathe a spirit
which recalls to us the sad smile of the Persian
Omar Khayyám, —

> "What boots it to repeat
> How time is slipping underneath our feet?
> Unborn to-morrow and dead yesterday, —
> Why fret about them if to-day be sweet?"

In one of the prettiest of them we read how the
heavy and gloomy pine, and the light poplar white
in the wind, love with their wedded boughs to
make a friendly shade, while the prattling brook
frets in its haste down its winding channel.   But
why this pretty picture?   To remind us that,
though now Nature smiles on us, death will soon
be on us all, both high and low.   Peace of mind
is to be gained neither by seeking rural scenes
nor by crossing wide seas.   Man carries happiness
and unhappiness with him wherever he goes, and
cannot fly from himself though he leave his fatherland far behind him.   His allusions to Nature do
not arise, I repeat, from any love of Nature, or
sympathetic observation of her various moods, but
from a desire to point philosophic reflections and
aphorisms.   Indeed, that very poem which of all

that Horace has written enters with most zest
into the delights of country life is, rightly viewed, a
clear proof of the poet's insensibility to these pleasures. It is nothing but an elaborate piece of ridicule directed against those who then were prone,
as some are now, to become ecstatic about the
country, though quite unqualified to appreciate its
charm sincerely. In the best of his Epodes, the
second, the work of his ardent youth, we have a
glorification of rural life which enters into every
detail of its joys with an enthusiasm hardly less
than that which inspires Virgil in the Georgics
and Eclogues. It is only after sixty-six verses of
high-wrought sentiment that we discover that the
speaker is not Horace but the usurer Alfius, and
that the moral of the poem is, that speculative enthusiasm has very little chance against a ruling
passion of a practical kind, and that many praise
the country who would be very unfit and very loth
to live in it. The best parallel one can recall to the
sustained irony of the Epode is the piece in which
Calverley describes the city clerk who left the
heat and noise and brass bands of Camden Hill to
enjoy his well-earned holiday. We read how he
laughed when he felt the cool breeze fanning his
cheek and the salt spray on his lip, and when
all the sights and sounds and fragrances of the
country, described with Horatian skill, were wafted
to him ; then how, when he remembered the dusty
streets he had left, —

> " At the thought
> He laughed again, and softly drew
>   That ' Morning Herald,' that he 'd bought,
>   Forth from his breast, and read it through."

There is not in literature a more musical or a more insincere glorification of the country ; and it differs from the spirit of many of his Odes only in this, — that here the poet shows his hand, and lets us see that he is laughing at what we should now call the Lake school of poets and their admirers.

It is with some diffidence that I have ventured to put forward some considerations, which, if they do not seem to convict Horace of a certain degree of insincerity, at all events would tend to show him as a mere restorer where he has been held to be a creator, and a literary *poseur* where he has been thought to be a poetical exponent of his real feelings. But for one department of his work it would be idle to claim the merit of sincerity. Even his warmest admirers have detected a false ring in his odes of love. Sir Theodore Martin writes : " His deepest feeling is but a ferment of the blood ; it is never the all-absorbing devotion of the heart." The most recent Continental criticism goes much further in the way of skepticism about the genuineness of his expressed feelings. In connection with it let us examine some curious features in the lyric poetry of Horace.

No reader of the Odes, however careless, can have failed to notice the extraordinary difficulty

Insincerity of his love poems.

of discovering in them anything like a connected train of thought. One may safely say that hitherto there has been no even moderately successful attempt to meet this difficulty. Bentley's method was, as might be expected, to have recourse to wholesale correction of the text. But his ingenuity addressed itself mainly to difficulties of expression and construction, and indeed hardly a correction of his is now accepted in constituting the text of the Odes. Peerlkamp, the most Bentleian of Bentley's successors, devel- *Peerlkamp.* oping the principle of his master, boldly declares : "I do not accept as the work of Horace anything but what is so exquisitely perfect that you cannot change it without spoiling it." The result is, that there is hardly an Ode in which Peerlkamp does not detect corruption and interpolation, hardly one in which he does not resort to emendation, excision, and transposition. The slightest deviation from the most exquisite taste, from the most natural and logical march of thought, from the most flawless accuracy and beauty of expression, is to him a complete proof that the offending passage could not have come from the hand of Horace. Goethe, going to the opposite extreme, held hardly anything to be unworthy of *Goethe.* Horace, to whom he denied all poetic gifts, unless deftness in the use of language, and skill in reproducing the Greek metres, could be so de- scribed. Hartman goes nearly as far as *Hartman.* the great German poet and critic. He regards the

Odes simply as exercises in metre, and thinks that
Horace did not trouble himself about consecutive-
ness of thought, provided the verses flowed
smoothly, and that he was always ready to surren-
der ease of transition and even correctness of expression, when the exigencies of his dainty metres
demanded the sacrifice. And truly in some cases
he has much to say for his theory. When we read
how "Virtue will refuse the name of *happy* to
kings, and will give (not the name of *happy*, but)
the kingly throne and diadem to him who, without
turning to gaze again, can look on huge heaps," [1]
we cannot help asking ourselves whether the poet
has really said what he wished to say. Heaps of
what? Of treasures, of course, say the commentators. But Horace has not written "heaps of
treasures," he has only written "heaps." Then,
Virtue, having refused the name of *happy* to kings,
grants that of *king* to him who has subdued cov-
etousness; and "eye unturned-back" is certainly
far from clear. Peerlkamp rewrites the stanza, inserting *auri;* the English commentators translate
as if Horace had written *auri acervos*, but leave the
words untouched. Hartman says Horace would
gladly have written *thesauros*, but unfortunately it
would not scan. It is this subservience of expression to metre which so often reminds us of the
work of the Irish Melodist, who is so much more
careful of the sound than of the sense.

[1] " Quisquis ingentes oculo irretorto
      Spectat acervos."— *Carm.* II. 2. 24.

" Fill the bumper fair !
  Every drop we sprinkle
 O'er the brow of care
  Smoothes away a wrinkle,"

runs very trippingly on the tongue, but *fair* is
a very poor epithet for a bumper, and *sprinkle* is
almost without meaning.

In point of fact, there would have been more to
excite our surprise if Horace had really Horace's
succeeded in producing genuine poetry attitude
towards
rather than exquisitely musical *vers de* poetry.
société, when we consider his own account of the
spirit in which he approached his task. He has
told us candidly that it was his poverty and not
his will which consented ; that he would look on
himself as an incurable lunatic if he would not
rather be asleep than writing verses, unless compelled thereto by the spur of actual want ; [1] and
he quotes the case of the soldier of Lucullus,
who could do prodigies of valor when destitute,
but declined to take any further trouble when he
no longer had his living to get. Horace does not
compare himself to a melodious nightingale or

[1] " Decisis humilem pennis inopemque paterni
     Et Laris et fundi paupertas impulit audax
     Ut versus facerem ; sed quod non desit habentem
     Quae poterunt unquam satis expurgare cicutae
     Ni melius dormire putem quam scribere versus ? "
                              Epist. II. 2. 50–54.

soaring lark ; he is, he tells us,[1] an industrious bee, and with infinite toil he fashions elaborate strains. He is not of those who can say, —

> " I do but sing because I must,
>   And pipe but as the linnets sing."

He is of those who sing for their supper. And what was his earliest song ? His own boast was that in his Epodes he gave to his fellow-countrymen a specimen of the vigor and versification of Archilochus, though he had not the materials or the motive of him whose lampoons drove Lycambes mad.[2] Hence we have in the fourth Epode a furious tirade against — nobody ! At least, nobody is mentioned by the lampooner, and not even the ancient scholiasts could identify the object of this *brutum fulmen*. It is to show how angry he could be if he were angry, — how he could tear in pieces a passion completely provided with every requisite save an object. It is —

> " A tale
> Told by an idiot, full of sound and fury,
>   Signifying nothing."

[1] " Ego apis Matinae
More modoque
Grata carpentis thyma per laborem
Plurimum circa nemus uvidique
Tiburis ripas operosa parvus
Carmina fingo." — *Carm.* IV. 2. 27-32.

[2] " Numeros animosque secutus
Archilochi, non res et agentia verba Lycamben."
Epist. I. 19. 25.

Pretty nearly the same account may be given of
the sixth Epode, in which, after heaping abuse on
some unknown offender, he bids him take care lest
he bring on himself the terrors of his (the poet's)
tongue, — "Venomous liar, fool, coward, hound,
look out, or I shall call you names!" We have already seen some reasons to believe that the tenth
Epode is no more than a Lucilian restoration; but,
whatever it is, it carries its insincerity on its face.
It is probably a Lucilian piece re-dressed in the
metre of Archilochus. In the Odes, too, we cannot help observing not only the prevailing shallowness of the sentiment, but an occa- Incorrect
sional sacrifice of correctness of expres- expressions
in the Odes.
sion when the metre, which is never
anything but absolute perfection, proves too ex-
acting. What is the meaning of to "join Libya
to the distant Gades"?[1] Surely, "to unite Africa
to Spain by a bridge." But what the writer meant
was, " to hold sway over both countries conjointly."
"This is the birthday of Maecenas" is expressed
by words which should mean "from this day forth
Maecenas revises the calendar."[2] In Carm. III.
8. 15,[3] what he intends to say is, "Keep the lamps
alight till dawn;" but Peerlkamp rightly contends

---

[1] " Libyam remotis | Gadibus jungas."— *Carm.* II. 2. 10.
[2] " Ex hac
Luce Maecenas meus affluentes
Ordinat annos." — *Carm.* IV. 11. 18.
[3] " Vigiles lucernas
Perfer in lucem."

that what we now read means "Endure (the glare
or smell of) the lamps until dawn."   "Neither Fa-
lernian vines nor Formian hills temper my cups"[1]
is as odd a fashion as could be devised of expressing the sentiment, "The wine I drink with water
is not of an expensive vintage."   Carm. II. 20,[2]
supplies a stanza which will compel each editor to
declare himself .a follower of Peerlkamp's or of
Goethe's method of criticism.   Every reader of
taste must be offended by the verse in which, after
comparing himself to a soaring bird, he goes on to
describe how the skin is shrinking and roughening
on his legs, and pursues the details of an actual
transformation into a winged creature.   "Furcht-
baren Realität!" exclaims the follower of Goethe.
"Horatio plane abjudicandum" is the verdict of
the disciple of Peerlkamp.   "An exercise in
metre," says Hartman, "and the metre is perfect."

The fifth Ode of the second book [3] contains figures and expressions which do not quite
conform to modern standards of taste,
but it would be a charming little piece
were it not for the last two stanzas.   Nothing

Examples
of uncer-
tain touch.

[1] "Mea nec Falernae
      Temperant vites neque Formiani
          Pocula colles." — *Carm.* I. 20, 10.
[2] "Jam jam residunt cruribus asperae
      Pelles, et album mutor in alitem
          Superne, nascunturque leves
              Per digitos humerosque plumae."
[3] "Nondum subacta ferre jugum valet," etc.

could be prettier than the comparison of the girl
Lalage, too young to be a wife, to a playful
heifer, or a cluster of grapes still unripe. The
too eager lover is assured that the years ripen-
ing Lalage will gallop for her and creep for him;
she will soon be old enough, and he will not be too
old. Lalage will presently be wooing him, and
the happy lover will meet her advances with a passion " greater than he felt for the shy Pholoë,
or Chloris, who is as brilliant as moonlight on the
sea, or as Gyges, who would be mistaken for a girl."
What a bathos! After sketching with a few exquisite touches the *piquante* unripeness of the girl,
he goes on to say: "When she is old enough for
you you will love her — better than shy Pholoë or
Chloris," comparing the latter to the moon, and to
Gyges, to whom he then devotes an elaborate
stanza. The runnel is exquisitely smooth, but its
shallow waters flow where they will, from their
natural channel, and end in a puddle.

The theory that the Odes are little more than
experiments in the Greek lyric metres, Type-
having little or no train of connected hunting
expounders
thought or feeling, becomes very tempt- of Horace.
ing when we consider the straits to which commentators have been reduced by their determina-
tion never to admit that Horace wrote mere *vers
de société*, or dashed off little *vignettes* in verse, intended only to show his felicity in the choice of
words, and his rare deftness in handling the metres
newly imported from ancient Hellas. That school

of expounders of the Old Testament, who insist on
finding symbolism even in the candlestick and "his
knops" in Leviticus, have not shown more ill-placed
industry than has been expended on the well-known
poem beginning, —

> " O navis referent in mare te novi
>   Fluctus," [1] —

in which Horace warns the bark which has just es-
caped the storm to put back into port : the wind is
rising again ; it cannot live in the sea, which is ever
growing angrier.   The bark, according to the type-
hunting editors,[2] is the Ship of the State.   The
masts, the sails, the Cyclades, the Pontic pine —
everything must be symbolical, and have its exact
counterpart in the thing symbolized.   His best
poems are really *vers de société*, or little *vignettes*
in verse, but the noble army of public school Hora-
tiolaters will not hear of such expressions, and the
ponderous German commentators play into their
hands.   For instance, one commentator suggests
that the *Pontic* pine points to Sextus Pompeius,
whose father was the conqueror of Mithridates
of *Pontus*.   He sees in every chance expression
more significance than Mr. Puff imported into
Lord Burleigh's nod in " The Critic."   " *Pontica
pinus !* " he cries ; " ah, there we have the clue.
Mithridates was king of Pontus ; Pompey the
Great conquered Mithridates ; the *Pontica pinus*
therefore refers to Pompey's son Sextus."   The

---

[1] *Carm.* I. 14.   [2] See Quintil. VIII. 6. 44.

meaning of the Ode, therefore, according to his
theory, is that Sextus Pompeius must not again
embark in a war with Octavian after the treaty of
Misenum, B. C. 39. As well might we discern in
the mention of a "Damask blade" an allusion to
the Crusades. Pontus was the traditional source
of timber for ship-building, as we learn from a
poem of Catullus,[1] and the Cyclades are proverbial
as presenting difficulties of navigation. Horace no
more had in his mind the Mithridatic wars when
he wrote *Pontica pinus* than Tennyson thought
of the Wars of the Roses when he wrote in "The
Talking Oak," —

> " She left the novel half uncut
> Upon the rosewood shelf."

On the same principle the next Ode, —

> " Pastor cum traheret per freta navibus," —

is by some maintained to be an elaborate allegory
of Antony and Cleopatra. Ritter draws the parallel in the minutest detail. Paris hidden by Venus
in Helen's chamber is Antony taking refuge in
Cleopatra's ship at Actium, and so forth. The
scholiast tells us that he is imitating Bacchylides
in this poem. Whether this be so or not, it is certainly remarkable that the Grecian heroes, with
whose prowess Nereus terrifies Paris as he flies
with Helen, are not those who were foremost in
the Achaean ranks ; not those who in the ancient
myths are said to have met the adulterer in com·

[1] *Dedicatio Phaseli*, IV. 13.

bat, to have put him to flight, or finally to have slain him; not Menelaus or Philoctetes; but — such heroes as have names which fit the Asclepiads in which the piece is written — Ajax the son of Oïleus, Laertiades, Nestor, Teucer, Sthenelus, Meriones, Tydides. It can hardly be a mere coincidence that we find Horace in another poem,[1] closely akin to this in subject, adducing, not the prominent heroes in both hosts, but Teucer, Idomeneus, Sthenelus, on the Grecian side; while from the Trojans no champion save Hector is named, but the metrically convenient Deiphobus.

It cannot be denied that Hartman's view of the nature and genesis of Horace's lyric poetry, based as it is on the massive authority of Goethe, accounts for a good many qualities in the Odes which it is hard to explain on any other hypothesis. To succeed in concealing the art which was requisite to accommodate the Latin language to a metre so *exigeant* as the Asclepiad, the Sapphic, or the Alcaic in the hands of Horace, it was often necessary to sacrifice the sense to the sound, to introduce superfluous tags, to omit a word essential to the meaning. Of the last defect we have had an instance above, where we have seen that the poet could only find room for "heaps," when "heaps of gold," or some such phrase, was demanded by the sense of the passage; and surely Horace was struggling in the shackles of his metre when, in warning Pollio how difficult and delicate was the

[1] *Carm.* IV. 9.

task of writing a history of the Civil War, he tells him that he is walking on treacherous ashes which conceal a fire beneath.[1] This ought in fitness of language to convey the sense that the task which Pollio essayed, though it looked easy and safe, was really dangerous and difficult; but this is plainly not his meaning, for the dangers and difficulties of writing the history of a recent civil war are obvious and unmistakable, and Horace has already dwelt on them in this poem. Indeed, any new theory, however daring, would be acceptable, if it were only to account for those extraordinary parenthetic accretions which disfigure some of the finest Odes, notably the fourth of the fourth book, which begins with such spirit with the words, —

"Qualem ministrum fulminis alitem," —

and in which the verses 18–22 [2] seem to be added by the poet in mockery of the art to which his poverty drove him, and which he considers it would be lunacy to practice if one could afford to be idle.

We have already referred to the ring of insincerity in the love poems of Horace, the false note

[1] " Incedis per ignes
Suppositos cineri doloso." — *Carm.* II, 1. 7, 8.
[2] " Quibus
Mos unde deductus per omne
  Tempus Amazonia securi
Dextras obarmet quaerere distuli,
Nec scire fas est omnia."

which sounds so cracked and thin amid the sighs
of Propertius and the groans of Catullus.

Further ex-
amples of
insincerity
in the love
poems.

He is merely playing the lover because a
lyric poet ought to be in love, and sometimes he misrepresents almost ludicrously
the signs of a real passion. " It is only three years
ago that I was mad about Inachia," he tells Pettius
in the eleventh Epode, " and here I am in love
again." Three years! Three days without love is
a lifetime to the real lover : —

" So thou hast come at last! Thrice night has followed the
    day.
  Three days longing! And one were enough to leave me
    gray ! " [1]

In another love-ditty (Epode XIV.) he tells Maecenas that he cannot write poetry because he is
in love — a strange reason — with Phryne, who,
however, is not satisfied with him alone, and has
other admirers ; but this does not seem to disturb
our philosophic lover, and only leads him to congratulate Maecenas on the greater happiness of his
lot because the girl he loves is — faithful to him
alone? No, because she is so very pretty. What!
Was Phryne, then, plain as well as faithless ? We
do not know; her lover seems to have forgotten
all about her before he finished the Epode, just
as he forgot all about Lalage when he began to
think of Chloris and Gyges. Then how sweetly

---

[1] ἤλυθες, ὦ φίλε κῶρε, τρίτᾳ σὺν νυκτὶ καὶ ἀοῖ.
ἤλυθες· οἱ δὲ ποθεῦντες ἐν ἤματι γηράσκοντ..
Theocr. XII. 1, 2.

but uncharacteristically reasonable is the lover who
bids his servant summon the charming Neaera in
all haste![1] adding, however : "If there is any difficulty about her coming, never mind ; return without her." In somewhat the same spirit Mercury
is summoned[2] to bring the magic of his lyre to
win the obdurate ear of Lyde ; but so little does
the lover really care about the success of his suit
that he fills a long Ode with the recital of the miracles music can work, telling how it can beguile the
pain even of the sufferers in the underworld, Ixion,
Tityus, and the Danaids, whose entirely irrelevant
story he tells with great command of language and
metre, but very little reference to Lyde.

Indeed, for this particular department of his
work it would be idle to claim sincerity, and even
his stanchest champions have abandoned the attempt. His love songs are bright, scentless flowers which charm the eye, but do not carry to the
heart that message of memory and association
with which the perfume of flowers is charged.
They are not wildwood violets hidden in the green,
but hothouse orchids or azaleas displayed in a *par-
terre*. One thinks for a moment that for Cinara he
had a genuine love in his young days, until we find
him boasting in middle age that he had found fa-

---

[1] " Dic et argutae properet Neaerae
    Murrheum nodo cohibere crinem:
    Si per invisum mora janitorem
        Fiet, abito." — *Carm.* III. 14. 21.
[2] *Carm.* III. 11.

vor in her eyes without pecuniary gifts, "insatiable as she was." His Odes afford no reason why we should believe that he was ever in love. Even such an advocate for Horace as the late Professor Sellar admits that his *liaisons* with the Leuconoës and Neobules of his Odes, whether they are of the *Dichtung* or of the *Wahrheit* of his life, seem to be as much inspired by an interest in human nature as by any more ardent feeling, and that his tone is more that of persiflage than of either passion or sentiment ; that in his lampoons the feeling was sometimes that of the imitative artist rather than the man ; and that even in his maturest art the thought is often obvious and commonplace. In his Odes Horace thought chiefly about felicity of expression, and deftness in the handling of new and dainty metres, and, provided the verses flowed smoothly and the phraseology showed his *curiosa felicitas*, did not much trouble himself whether the train of ideas was consecutive, or indeed whether there was any regular march of thought at all.

Horace as a literary critic is often instructive, and always highly suggestive, but is occasionally a very unsafe guide. His view of the function of the Greek chorus is perhaps not more inadequate than might have been expected in his day. But a not very deep study of the Greek drama might have shown him that the *Deus ex machina* in many of the plays of Euripides (notably the "Bacchae") has no knot

Horace as a literary critic.

whatever to untie by his intervention, the action being completed before the god appears. Some of his comments on the moral purport of the "Bacchae" would seem to show that he had never read the play; and it naturally struck Macaulay, a great admirer of Horace, as remarkable that he should have mentioned Aeschylus only as the introducer of certain mechanical improvements in stage properties. Professor Jebb (" Classical Greek Poetry," p. 43) makes an interesting comment on his conception of the character of Achilles. " Modern readers have too often taken their idea of the Homeric Achilles from the misleading summary of his character by Horace, ' Let him deny that laws were made for him, and acknowledge no umpire but the sword.' The very keynote in the character of the Homeric Achilles is his burning indignation at a wrong, at a gross breach of justice; he does not represent the sword as against right, but right as against tyranny." Finally, Horace tells us that Homer put before us in the person of Ulysses an example of what virtue and wisdom could do, and especially refers to the episode of Circe. Horace contrasts the greediness of the crew with the self-restraint of Ulysses. But in the incident as described in the Odyssey neither the praise nor the blame finds any countenance. The companions of Ulysses follow the universal practice in accepting the hospitality offered to strangers, the fatal consequences of which they could have no ground for suspecting. Ulysses is preserved from their fate, not by any self-command on his own part, but by a previous divine warning and a special antidote which had not been vouchsafed to the rest. To ascribe a didactic purpose to the Odyssey — except in so far as any series of adventures admirably told may imply a lesson though the narrator is unconscious of it — is to misconceive completely the character of the poem.

I have dwelt chiefly on the limitations of Horace's art because they are so much less obvious than his excellences, which are easily recognized and more likely to be exaggerated than unduly depreciated.

Chief source of his popularity with the modern world.

The gaiety of his spirit and the music of his lyrics will ever fascinate the young; his shrewd common sense will attract the man of the world, whatever be his time of life, his country, or his epoch ; and he will always be the most perfect exponent of the actual life and movement of the Augustan age. But may we not detect in him some more special and individual quality of character which has endeared him so universally to gentlemen of every race and every period, so that one can hardly conceive the time when Horace will have ceased to form part of the mental furniture of, at all events, every English-speaking gentleman ? I think the quality is not hard to find. It is that Horace was essentially a gentleman himself. Lord Shaftesbury called him the most gentlemanlike of the Roman poets, and I do not think he has ever been better described. As far as birth

goes, none of the great Roman poets — if we except
the dramatists — *less* deserves the grand old name
of gentleman.   Catullus and Calvus belonged to
the aristocracy; Lucilius was a knight; and Tibullus, Propertius, and Ovid were of equestrian rank ;
Virgil's father was a man of property : but Horace was the son of an emancipated slave.   Yet
never was the name "gentleman" less "soiled with
ignoble use" than when it was applied to Horace
by the author of the "Characteristics."   Béranger
boasted of his lowly origin ;[1] Horace neither conceals it nor boasts of it.   He is

> "Too proud to care from whence he came."

The gentlemanliness of Horace's style is of one to
the manner born.   He often reminds us of Addi-
son, and still oftener of Thackeray, especially when
he laughs at himself, and holds up his own follies
and weaknesses to ridicule in a way which disarms
hostile criticism, and blunts the shaft even of ma-
lignity.   And who has not called to mind Horace's
genial acceptance of the calm joys of middle age,
with his "lenit albescens animos capillus" and a
hundred like sentiments, in reading some of Thackeray's ballads ?   I know no poem in English — not

[1] The "Je suis vilain et très vilain" of Béranger is almost
as alien from the refined indifference of Horace as is the
obsequious coxcombry of Moore, or the petulant self-con-
sciousness of Pope.   Burns has more in common with Horace : —
> "My freedom's a lairdship nae monarch can touch"

is quite in the manly tone of the Roman.

professedly an imitation — more Horatian in tone than Thackeray's "Age of Wisdom:" —

> " Forty times over let Michaelmas pass —
>   Grizzling hair the brain doth clear —
> Then you know a boy is an ass,
> Then you know the worth of a lass,
>   Once you have come to forty year.

> " Gillian 's dead — God rest her bier !
>   How I loved her twenty years syne !
> Marian 's married, but I sit here,
> Alone and merry at forty year,
>   Dipping my nose in the Gascon wine."

Horace is at the very opposite pole to snobbishness. There is not a trace in his writings of mean admiration of mean things, nor is there a sign of sycophancy or subserviency in his character and conduct. In his time a patron was an absolute necessity to a man of letters. The rewards of literature were to a large extent indirect, and took the form of presents, appointments, and endowments of various sorts, in an age when there was no copyright, and every wealthy Roman who aspired to be a man of taste kept an establishment of literary slaves for the purpose of copying popular works, and was not withheld by any statute or sentiment from multiplying copies of his favorite author for presentation, or even for sale. A publishing firm would not give much for a work which would be public property as soon as a few copies came into the hands of a few rich men. Martial tells us that his poems are on the lips of every one, — that even in remote Britain he is quoted and recited. "But," he adds, "what good to me? My purse never discovers how popular they are."

In these circumstances a patron was indispensable to one who aspired to live by his pen. The friendship of Maecenas was the greatest boon that could have been

His relations towards Maecenas.

conferred on Horace. Observe, then, the growth of their friendship. On their first interview Horace's words were few and hesitating, the replies of Maecenas were curt and commonplace. Horace did not at once make a strong impression. The patron and the poet did not meet again for nine months, but thenceforth the intimacy ripened naturally and rapidly. Within a year Maecenas took Horace with him on his journey to Brundisium, and about three years afterwards he presented him with the Sabine farm. But during all this time the independence of Horace is absolute. There is not a word of sycophancy. Maecenas was a poet — a bad poet — to whom a word of commendation from Horace would no doubt have been grateful, but no such word did he ever get; indeed, we find no reference at all to any literary projects of Maecenas except a prose history of the achievements of Augustus not at the time begun, and probably never actually written. One day in August Horace went to the country, intending to stay a week. His sojourn extended over a month, and Maecenas, impatient of the prolonged absence of his friend, seems to have remonstrated with him

somewhat sharply, and to have reminded him of
the obligations which he had incurred. We have
a perfect proof of the spirit of Horace in the reply [1]
in which he firmly but courteously denies the right
of his patron to abridge his stay in the country and
order him back to Rome. He distinctly declares
he will not return till the spring. "Your poet,"
he writes, "will come back, my kind friend, with
the zephyrs and the first swallow." Even his Sabine farm would be bought too dear at the price of
his independence. "Sooner than that," he boldly
writes, —

> "I 'll give up all I have without a sigh."

If a man finds his liberty in danger, his first duty is
to secure it. No matter what he has gained by its
sacrifice, —

> "When he finds out he 's changed his lot for worse,
>   Let him betimes th' untoward choice reverse."

Surely there never was a more manly declaration of
the limits within which a patron's influence ought
to be exercised, nor one more likely to endear its
propounder to the land

> "Which sober-suited Freedom chose, —
>   A land where, girt by friends or foes,
>   A man may speak the thing he will."

The dignity which Horace maintained in his relations with Maecenas was the more remarkable
because dignity was not a virtue of his age, and
because Maecenas does not appear to have been

[1] *Epist.* I. 7.

one of those happy natures with whom it is easy to live and difficult to quarrel.   He is per- haps the most decidedly eccentric charac- ter that meets us in Roman history.   Though descended from Etruscan kings, and holding the first place in the confidence of the sovereign, he refused to accept any dignity, and lived and died a simple knight.   Yet his contempt for honors and titles can hardly have arisen from exceptional strength of mind.   There was one thing at which he trembled, and which many an ordinary man can meet with firmness, — death ; and, what is more singular, he was brave enough to own his tremors. Among the few verses of his that have come down to us, there are some half dozen glyconics which enshrine the most craven wail in which a man ever confessed his desire "to sweat and grunt under a weary life," — to cling to existence however insupportable : —

> " Paralyzed in hand and thigh,
>   Toothless, humpback'd, lame,
> Only bid me not to die, —
>   Life is all I claim.
> Give me, powers above me, give,
>   Be it on the rack, to live ! "

Yet, though he thus recoiled from death, he was as indifferent as Lucretius to death's sequel.

> " No useless sepulchre I crave :
>   Nature gives all her sons a grave,"

has been transmitted to us by Seneca as an utterance of Maecenas, who perhaps took a cynical

pleasure in thus mocking the forlorn dignity of the
great nobles whose ashes were stored in the urns
that lined the Latin and Flaminian roads.

The eccentricity of this Etruscan's literary style
was so marked that Augustus gave the name of
calamistri, or "curling pins," to his contorted
phrases; and similar singularities marked his life
and conduct. His slovenly dress provoked the
laughter of the passers-by; and his quarrels and
reconciliations with his wife Terentia were so
incessant that Seneca said of him that he was
married a thousand times, though he never had
but one wife. It was the Etruscan eccentric who
bought up the hideous purlieus of the Esquiline, —
described by Horace as the haunt of obscene hags
and desperate criminals, the place where slaves
were buried and convicts executed, — and trans-
formed them into those gardens which afterward
became celebrated as containing the tower to which
one emperor, Augustus, used to retire to recruit
his failing health, and from which another, Nero,
gazed on the spectacle of burning Rome.

Such was the patron with whom Horace lived
on terms of perfect equality and social
friendliness; and we leave our consideration of the poet's genius and character
with the pleasant feeling that we have been con-
templating two natures presenting each a type
very uncommon in Augustan Rome, and both in
a different way very attractive. It is a rare and
an interesting sight to observe ability and real

Horace and
Maecenas
both rare
types.

power despising the *insignia* of office and the rib-
bons of court distinctions; it is as pleasant and
almost as rare to meet an honest, manly, cultured
spirit in which genial friendliness, sound common
sense, and refined self-respect are equally fused
and mingled.   Still seldomer and with still greater
satisfaction do we witness a warm and manly
friendship between two representatives of rare
types, — a friendship equally creditable to both,
that grew up naturally, and was only interrupted
by death, which, strangely fulfilling a half-playful
prophecy of the poet, claimed the two victims
within one year.

VII.

LATIN SATIRE.

THERE was a moment when the primitive simplicity and austerity of Roman life began
to undergo a softening process, and to
become polished by contact with Greece.
This was the moment seized by Lucilius for the
creation of what was in effect a new form of art.
For, though *saturae* were written by Ennius and
others, Lucilius really originated this form of composition, so interesting because it is the narrow
pedestal on which the Roman claim to originality,
in the department of poetry at least, takes its
stand. In prose Rome may claim to have been
the first to have raised familiar correspondence
to a branch of literature in which she is still
unrivaled; and she has certainly stamped her
mark on history, and made jurisprudence altogether
her own. In poetry she can claim nothing save
satire; but the boast of Quintilian, " Satira tota
nostra est," is as just as are most of the utterances
of that eminent critic. When Horace adverts to
the affinity of satire to the Old Comedy of Greece,
he makes an instructive literary comment; but it
would be a mistake to refer the origin of Latin
satire to any such source. A still greater error
would it be to connect it in any way with the

Rise and
source of
Satire.

Greek satyric drama. Such a theory has been put forward, but one has only to read the "Cyclops" of Euripides to see that to the Latin *satira* and the Greek satyric drama there is nothing common but a fortuitous resemblance in sound between the names of two very different things. As the Greek drama, which is the mightiest product of the human spirit, took its rise from the primitive worship of Dionysus, so the only form of art which the Latin mind struck out for itself had its birth in what was essentially an act of worship, the thanksgivings and rejoicings for the harvest-home, in the course of which the peasants of agricultural Italy bantered each other in rude Fescennine strains. To the Fescennine masque, no doubt, we are to look for the common source of comedy, of satire, and of pastoral amoebaean poetry.

We do not know whether the interlocutors in the Fescennine dialogues spoke each in his own person, or assumed that of some one else, and so became actors on a petty scale. But we learn from Livy [1] that, in the consulship of C. Sulpicius and Licinius Stolo in 389, some Etruscan artists in an expiatory ceremony executed dances to the music of a flute, and thus gave the idea of a performance composed of mingled music and acting, and hence named "a medley," *satura*. From this was developed in one direction Latin comedy through the Atellane farce and the mime; in the other, that *medley* of topics and metres with which Lucilius

[1] VII. 2.

lashed the town in those open letters to the public, which were very similar in scope to the modern weekly press.

It is interesting to notice how Latin satire re-
Relation
to Atellane
plays and
mimes. produces some of the characteristic features of the Atellane farce and the mime, which were offshoots from a common stem. From the latter it has taken its coarseness, from the former a tendency to hold up to ridicule provincial oddities. The favorite butts of Atellane raillery in the hands of Pomponius and Novius seem to have been municipal eccentrics, as has been already observed in the first lecture. And the affectations of country magistrates is a constant theme of Latin satire. These moved the mirth of Horace and his city friends on the journey to Brundisium, when they laughed at the decorations of the ex-clerk who was Praetor of Fundi, and who was so proud of his purple robe, his broad stripes, and his pan of coals. Persius [1] ridicules one "who thinks himself somebody, forsooth, because, once stuck up with provincial dignity, he has broken short half-pint measures officially at Arretium." Juvenal, after describing the fall of Sejanus,[2] asks : —

[1] " Sese aliquem credens Italo quod honore supinus
      Fregerit heminas Arreti aedilis iniquas." — I. 129.
[2] " Hujus qui trahitur praetextam sumere mavis,
      An Fidenarum Gabiorumque esse potestas,
      Et de mensura jus dicere, vasa minora
      Frangere, pannosus vacuis aedilis Ulubris ? "

X. 99.

" Wouldst don the purple of that wretched corse,
   Or be the Mayor of Gabii or Fidenae,
   Give laws upon short measures, and smash up
   Pint pots below the statutable size,
   A ragged Aedile 'mid Ulubrae's wastes?"

One kind of satire is as old as human nature, and arises partly from a certain cruel disposition to ridicule our fellows, partly from a sentiment of justice and a feel- Originality of Latin Satire. ing that there should be a social tribunal before which to hale those whom the civil tribunal cannot reach, and partly even from a more or less sincere desire to improve society. But such feelings and beliefs may find expression in the drama, as they did in the Old Comedy at Athens, or in the newspaper press and the society novel, as they do at the present time. The one original feat of Latin poetry was to develop from the Fescennine allusion the versified letter to the public, which was unknown to Greek literature, and which has ever since given its distinctive character to satire. Horace, whose literary judgments are seldom sound, erred in referring to the Old Attic Comedy the origin of satire ; Quintilian, who is seldom wrong, took the right view when he said, " Satire is all our own." This was the way which Rome chose in which to " hold the mirror up to Nature, to show Virtue her own feature, Scorn her own image, and the very age and body of the time his form and pressure."

Horace himself, perhaps somewhat inconsist-

ently, recognizes the substantive character of Roman satire when he alludes to it as "a kind of
poetry untouched by the Greeks." Yet that marvelous people often came near to the idea of such
a form of art. We can hardly recognize a nu-
cleus of it, as some critics have done, in the Homeric picture of Thersites, but the travesty called
"Margites" was a nearer approach. The satirical portraiture of various types of women under
the figure of various brutes, the fox, the mare, and
so forth, — by means of which Simonides of Amor-
gos paved the way not only for the fierce denuncia-
tions of Juvenal's Sixth Satire, but also for the
Mrs. Nicklebies and Mrs. Proudies of our own
day, — took a further step in the same direction.
When Aristophanes figured Demos as an old im-
becile led about by his flatterers, he was on the
threshold of satire ; and the recently discovered
mimes of Herondas want little but a freer form and
more unity of purpose to make them such pictures
of society as we have in Lucilius, Horace, Persius,
and Juvenal. The "Characters" of Theophrastus
present us only male portraits, — a significant proof
that the Greeks did not feel how powerful an
instrument satire could be made. The Greek
novelists actually turned their backs on the portraiture of character, and quite failed to realize the
opportunities presented by the novel to take up
the work of satire, and enlist the interest which it
always commands.

The delight with which the Roman satirists

approached their task finds full expression in Horace and Persius. The former tells us : —

> "T is my delight to build the homely rhyme,
> Like that in which Lucilius lash'd his time."

The latter exclaims, " This jape of mine, trumpery as it seems, I would not sell for any Iliad ;"[1] and though Persius kindly says that Horace's victims smile under his lash, and that Horace plays round the heart to which he finds so ready an entrance, yet we, less prejudiced, must admit that the Matinian bee can sting, and that Horace enjoys his mockery of the world at least as much as his successor and imitator. *The Roman satirists enjoyed their work.*

We read that when Lucan, who was by eight years the junior of Persius, was taken, a very young man, to hear some poems of the satirist recited, he could not restrain an exclamation. One would have been glad to know what this exclamation was, but unfortunately time has robbed us of it. Nothing re- *Discrepant estimates of Persius.*

---

[1] " Hoc ridere meum tam nil nulla tibi vendo Iliade."
— I. 122. My quotations of Persius cannot be taken from any of his metrical translators, who are quite unsuccessful. They will come from the admirable prose version of Conington, slightly remodeled occasionally, merely for the purpose of bringing out some point which I may desire to make, and which the translator naturally did not bring into prominence Persius loses little by being rendered into prose, but his style has completely evaporated in the metrical versions which I have seen, especially in that of Gifford, who sometimes succeeds well enough with Juvenal.

mains but a mere smudge in the manuscript of the biographer.[1] I must own that I think time has dealt kindly with the reputation of Lucan as a literary critic. If his exclamation had survived, it would certainly have been quoted by one class of critics as a proof of Lucan's utter blindness and obtuseness, though no doubt by another it would have been hailed as a new proof of the unerring perspicacity of the future author of the "Pharsalia." For about the merits of no ancient author is opinion so sharply divided. Quintilian, indeed, has declared that "much real glory Persius earned by a single work;" but after all this does not give us the actual opinion of the great critic himself. Glory may be real (*vera*) and yet not deserved. Persius was certainly admired enthusiastically in the Middle Ages for his moral elevation, and the Fathers teem with quotations from his little book. But after the revival of learning he found few admirers save Casaubon, of whose edition of Persius Scaliger said that the sauce was better than the fish. Turnebus thought little of him, and Jerome threw his Satires into the fire. In modern times he has been edited oftener than estimated. To show that the question of his literary merit is not yet settled, I will cite two rival judgments by two eminent French critics, both characterized by the elegant pointedness and uncompromising decisiveness which the French school of criticism has made all its own. M. Constant Martha sees even

[1] Suetonius, *Vita Persii.*

in the tortuous obscurity of Persius the sacred gloom of some hallowed grove; even when he despairs of catching his meaning, he regards his text with veneration and awe, and, quoting finely from Virgil,[1] exclaims in rapture : —

"Surely a God is here: what God I know not."

On the other hand, his eloquent fellow-countryman, M. Nisard, has protested that Persius spoiled the beautiful language in which he wrote by trying to say *précieusement* what had often before been said naturally but excellently well. Bad writing, he insists, comes from want of ideas. There cannot be a clear style if the thought is unformed and confused. Persius uses contortions of language to disguise the fact that he has nothing to say. If he gets anywhere a bit of gold, he is forced to beat it out thin; for it will be long before he lights on another. Hence he is really verbose, while apparently conciseness itself; diffuse and yet cramped to the verge of unintelligibility. The precision is only in his words, but it gives to his thoughts an appearance of virility which does not really belong to them. His gait is naturally short and tripping, but he rarely forgets that he ought to have a manly stride. He declares with Rosalind : —

"We 'll have a swashing and a martial outside."

But, while he poses, he reminds us of an old-fashioned child who is playing at being grown up.

[1] "Quis deus incertum est : habitat deus."
Aenëid, VIII. 352.

If we consider only the vehicle which Persius has
His style and diction. chosen for his fine and sometimes sublime
thoughts, we must admit that we have in
him an example of deliberate eccentricity and elaborate tortuousness quite alien from the ancient
world, and hardly to be paralleled even in the present age of recoil from simplicity, in which to have
a style is to be consistently and invariably affected.
It is a remarkable fact that in Roman literature we
have only two Etruscans, Persius and Maecenas,
and both are signalized by the willful obscurity and
involution of their style. In the lecture on Horace
I have already referred to the eccentricity of the
life and character of Maecenas. This eccentricity
invaded his literary style as well, and Augustus
compared the tortuous phrases of his minister to
curling-tongs (*calamistri*). But in this respect his
fellow-countryman Persius altogether surpassed
him. For instance, he wishes to say of a man that
he is so greedy of gain that his mouth waters at
the sight of gold : what he writes is, that he " gulps
down Mercurial spittle ; "[1] a phrase in which we
can barely grasp at a shred of meaning if we remember that Mercury was the god of treasure-
trove, or unexpected gain. Again, "You are a
good Stoic" is not a very recondite sentiment ;
but how does he express it? He must needs
make a subtile allusion to the fact that the letter
Y was a symbol in the Pythagorean philosophy,
the stem standing for innocent childhood, and

[1] " Sorbere salivam Mercurialem." — V. 111.

the divergent branches figuring the alternative paths of right and wrong presented to the choice of the responsible adult. How, then, does the simple thought, "You are a good Stoic," frame itself in words? We have to remember that Pythagoras came from Samos, and that the Porch borrowed the Pythagorean letter to symbolize the divergent paths of right and wrong, and then we can just see how Persius persuaded himself that he had conveyed the sentiment, "You are a good Stoic," when he wrote down such a portentous expression as "The letter which spread into Samian branches has pointed out to you the steep path which rises to the right."[1] In comparison with this, he is almost lucid when he speaks of philosophers "mumbling mad-dog silence and balancing words on the pivot of their shot-out lip;"[2] or of "coins nursed at a modest five per cent till they go on to sweat a greedy eleven;"[3] or when he exclaims, "Oh that the grandeur of my rich uncle would boil over into a sumptuous funeral;"[4] or describes

---

[1] "Et tibi quae Samios diduxit littera ramos,
   Surgentem dextro monstravit limite callem."

III. 56.

[2] "Murmura cum secum et rabiosa silentia rodunt,
   Atque exporrecto trutinantur verba labello."

III. 81.

[3] "Ut nummos quos hic quincunce modesto
   Nutrieras, pergant avidos sudare deunces."

V. 149.

[4] "O si
Ebulliat patruus, praeclarum funus!" — II. 9.

students of the Old Comedy as "paling o'er indignant Eupolis and the grand old man." [1] Not many,
probably, of the many admirers of Mr. Gladstone
are aware that there was so ancient a claimant as
Aristophanes of a name so familiar of late years in
England.

It will be a good study in the style of this young

Horatian passages how modified by Persius.

philosopher, who seems to have labored
under a failing rife in our own literature
at present, and to have been physically
incapable of saying a plain thing in a
plain way, if we examine the process to which he
has subjected a few of the expressions which he
has borrowed from Horace, and which have been
brought together by M. Nisard. The older poet [2]
writes, "Men cry out that shame is extinct;"
this, expressed *précieusement*, becomes "The world
has lost its forehead," [3] that being the supposed
seat of shame. Horace [4] gives the excellent advice to a tragic poet, "If you want me to weep, you
yourself too must first feel sad;" in Persius [5]
this is twisted into "He will weep who would
have me bow'd down under his piteous tale."
Horace talks of one who is like a perfect sphere

[1] "Iratum Eupolidem praegrandi cum sene palles."
I. 124.
[2] "Clamant periisse pudorem." — *Ep*. II. 1. 80.
[3] "Exclamet Melicerta perisse
Frontem de rebus." — V. 103.
[4] "Si vis me flere dolendum est
Primum ipsi tibi." — *A. P.* 102.
[5] "Plorabit qui me volet incurvasse querella." — I. 91.

on the smooth surface of which no speck of dust
can rest:[1] Persius' test of an elaborately perfect
composition is that "every joining should spill
o'er the smooth surface the critical nail,"[2] that is,
should allow the nail to pass over the surface as
smoothly as if it were water. The idea of a joining
shedding (or spilling) over it a critical nail seems
quite worthy of being made the subject of an essay
to be read before some of those societies which
profess to explain expressions in modern poetry
which have puzzled the authors of them. It possesses all that "divine crookedness" and "holy
awkwardness" which the cinquecettists claim for
their favorite poets. These very epithets are applied with pride (but, as it seems to me, quite without reason) to Dante Gabriel Rossetti in a recent
eulogy on him by an aesthetic admirer. Too well
has Persius described his own style when he speaks
of the poet who "thumps his writing-desk and
knows the taste of his bitten nails."[3]

But it is pleasant to leave the literary contortions of a young man who was a fit type　Home life
of an age in which there was hardly any　of Persius.
originality, but countless teachers of the art of
being original. Let us turn from the young rheto-

---

[1] "Teres atque rotundus
Externi ne quid valeat per leve morari."
Sat. II. 7. 86.

[2] "Ut per leve severos
Effundat junctura ungues."—I. 64.

[3] "Pluteum caedit . . . demorsos sapit ungues."—I. 106.

rician, whose style was tortured into such fantastic convolutions by the curling-tongs of Verginius Flavus and Remmius Palameon, to the precocious philosopher whose gentle nature expanded under the influences of a cultured home circle, and friends like Cornutus and the truly noble Thrasea. Persius is chiefly interesting as the enthusiastic disciple of a philosophy in which under the Roman Empire the human conscience sought and found an asylum. Stoicism had now ceased to be a philosophy, and had become a religion, appealing to the rich and great as Christianity appealed to the poor and humble. On assuming the garb of manhood, Persius threw himself at once into the arms of Cornutus, and perhaps his confession of his own distrust of himself and lively personal devotion to the Stoic philosopher is the least affected passage to be found in his work : —

"When first the guardianship of the purple ceased to awe me, and the boss of boyhood was hung up as an offering to the quaint old household gods, while my toga of manhood yet unsoiled left me free to cast my eyes at will over the whole Saburra ; when the way of life begins to be uncertain, and the bewildered mind finds that its ignorant ramblings have brought it to a point where roads branch off, — then it was that I made myself your adopted child, Cornutus. You at once received the young foundling into the bosom of a second Socrates. Anon your rule with artful surprise straightens the moral twist that it detects, and my spirit becomes moulded by reason, struggles to be subdued, and assumes plastic features under your hand. Ay, I mind well how I used to wear away long summer suns with you, and with you pluck the early bloom of the night for feasting.

We twain have one work and one set time for rest, and the enjoyment of a moderate table unbends our gravity. No, I would not have you doubt that there is a fixed law that brings our lives into accord, and one star that guides them." [1]

The Stoics did not seek to soften their teaching. The society in which Persius grew up is described by his biographer as one of high and hard thinking (*acriter philosophantium*), — a society having what would now be called a Puritanical bias, and an aversion for the court, its morals and ambitions. A notable figure in this set was Cornutus, who owed his banishment to an uncourtier-like reply to the emperor, which I confess seems to me to have been not only rude, but silly. The story goes that Nero had formed a design of writing a history of Rome in verse, and was desirous of learning the opinions of his friends as to the length to which the poem should run. "At least four hundred books," suggested his courtiers with one voice. Cornutus, being consulted, opined that no one would read a work so voluminous. "But," retorted the courtiers, "has not your master Chrysippus written as many or more?" "True," said Cornutus, "but they are of use to the world." I own I think that any history of any place, even though it should be by an emperor and in verse, would have a better chance of doing good to humanity than such precepts as those which Cicero has culled from Chrysippus in his speech for Murena, — precepts such as, "The wise man ought never to par-

[1] V. 30 ff.

don any fault in another, and never to repent of
any sin of his own ; " " All faults are equal, and it
is as criminal to kill a chicken needlessly as to
murder your father ; " " The wise man is beautiful though he be a hunchback, rich though he be
dying of want, a king though he be your slave." I
think the four hundred books of Nero's poem could
hardly have contained any less useful propositions
than these.

Another member of this coterie was Caesius
Bassus, who is said to have edited the poet's
work after his untimely death, and of whom we
know nothing else except that Quintilian has pronounced him the only one of his age whom he
could think of putting in comparison with Horace
as a lyric poet. But by far the noblest of his associates, and the most inspiring, more by example
than precept, was the heroic Thrasea, " in whose
person," says Tacitus, " Nero tried to murder Virtue herself." Probably Persius had him before
his mind when he wrote the noble curse on tyrants,
" Let them look on Virtue and die of the thought
that they have lost her forever." [1] At Thrasea's
house the young poet met Arria, the wife of the
philosopher, and the daughter of the heroic Arria,
who plucked the sword from her bleeding breast
and handed it to her husband with the words, "I
feel no pain but from the blow you are going to
deal to yourself." Such a woman knew how a
Stoic should die at a tyrant's behest, and knew

[1] " Virtutem videant intabescantque relicta." — III. 38.

how to lift philosophy from the ridicule to which the paradoxes of Chrysippus exposed it. The short life of the poet was spent in the bosom of religious and aristocratic families, in which women were beginning to be able to exert their influence for good, as Agrippina and Messallina exercised theirs for evil. The only weakness of the whole society was a thirst for fame, " that last infirmity of noble minds." " The last weakness," says Tacitus, " of which even the sage divests himself is the love of glory." [1]

If we think of Persius, brought up in this refined atmosphere, young, very handsome, deli-cate, admired for his character as well as for his talents, kept far from the contact of vice not only by the natural elevation of his character, but also by his physical weakness, surrounded by high-souled and admiring women, and utterly inex-perienced in life, we may well expect that his work will be something peculiar and rare ; and we are not disappointed. We find in him the roughness and spiritual brusqueness of one who broods much in solitude ; the obscurity of one who speaks but for his own circle, which will understand what is only half said ; the exaggerations of a neophyte who looks out at an unknown world from a Stoic clois-ter, — in a word, we find the creed of a coterie set forth with more dry light than tempting fruit, a catechism of Stoicism which is in equal parts the

Its effect on his writings.

---

[1] " Etiam sapientibus cupido gloriae novissima exuitur."
Hist. IV. 6.

poetical exercise of a too painstaking and quite
over-taught pupil of rhetoricians and grammarians,
and the confession of faith of an aristocratic and
high-minded but very limited society.[1]   Persius
was a conspicuously pure and good young man,
who took his knowledge of vice from books, and
who was only the versifier of a philosophical system which commanded his sincere intellectual assent, but did not inspire his heart and soul, as
Epicureanism inspired the heart and soul of Lucretius.   Hence Persius is not a good hater like
Juvenal, though he says of himself that he " wears
the grin of a petulant spleen." [2]   The only class
which seem able to make him lose his
temper are the officers of the army.   It
was no doubt because they encouraged discontent
with the military régime that Domitian banished
the philosophers from the city ; and, indeed, from
the Stoic porch was most likely to emerge anything
that was left of the spirit of old Rome, — all who
dared to band themselves against tyranny, and did
not fear to die.   Hence we find Persius so far for-
getting the sweet reasonableness of a philosopher
as to apply such a Carlylian epithet as "unsavory "
(*hircosus*) to the centurions.   One might fancy the
epithet to be more applicable to the ragged philosopher with flowing, uncombed beard, who "mum-

His Philis-
tines.

---

[1] M. Constant Martha, *Les Moralistes*, p. 123.   He further
describes his *entourage* as a company of Jansenists, a kind
of Roman Port Royal waging incessant war with the court.

[2] " Sum petulanti splene cachinno." — I. 12.

bles mad-dog silence " in a passage already quoted.
The centurions represent to Persius the class most
opposed to his teachings, and are to him what the
world is to the Puritan, the *bourgeoisie* to the *beau
monde*, the Philistine to Culture.

The literary ideas of Persius are much colored
by his age. When the suppression of Subjects of
political eloquence carried in its train a his Satires.
general decline in the higher walks of literature,
poetry was encouraged by the court, and hence
that " itch for the pen " (*scribendi cacoëthes*) of
which Juvenal, too, complained. Persius ridicules
in the first Satire the popularity of the poet, his
affectation of archaism, and his unceasing struggle
to attain to the sublime, " something in the grand
style to come from the heart with mighty gusts of
breath ; "[1] but he is happiest when he is dealing
with the incompetence of the critic, — a theme
which possesses in every age an irresistible charm
for the literary aspirant. His religious thoughts
are put forward in the second Satire, " On Prayer."
They are protests against that kind of religion
which treats the gods as persons with whom a
bargain may be struck, or who might even be
made accomplices in crime, or at least accesso-
ries after the fact. His teaching broadly resembles that which the Hebrew Prophet[2] sums up in
the words, " I desired mercy, and not sacrifice ;

[1] " Grande aliquid quod pulmo animae praelargus anhelet."

I. 14.

[2] Hosea vi. 6.

and the knowledge of God more than burnt offerings;" and we cannot but recall " Ho, every one that thirsteth, come ye to the waters,"[1] when he bursts into an impassioned appeal to the world to come and eat of the corn of Cleanthes. "From this," he cries, "seek ye all, old and young, a limit for your desires, a provision for the sorrows of old age."[2] Persius beseeches his contemporaries to live in the use of prayers to which all may listen. Christ told his followers not to court the observation of men, but to seek the throne of God from their closets. But the worshiper to whom Persius spoke sought his closet, not from unostentatious humility, but because he blushed to disclose to man the vile proposals which he made to his god: "Grant me the death of my rich uncle or my sickly ward; look at Nerius with his third wife: grant this, and all my due observances will never fail." "If you made such a proposal," says Persius, "to the most unworthy of your acquaintance, he would cry shame on you: and what do you think Jupiter will say?"[3] In one place the Satirist falls into an implied limitation of the omnipotence of Heaven. The gourmand prays for health, "but rich dishes and thick gravies forbid the gods to

---

[1] Isaiah lv. 1.

[2] "Juvenum purgatas inseris aures
Fruge Cleanthea. Petite hinc puerique senesque
Finem animo certum miserisque viatica canis."

V. 63.

[3] II. 9–23.

grant it, and lay a veto on Jupiter himself." [1] One is reminded of the Irish judge who on reading a Fenian proclamation, was heard to remark, "Ay, *God save Ireland;* that's the way they always begin; and that's the very thing they are making it downright impossible for Him to do."

The Christian tinge of some of the expressions of Persius has been noticed, as for instance in "this sinful flesh" (*scelerata pulpa*). It is extremely unlikely that Persius borrowed these from Christian writers, and far more probable that both he and the Christian writers adopted them from the philosophy of the time. But certainly the whole tone of some passages in Persius is eminently Christian: —

His Christian tone.

> "Give *we* to the gods such offerings as great Messalla's blear-eyed son cannot give, be his dish never so ample, — duty to God and man well blended in the mind, purity in the heart's shrine, and a bosom full of the inbred nobility of goodness; let me have these to take to the temples, and a handful of meal will justify me in the eyes of Heaven." [2]

Such doctrine as this is startling in its originality in a pagan philosopher, and would strike us still

---

[1] " Sed grandes patinae tuccetaque crassa
  Adnuere his Superos vetuere Jovemque morantur."
  II. 42.

[2] " Quin damus id Superis, de magna quod dare lance
  Non possit magni Messallae lippa propago :
  Compositum jus fasque animo, sanctosque recessus
  Mentis, et incoctum generoso pectus honesto :
  Haec cedo ut admoveam`templis et farre litabo."
  II. 71.

more powerfully, were it not that Christianity has made such teachings as familiar to us as household words during all the ages which separate us from the time of Persius.

The morality of Persius is, as a rule, simply that of Stoicism, — the Stoic war against the passions, love, ambition, luxury. But he adds something to it when he expresses his craving after true liberty. The fifth Satire has a fine description of true liberty as distinguished from that merely material freedom which Dama can get from the praetor's wand : —

His ethics.

" The thing we want is Freedom, not that by which every new recruit for citizenship enlisting in the Veline tribe gets a quota of spoiled corn for his ticket. What a pinchbeck age, when a single twirl makes a citizen of Rome ! Look at Dama, a stable slave not worth twopence, blear-eyed from low tippling, and ready to tell a lie about a single feed of corn. Let his master give him a turn, and, presto ! by the mere act of twirling he is converted into Marcus Dama. Prodigious ! What ! Marcus surety, and you refuse to lend money ? Marcus judge, and you feel uneasy ? Marcus has given his word : it is so. Pray, Marcus, witness this document." [1]

This is the liberty the praetor's wand can give. The liberty that is of Stoicism and the spirit is far higher and far harder to achieve. And — worse still — the world wants it not, and will not don the Phrygian cap : —

" Talk in this way among the varicose centurions, and huge Pulfenius breaks into a horse laugh, and says he would

[1] V. 73–81.

not give a clipped *centussis* for a hundred of your Greek philosophers." [1]

The last really weighty utterance of Persius is
the expression of his conviction that the spiritual
condition of the Philistine is desperate.

Juvenal offers in many ways a marked contrast
to Persius, though the two are so often
coupled together in editions, lectures,
and histories of literature. The latter *Juvenal and Persius con-trasted.*
was of noble family ; began to write his satires
when little more than a boy ; and died before he
had reached his twenty-eighth year. The former,
the adopted (if not the real) son of a freedman,
spent all his life up to past middle age in declamation ; in urging Sulla to go into private life ; or
bidding Hannibal to think what a blessed thing
it would be to pass his life in the advocacy of
platitudes and die a good old man ; or taking a
part in resolving some of those hard cases which,
Quintilian tells us, were devised to exercise the
powers of rival declaimers. Juvenal probably did
not compose anything, except mere rhetorical exercises, until he had reached twice the age at which
Persius died, and did not publish until he was an
old man. Again, Persius was a philosopher and
nothing but a philosopher, while Juvenal belongs
to no sect, and says that the only difference be-

[1] " Dixeris haec inter varicosos centuriones,
   Continuo crassum ridet Pulfenius ingens,
   Et centum Graecos curto centusse licetur." — V. 189.

tween the Stoics and the Cynics is in their tunics.
Lastly, while the literary position of Persius is still
in the scales of criticism, and his claims to the
name of poet are denied as stoutly as they are af-
firmed, the dazzling magnificence of Juvenal's language, his strength which is sometimes fairly bru-
tal, and his scathing fury of invective, have silenced
criticism and drowned the voice of protest. The
arrows of his speech, headed and winged with
flame, have so fierce a flight that they mock the
eye which strains itself after them. The flood of
indignation, pent up in furious silence for forty
years, once loose carried away on its current or
tossed aside every obstacle that impeded its onward
rush.

While the literary merits of Juvenal are far
beyond and above criticism, — for who can call
these in question who has not utterly forgotten the
amazement with which he first read the eighth,
tenth, and thirteenth Satires? — yet there are
questions about certain qualities in his work which
invite and have often provoked discussion.

Was Juvenal a satirist in the truest sense of the
In what word? Did he really abhor the vices
sense was which he lashed, or was he like the rich
Juvenal a man in his own satire, who looked on
satirist? with pleasure at the burning of his house, because
he knew that it would be to him in the end a
source of profit? Did he regard the smouldering
fires which were eating away the heart of old
Rome with the pleasure with which Nero contem-

plated the flames that preyed upon her streets and colonnades? Did Juvenal congratulate himself that there was such an abundant harvest for him to reap? Does the fearful realism with which he depicts vice show the extreme of fervid abhorrence, or a secret pruriency and pleasure in dwelling on the details? Some of these questions are such as could only be tried *in camera*, and fortunately we are not bound to be the judges. We cannot get much good now out of fierce invectives against vices which do not allure but only disgust, and which, we may fairly say, have died with the Roman Empire. But we may well feel that it would have been better if some of his satires had never been written. Though he has given us the noble sentiment that there is no debt so sacred as that which we owe to the purity of the young,[1] yet no writer has more freely outraged modesty, or done so with more apparent gusto.[2]

[1] " Maxima debetur puero reverentia : si quid

Turpe paras, ne tu pueri contempseris annos."— XIV. 47.

[2] From this point of view M. Gaston Boissier is the most formidable assailant of the character of Juvenal. Professor Mayor has put the rebutting case strongly and brilliantly in the advertisement to his edition of 1886, but I must confess myself unable to accept his conclusions, that "from the first page to the last breathes one spirit of homely manhood," and that " his standard is that of the 'Gospels and of St. Paul." Professor Mayor admits that there is at least one passage (XI. 186–189) to which a virtuous motive cannot be ascribed. It is hard to resist the feeling that there are many such passages, which betray a desire to dwell on impure topics, rather than to show up the ugliness of vice.

The little we know about his life does not afford
much material for building up the poet's
character from his environments, — always a hazardous attempt.   He saw eleven emperors, — from Claudius to Hadrian, — but probably
he began to write only under Domitian, and to
publish under Hadrian.   The most important fact
which we learn from his biographer is, that he spent
much of his life in oratorical exercises, though
he did not become a professional advocate, —in
declaiming for declaiming's sake.   Under Domitian he wrote some verses on a favorite actor,
Paris.   These verses, when published under Hadrian, were thought to reflect on another popular artist of that day, and they brought about his
fall.   The court paid back the satirist in his own
coin by giving the octogenarian scoffer the command of a legion in Africa, an ironical recognition
of misapplied ability, which really amounted to a
sentence of exile.

His life.

"Easy," cries Juvenal, "is Democritus' smile of
derision, but where did Heraclitus, the
weeping philosopher, find tears enough
for the folly of man?"   Yet Juvenal himself has a
far larger supply of tears and indignation than of
laughter and gibes.   He is always in a rage, and a
laugh seems to sit strangely on his lips.[1]   But his

His attitude toward vice.

[1] Dr. Johnson said that the peculiarity of Juvenal was a
mixture of gaiety and stateliness, but his gaiety is never
more than a slight and momentary relaxation of his prevailing sternness.   "Raro jocos," observes Lipsius, "saepius

furious indignation against vice seems to have had its source rather in the head than in the heart. He is like the lion in Homer that lashes his sides with his tail, "and mightily stirreth him up to fight." Perhaps it may be urged that, if he really thought

> " Vice is a monster of such hideous mien,"

he would not have taken such pains to paint her every feature in colors that will never fade ; nor would he, perhaps, have been so intimate with Martial ; nor would that poet have addressed to him three epigrams, two of which contain gross and irrelevant impurities. Nor yet would he, if his hatred of vice had been as real as it seems, have laughed in his sleeve at his own fervor, and wound up an impassioned invective with a sneer, as when he ends the catalogue of Nero's crimes and his comparison with the matricide Orestes by saying that Orestes never sung on the stage or wrote a *Troica*. In some cases, so artificial is the passion into which he has worked himself that he seems completely to forget its existence for a moment. The act of cannibalism at Ombi in Egypt described in the fifteenth Satire is the occasion of a good deal of "fine frenzy," and many beautiful verses and pathetic passages, such as —

acerbos sales miscet." It is with a sympathetic pen that he portrays the moody and saturnine cynicism of Domitian in the tale of the Council of the Turbot, so matchlessly told in the fourth Satire.

" But serpents now more links of concord bind:
  The cruel leopard spares the spotted kind; " [1]

and —

" Nature, who gave us tears, by that alone
  Proclaims she made the feeling heart our own;
  And 't is her noblest boon: this bids us fly
  To wipe the drops from sorrowing friendship's eye,
  Sorrowing ourselves; to wail the prisoner's state,
  And sympathize in the wrong'd orphan's fate,
  Compell'd his treacherous guardian to accuse,
  While many a shower his blooming cheek bedews,
  And through his scatter'd tresses, wet with tears,
  A doubtful face, or boy's or girl's, appears.
  As Nature bids, we sigh when some bright maid
  Is ere her spousals to the pyre convey'd;
  Some babe by fate's inexorable doom
  Just shown on earth and hurried to the tomb." [2]

But all this beautiful writing leads up to the incredibly frigid question, what would Pythagoras

---

[1] " Sed jam serpentum major concordia: parcit
      Cognatis maculis similis fera."— 159.

[2] " Mollissima corda
      Humano generi dare se Natura fatetur
      Quae lacrimas dedit; haec nostri pars optima sensus:
      Plorare ergo jubet casum lugentis amici,
      Squaloremque rei, pupillum ad jura vocantem
      Circumscriptorem, cujus manantia fletu
      Ora puellares faciunt incerta capilli.
      Naturae imperio gemimus cum funus adultae
      Virginis occurrit, vel terra clauditur infans
      Et minor igne rogi." — 131.

I avail myself of the spirited version of Gifford when it is
not too diffuse.   Sometimes I modify it, or attempt a version
of my own, where the usually vigorous rendering of Gifford

have thought of cannibalism? — Pythagoras, who
abstained from all meat, and did not even treat
himself to every kind of vegetable! How strangely
and suddenly the fire of indignation has gone out!
Moreover, furious though he always appears to be,
there is method in the madness which announces
in the very first Satire that he will assail only those
whose ashes fill the funeral urns which line the
Flaminian and Latin roads.[1]

Vice may be lashed from the pulpit or the stage.
Horace, of whom Quintilian says that he was without a rival in his sketches of character, chose the methods of the stage. Juvenal was driven back chiefly on the resources of the pulpit when he made the resolution that his puppets should only represent the dead. Not that it made much difference. Society in the time of Horace was decaying, in the time of Juvenal was rotten to the core. If Juvenal had attacked the living, it may be doubted whether he would have done them much good, while it is certain that he would have done himself much harm. It would

Juvenal a preacher,

seems either to misrepresent the meaning of the text, or to
wander too far from the sentiment.

[1] When he refers to persons still living, they are either
quite obscure and therefore not formidable, like Machaera
the auctioneer (VII. 9), or Basilus the pleader (VII. 145), or
else men once powerful but subsequently disgraced or exiled,
such as Marius Priscus (I. 41, VIII. 120). Of the deceased
objects of his satire, most are taken from the reigns of Nero
and Domitian. The freedmen come from the reign of Claudius.

be a mistake to credit Juvenal with any heroic independence in spite of his brave words. "What a
fine contumacy and fearless boldness of speech!"
we are disposed to exclaim when we meet the furious verses which tell how Domitian,

> "drunk with fury, tore
> The prostrate world which bled at every pore,
> And Rome beheld in body as in mind
> A bald-pate Nero rise again to curse mankind." [1]

But we must remember that attacks on dead
emperors were not attended with any
appreciable danger in Juvenal's time.
Though the Caesars, as long as they all belonged
to the one Caesarean house, resented unfavorable
criticism on deceased princes, yet we know that
even then poets referred with eulogy to the open
enemies of the founder of the Empire. How often
has Cato been glorified by Virgil, Horace, Lucan,
even Seneca, the minister of Nero! But in the
time of Juvenal, to traduce a dead emperor was
sometimes the best road to the favor of the living
wearer of the purple. Pliny's Panegyric on Trajan
is a detailed indictment of his predecessors. The
most acceptable offering to Domitian was the
wounded name of those who reigned before him.
The successors to the Twelve Caesars who came
to the throne through adoption or election set up
the claim that they had restored the liberty of the
ancient régime. Pliny compares Trajan to the

but not a martyr.

---

[1] " Cum jam semianimum laceraret Flavius orbem
    Ultimus, et calvo serviret Roma Neroni." — IV. 37.

Brutus who drove the kings from Rome. Attacks, moreover, on despots were the licensed and chartered themes of declamation. Juvenal tells us that he, too, had in his salad days given advice to Sulla to retire into private life, and draws a moving picture of the poor teacher of rhetoric ready to expire with weariness while a droning class does to death inhuman tyrants.[1] Philostratus of Lemnos met Aelian, a Roman sophist, with a book in his hand, which he was reading with great apparent satisfaction. Being asked what it was, "It is," said Aelian, "a furious attack on the tyrant lately slain, whom I have dubbed Gymnis, to indicate the profligacy by which he has disgraced the Roman name." "If you had accused him in his lifetime," said Philostratus, "I should have admired you. A man was needed to smite a living tyrant; any coward could trample on his corse."

Decidedly the most astonishing quality in the style of Juvenal is his amazing faculty for suggesting a picture to the mind. *His picturesqueness.* Let us observe how his fancy ever dips its wings in all the hues of the rainbow, and turns descriptions into pictures. The poet has to say, "after the victory of Marius over the Cimbri," but the reader must be made to think of the huge stature of these northern warriors, and of the terrible slaughter of Vercellae, and so we have, not words, but a word-picture : —

[1] " Cum perimit saevos classis numerosa tyrannos."
VII. 151.

> "When carrion crows flocked to the Cimbrian slain,
> Crows that had never rifled huger corses."[1]

Was there ever a more hideous portrait than that in the sixth Satire of a Jezebel who seeks in vain, by paints and cosmetics, to repair the ravages of time?—

> " But tell me this : this thing thus daub'd and oil'd,
> Thus poulticed, plaster'd, baked by turns and boil'd,
> This thing veneer'd and vamp'd and lacquer'd o'er —
> Is it a face, Ursidius, or a sore?"[2]

We see the very race-course itself when we read of the winning horse,—

> " Under whose flying feet
> Dances the foremost whorl of trampled dust."[3]

And what pencil or brush could more vividly bring before our eyes the famished and mangy hound that

> "Licks the dry lamp for but a drop of oil"?[4]

[1] " Postquam ad Cimbros stragemque volabant,
Qui nunquam attigerant majora cadavera corvi."

VIII. 251.

[2] "Sed quae mutatis inducitur atque fovetur
Tot medicaminibus, coctaeque siliginis offas
Accipit et madidae, *facies dicetur an ulcus?*"

VI. 471.

[3] " Cujus
Clara fuga ante alios et *primus in aequore pulvis.*"

VIII. 60.

[4] " Canibus pigris scabieque vetusta
Levibus et siccae lambentibus ora lucernae."

VIII. 35.

A part of his terrible indictment of old age may be quoted; the rest is too horrible : —

> " The face a parody of its former self,
> Instead of skin a hideous hide, and cheeks
> That flaccid hang, networks of lines and wrinkles
> Such as in Tabraca's woods the grandam ape
> Sitting at squat scrapes on her leathern jowl.
> Between the young there 's many a difference,
> Some comelier, some stronger; but the old!
> The old are all the same, the piping voice,
> The tottering limbs, the hairless head, the nose
> Drivelling, — babyhood is come again." [1]

For Juvenal every conception clothes itself with color and shape. He cannot think of Hannibal without fancying what a picture would be the one-eyed general borne on his Gaetulian beast.[2] Marius comes before his mind's eye as stepping down from the car that bore him in triumph for Aquae Sextiae,[3] and Vulcan as washing the grime

[1] " Deformem et tetrum ante omnia vultum
Dissimilemque sui, deformem pro cute pellem
Pendentesque genas, et tales adspice rugas
Quales, umbriferos ubi pandit Tabraca saltus,
In vetula scalpit mater jam simia bucca.
Plurima sunt juvenum discrimina : pulchrior ille
Hoc, atque ille alio : multum hic robustior illo :
Una senum facies, cum voce trementia membra,
Et jam leve caput, madidique infantia nasi."
X. 191.

[2] " O qualis facies et quali digna tabella,
Cum Gaetula ducem portaret bellua luscum."
X. 157.

[3] " Cum de Teutonico vellet descendere curru."
X. 282.

of his Liparaean workshop from his brawny arms.[1]

Juvenal would have been more than human if Defects arising from it. the possession of such marvelous powers of description had not sometimes led him astray. And sure enough we find that some of his most graphic tableaux, however matchless for power, are irrelevant where they are introduced, and have the worst fault that an illustration could have, — the fault of not illustrating. Nothing, for instance, could surpass his well-known picture of the fall of Sejanus, and the comments thereon in Rome.[2] But does it illustrate the vanity of human wishes? Not, except in so far as every reverse of fortune in history may be said broadly to exemplify the theme. It would rather serve to illustrate a proposition unfortunately not always true, and less true perhaps in Juvenal's age than in any other, that a life of the blackest infamy is likely to issue in disaster. Sejanus was no doubt ambitious, but he was also a villain without a redeeming trait. To quote his fall as an instance of

> "Vaulting ambition that o'erleaps itself
>   And falls o' the other,"

would be like citing as an instance of Sabbath-breaking an atrocious murder perpetrated on Sun-

[1] " Tergens
Brachia Vulcanus Liparaea nigra taberna."

XIII. 44

[2] X. 56–97.

day, or condemning as want of punctuality a soldier's desertion on the eve of battle.

Another defect, arising from his very brilliancy,
is that hyperbole with which Boileau charged him,
and which makes him, in the words of Horace,
" assail with the terrible knout offenses worthy
only of the light cane." For instance, in dealing
with the nobility in the eighth Satire, he pursues
with mingled curses and tears the theme of " How
are the mighty fallen ! " There is nothing new in
this subject, which was indeed one of the commonplaces of rhetoric and philosophy. Sallust handles
it finely in the speeches of Memmius and of Marius
in the " Jugurthine War ; " and Seneca had already
said, " Nobility does not lie in a hall full of family
portraits dimmed by the hand of Time." There is
nothing peculiar to Juvenal's work save its amazing brilliancy. But the vials of his wrath contain
no tempered liquor, and they cannot be poured
out drop by drop. Hence the unmeasured and
unproportioned fury of the satirist. Hence the
furious diatribe against Damasippus, the " ostler-
consul," [1] who with his own hands drives his horses

---

[1] " Ipse rotam astringit sufflamine mulio consul." — VIII. 148.

This is the recent and certain emendation of the verse,
which has hitherto stood : —

" Ipse rotam astringit multo sufflamine consul."

No doubt *mulio* was originally misread *multo*, and then
multo was placed before *sufflamine* for the sake of the metre.
Mulio consul at once makes a weak line thoroughly worthy
of Juvenal. The emendation is due to Bücheler, who elicited

past the ashes of the mighty dead, his ancestors: the Sun, fortunately, sees him not, but the Moon, the Moon looks down on the abominable thing, and the fires of Heaven bend on it their attesting eyes. The ostler-consul's crime of taking the place of his coachman is put beside forgery and adultery, and is one of those before which

> "The lofty pride of every honor'd name
>   Shall rise to vindicate insulted fame,
>   And hold aloft the torch to blazon forth its shame." [1]

We must make allowance for the strange potency of Roman *gravitas*, and we must remember that Tacitus, as well as Juvenal, tells how Nero sang on the stage, in a tone only a little less awful than that in which he narrates his incest and matricide. We must recall, too, the indignant protest of Laberius, in republican Rome, when Julius Caesar compelled him to take part in one of his own mimes. But when every allowance is made which far different times and circumstances can suggest, we cannot help feeling that in this passage Juvenal is breaking a butterfly on the wheel, and violating by exaggeration, which however eloquent is certainly excessive, the fundamental canons of sober art.

Roman traits in Juvenal.

it from the note of the scholiast and the "Florilegium San-gallense." It has been heartily accepted by Professor Mayor and all the editors.

[1] "Incipit ipsorum contra te stare parentum
      Nobilitas, claramque facem praeferre pudendis."
                                                    VIII. 138.

Another curiously Roman trait is his indignation against the patrician gladiators, when set beside his apparent tolerance of the bloody sports of the circus. Pliny, it is true, congratulates Trajan on the revival of the spectacles ; but Cicero, more than a century before the time of Juvenal, had condemned the games, and Seneca had uttered the fine sentiment, " Man's life to man is sacred." [1] Juvenal finds nothing shocking in the lavish sacrifice of human life. It is not human blood, but patrician blood, which is sacred in his eyes. What shocks him is that the gladiator is a patrician, noble, and (worst of all) that he chooses, not the part of the *mirmillo* or assailant, but that of the *retiarius*, or lasso-man, who seeks to baffle his armed adversary by casting a net over his head. And why is this so shocking ? Because the *mirmillo's* face was covered, but as *retiarius* the noble gladiator displayed his patrician features to the gaze of the common crowd. This is desecration, this is indeed profanation of that which should be inviolate. [2]

Though Juvenal tells us that he takes all life, all the world, for his text, —

> " Whatever passions have the soul possess'd,
> Whatever wild desires inflamed the breast,
> Joy, Sorrow, Fear, Love, Hatred, Transport, Rage,
> Shall form the motley subject of my page," [3] —

[1] " Homo sacra res homini."

[2] M. Constant Martha, *Les Moralistes*, p. 292.

[3] "Quidquid agunt homines, Votum, Timor, Ira, Voluptas
Gaudia, Discursus, nostri est farrago libelli."

I. 85.

yet we find him curiously blind to social tendencies

His blindness to social tendencies. which were unfolding themselves under his eyes. If one were asked what class in society was the most characteristic product of imperial Rome, one would say, without hesitation, the Freedmen ; and the more especially because this was the class with which the emperors seem to have dealt according to the dictates of a fixed and settled policy, and with some just appreciation of the social force which they represented. This social force was nothing less than commerce and enterprise, and all the arts by which a man might grow rich in Rome, save only war and eloquence, which were the monopoly of the nobility. The emperors encouraged this class as a counterpoise to the nobles, just as Louis XI. sought to create a middle class between the feudal barons and the serfs. The influence of the freedman expanded quickly. Even under Tiberius, Pallas was so powerful that, as Tacitus tells us,[1] "it was counted a proud boast to be known even to his lackeys." The development of this particular ingredient in the formation of a middle class was really a step in advance for civilization, and started the reform which ended in the abolition of slavery. But Juvenal sees in the freedman, be he never so rich or enterprising, nothing save what is contemptible. In the first Satire he tells us, with indignation, how the very *Trojugenae* are thrust aside

[1] " Libertis quoque et janitoribus ejus notescere, pro magnifico accipiebatur." — *Ann.* VI. 8.

for the freedman, whose ears bored for the ring
proclaim that his birthplace was on the other side
of the Euphrates, but whose five freeholds enable
him to live in a splendor denied to the purest representatives of the old Roman stock.[1] In the third
Satire, 29–40, he thus describes them : —

> " Here, then, I bid my much-loved home farewell,
>   Ah, mine no more !   There let Arturius dwell
>   And Catulus ; knaves who in truth's despite
>   Can white to black transform and black to white,
>   Build temples, furnish funerals, auctions hold,
>   Farm rivers, ports, and scour the drains for gold.
>   Once they were trumpeters, and ever found
>   With strolling mummers in their annual round,
>   While their puff'd cheeks, which every village knew,
>   Called to high feats of arms the rustic crew :
>   Now they give shows themselves, and at the will
>   Of the base rabble raise the sign to kill."

The colluvies of foreign nationalities which were
pouring into the Imperial City with their strange
rites and outlandish gods, and were changing the
face of society not only morally but even artistic-
ally, found in Juvenal a supremely brilliant but
by no means profound critic.   We read how the
Syrian Orontes has been flowing into the Tiber,
and how the morals of the foreigners that flock to
Rome are as crooked as the strange dulcimers and
sistra which they carry in their train.   Who does
not remember his sketch of the Greeks, that nation of play-actors who will rejoice with them that
do rejoice and weep with them that weep ; who,

[1] I. 100–111.

like Osric with Hamlet, will exclaim, "It is very hot," and anon, " It is indifferent cold, my lord, indeed ; " nay, more, who, when you say, " It is burning hot," can actually burst into a sweat ? The picture is, indeed, vigorous, and reflects the opinion of the time. Contempt for the Greeks had already found its way into the very tongue of Rome, in which *Graeca fides* meant "dishonesty" and *pergraecari* "to be an arrant knave." But one would have expected that Juvenal should have been able to see how the Greeks by their philosophy were changing the face of Roman society. He speaks of it with contempt in a passage already referred to, where he says the difference between the Stoic and the Cynic was merely one of dress ; [1] and he even sneers at their art in another place, where he glorifies the times when soldiers smashed up priceless miracles of Greek workmanship to adorn their steeds, — a contempt for the arts of civilization which would have been a ridiculous anachronism in the Imperial City of his time.[2] " I cannot bear," he cries, " this Graecized Rome." [3] Again, he tells us that the Jews worship the skies, and will not guide a Gen-

His contempt for the Greeks,

[1] " Nec Cynicos nec Stoica dogmata legit
A Cynicis tunica distantia." — XIII. 121.

[2] " Tunc rudis et Graecas mirari nescius artes
Urbibus eversis praedarum in parte reperta
Magnorum artificum frangebat pocula miles
Ut phaleris gauderet equus." — XI. 100.

[3] " Non possum ferre, Quirites,
Graecam urbem." — III. 61.

tile to the fountain or tell him his road.[1]   Seneca
had testified of this despised race that   and the
the vanquished gave laws to their victors,   Jews.
— "victi victoribus leges dedere," — a reflection
on the moral influence of Rome's subjects fit to be
placed beside Horace's oft-quoted estimate of the
literary influence of Greece on Rome.[2]

As to religion, Juvenal laughs at it, though he
ascribes to its neglect most of Rome's
disasters.   In Satire XIII. 38–48 he   His attitude
toward
jestingly refers to the age of Belief : —   religion;

> " There was, indeed, a time
> When the rude natives of this happy clime
> Cherish'd such dreams.   'T was ere the King of Heaven
> To change his sceptre for a scythe was driven;
> Ere Juno yet the sweets of love had tried,
> Or Jove advanced beyond the caves of Ide.
> 'T was when no gods indulged in sumptuous feasts,
> No Ganymede, no Hebe served the guests,

[1] " Nil praeter nubes et caeli numen adorant . . .
      Non monstrare vias eadem nisi sacra colenti,
      Quaesitum ad fontem solos deducere verpos."
                                        XIV. 97.

[2] Dean Merivale (*History of the Romans under the Empire*, vol. viii. ch. lxiv.) commends Juvenal and Tacitus
for their protest against the encroachments of foreign ideas
and sentiments, and for their hostility to everything which
might seem to threaten the old principles and traditions of
Rome: " No Roman writers are more thoroughly conservative than these last of the Romans.   Tacitus and Juvenal
are more wholly Roman than even Cicero or Virgil.   They
maintain the laws, the manners, the religion of their fathers
with more decision than ever, as they feel more than ever
how much protection is required for them."

> No Vulcan from his sooty labors foul
> Limp'd round officious with his nectar bowl,
> But each in private dined : 't was when the throng
> Of godlings, now beyond the scope of song,
> The courts of Heaven in spacious ease possess'd,
> And with a lighter load poor Atlas press'd."

In his sentiments with regard to slaves, Juvenal
toward
slaves; is almost Christian. In the fourteenth
Satire he proclaims the doctrine that the
slave is a man and a brother, and asks where are
those who will

> " Instill the generous thought that slaves have powers,
> Sense, feeling, all as exquisite as ours." [1]

And one cannot forget the indignant tone of the
passage in the sixth Satire, where the Roman lady,
who has hired by the year a man whose sole duty
is to scourge the slaves, chats with her female
friends, applies her face-wash, reads her accounts,
and discusses the gold border on her dress, while
the eternal thong is being laid on, until the exe-
cutioner, wearied with his scourging, flags in his
work, and at last reluctantly she thunders his dismissal, " Begone ! " [2]

[1] " Animos servorum et corpora nostra
Materia constare putat paribusque elementis."

XIV, 16.

[2] " Sunt quae tortoribus annua praestent.
Verberat, atque obiter faciem linit, audit amicas,
Aut latum pictae vestis considerat aurum,
Et caedit : longi relegit transversa diurni,
Et caedit : donec lassis caedentibus *exi*
Intonet horrendum." — VI. 480.

Juvenal's sympathy with the poor is but a commonplace of his time. And what rem- toward
edy does he suggest for their hard case? the poor;
In the third Satire (169) he urges emigration.
Seneca would have made a better suggestion and
said *death*. Indeed, we have very little comfortable or even positive advice in Juvenal. Instead of
the thousand little precious maxims which Horace
has given us for the regulation of our lives and the
cleansing of our hearts, what have we from Juvenal? The cold platitude in the end of the tenth
Satire, that the path to peace is Virtue. But Virtue could do little for men in Juvenal's time, save
help them to die, and " make a libation of their
blood to liberty," like Thrasea.[1]

The only class which had a sincere and serious
answer ready to the question " What and Chris-
must I do to be saved?" was hardly tianity.
recognized as existing. Seneca does not dare to
praise them, though he thinks well of them. Tacitus calls them enemies of the human race. Suetonius counts their persecution among the few redeeming traits of Nero's wicked reign. Quintilian
never mentions them. Pliny accords to them a
cold defense, and commends Trajan for recogniz-

[1] " Porrectis utriusque bracchii venis postquam cruorem
effudit, humum super spargens, propius vocato quaestore,
'libamus' inquit 'Jovi liberatori. Specta, juvenis: et omen
quidem Di prohibeant, eeterum in ea tempora natus es quibus firmare animum expediat constantibus exemplis.'"
Tacitus, *Annals*, XVI. 35.

ing in them varying degrees of criminality, for distinguishing hardened cases from those on whom their religion sat more lightly, — *robustiores* from *teneri*. It is strange how little justice Christianity received from minds so cultivated and so amply furnished as those of Tacitus and Juvenal, Seneca and Pliny. After all, historical fairness, like self-knowledge, is perhaps better achieved by the will than by the understanding.

The fortunate side of Juvenal's rhetorical training is (as M. Constant Martha observes) to be found in the fact that it made his style an excellent representative of the spirit of his age. Had it been formed in the schools of philosophy, like Seneca's, it would probably have been in advance of his time. But in the schools of rhetoric we meet only ideas which are firmly held and widely diffused. Thus we are able to see reflected in the pages of Juvenal a jealous and exclusive patriciate crushed by the emperors, and giving place to a middle class resting mainly on the energy of freedmen and the development of commercial enterprise. Rome becomes the home of every foreign people and cult. Among these the most finely touched are the Greeks, who succeed in imposing on Rome not only their manners but even their language, — a literary phenomenon to which the works of Apuleius and Fronto bear witness. Foreign religions germinate chiefly in the slums of the Imperial City, but they gradually work into the very heart of the whole system of government and

The spirit of his age.

life. The prejudice against the slave begins to lose some of its force, and he begins to find sympathy at least, if no more solid blessing. The body politic is in outward semblance the same, but it contains within it seeds which are slowly fructifying, and which in the fullness of time will bring on the throes of a new birth.

VIII.

LATIN POETRY OF THE DECLINE.

Phaedrus.

IF we look at the Augustan Age from the spiritual point of view, Ovid may be regarded as the poet of the Transition. The Silver Age is the age of words. Ovid is to Virgil as Euripides to Sophocles, and we find that Ovid is imitated more than Virgil by the poets of the Decline, — by Lucan, Statius, Seneca, and Valerius Flaccus. But if we view the question merely materially as one of chronology, Phaedrus will be the connecting link. He lived from Augustus to Nero, and is the only writer who fills the interval. There was between the Golden and the Silver Age half a century of literary darkness, illumined only by the trifling contributions to literature which Phaedrus has made. He is not mentioned by a single writer of the Empire but Martial under Domitian and Avianus under Theodosius. Phaedrus no doubt chose the rôle of a fabulist because it was a vein hitherto neglected by the Latin poets. We know hardly anything about his life, but we are told that he incurred the resentment of Sejanus and was imprisoned. There is certainly much in his work which seems to be directed against Tiberius and Sejanus, and we must admire the bold outspokenness of many of his fables as

well as the ingenuity of one ambiguous criticism
on his times : —

" Utilius homini nihil est quam recte loqui," —

a phrase which may mean quite equally well either
" Nothing is more truly a man's interest than to
speak honestly," or " It is more a man's interest
to say nothing at all than to speak the straightforward truth." Whether we believe or not that his
sarcasms were resented, we may safely discredit the
statement that, if resented, they were visited only
with incarceration, — an incredibly light sentence
on blasphemy against the emperor in an age when
death was often the punishment of mere silence.
Phaedrus is rather a *raconteur* than a fabulist. He
is best when he is only telling a story. His ani-
mals are but vehicles of moral reflections. One of
his fables tells how there were two mules, one of
which bore a great treasure and the other only a
load of barley. The former is despoiled of his load
and wounded by robbers ; the latter is unhurt, and
bears his burden safely to its destination. But we
read that the first stepped along proudly with his
head in the air, while the other trudged on his way
dejected and humble. Now these (as has been remarked) are the traits, not of the beasts in the
story, but of the human beings there symbolized,
and the human qualities and conditions illustrated,
luxury and poverty. Aesop never makes Compared
such a mistake. His fable and his moral with Aesop.
leap together from his brain. In Phaedrus the

moral comes first, and then he attaches an animal to it. Phaedrus is signalized by an overweening vanity and self-esteem. He constantly plumes himself on his originality, or at least on his superiority to his model, Aesop. Like Cicero, another Transition Poet, he is jealous of his fame and covetous of praise. He is very concise, but never to the point of obscurity like Persius. He strongly resembles the Augustan writers in his cultured taste, his familiarity with Greek literature, and his ambition for a place in the regard of posterity.

Poetry revives under Nero, and its chief representatives in that reign are Lucan and Seneca. Like Catullus and Persius, Lucan died very young, in his twenty-sixth year; but, unlike them, he found not only an untimely but a dishonorable grave. He is a black spot on the goodly fellowship of Stoics which Persius adorned. He halted between the life of a courtier and the death of a Stoic, and faced the latter only when he could no longer preserve the former. He tried unsuccessfully to make the best of both worlds, and finally gave up his life only after the failure of a vile attempt to save it by the sacrifice of his mother's. And yet he was a member of that eminent Stoic family which shed such lustre on the dark days of Nero's reign. His father was M. Annaeus, a son of Seneca the elder, and his uncle was Seneca the younger, who was high in favor at the court of Nero. Lucan himself displayed extraordinary precocity. So the in-

Lucan.

His precocity.

fant prodigy was sent from Corduba to Rome, and
put into the mill of Palaemon and Flavus, who had
just finished their task of ruining the style of Persius, and were now ready to take in hand a fresh
victim. The story that bees settled on his lips in
infancy is one which is told of many poets, but of
none surely more inappropriately than of Lucan.
The bee takes its fragrant store from Nature herself, and never did a poet owe so little to Nature
as Lucan, or possess more wearisomely perfect
skill in embroidering ideas which he has not completely grasped, pleading with feverish earnestness
causes in which he has no interest, and making
the most emphatic pronouncements on subjects on
which he has no knowledge and not even preju-
dices.

As Ausonius, the poet of Bordeaux, owed to the
favorable horoscope which fired the am- His early
bition of his parents that start in life training.
which he used so well that, beginning as a teacher
of rhetoric, he finally became consul, verifying the
verse of Juvenal, —

"Si fortuna volet fies de rhetore consul," —

so Lucan owed to the chance, that he possessed a
relative influential at court, his early introduction
to Roman life and fashion. But the young Spaniard would have profited far more by the curb than
the spur. The precocious bud of his genius needed
pruning, to prevent its blowing into a flower too
soon. His teachers and admirers would not even

leave the bud to Nature, but tried to pull open the leaves and make it look like a flower before its time. Thrust while still a child into a position which Lucretius, Virgil, and Horace with difficulty achieved for themselves, and with all his worst tendencies not corrected but fostered, did not the young genius afford a perfect illustration of that saddest and truest of sayings, *Corruptio optimi pessima?* At first he enjoyed high favor with the emperor, who made him a quaestor. It is true that by statute he was not yet eligible for the office. But what matter? In those days it often happened that the first time one heard of a law was when it was set aside by the emperor. But jealousy soon troubled the smooth current of Lucan's prosperity. The emperor and he were equally prolific poets, but the emperor's "Mimallonean boomings"[1] commanded only enforced applause, while those of his young rival were received with real enthusiasm. It is singular that, though Nero was so proud of his poetry, he so utterly failed to bring about its survival. Few even of the titles of his poems have come down to us. It seems as if a great reputation, either for good or for evil, in the sphere of action is unfavorable to survival in the realms of art. The hand of Time has smeared out the imperial boomings in the blood of his innocent victims. Lucan was forbidden to read his verses in public. One might as well have taken away books

The emperor's jealousy.

Its result.

[1] " Mimalloneis bombis." — *Pers.* I. 99.

from Cicero, rich meats from Vitellius, or men from Cleopatra. The applause of the salôn was the air which Lucan breathed. Full of bitterness, he threw himself into the conspiracy of Piso, resenting not so much the suppression of the liberties of his country as of his own right to thrill the ears of the applauding public. By no writer has the Republic been more ardently beloved than by Lucan, but he loved it, not as a form of government, but as a subject for rhetoric ; not as the creation of the Roman people, but as the theme of the " Pharsalia." If Martial is to be believed when he tells of the profits earned by that poem,[1] we may say that few have sold their country more advantageously than Lucan. He was a political economist, too : Roman citizenship was at a discount ; he bought it in the cheapest market, the Comitia, and sold it in the dearest, the Argiletum, or Booksellers' Street, of Rome. What did a Spaniard care about Rome ? He would never have come near it, but that it was the best opening for a young man of talent, and the best market for the gaudy wares which he had to sell.

We know how Piso's conspiracy was discovered, and how, among all the nobles and poets that took part in it, there was not one who was not as ready as an Irish Invincible to purchase his own safety by denouncing the rest, save

Lucan's death.

[1] Martial, XIV. 194, makes Lucan say of himself : —

> " Sunt quidam qui me dicunt non esse poetam :
> Sed qui me vendit bibliopola putat."

one poor harlot, Epicharis, whom, perhaps, some womanish weakness, maybe indignation at the judicial murder of a lover, had driven into the plot, but from whom, in the words of Tacitus, "neither scourge nor fire, nor the fury of the torturers, who were loth to be beaten by a woman," could extort one word of confession, betrayal, or retractation. Lucan surpassed the rest in his eagerness to save his life even by denouncing his own mother, an act which gives a new and literal meaning to Juvenal's scathing line, —

> " Et propter vitam vivendi perdere causas."

But the imperial matricide was not impressed by the sacrifice of a mother, and Lucan was forced to confront what he calls "the greatest of horrors," the face of Death. He bled to death at the age of six-and-twenty, reciting some verses from the "Pharsalia." He can hardly have been in love with death, which he tried so basely to shun; yet he is never tired of glorifying it. Of facing death he writes : —

> " Happiest who can, next happiest he who must."[1]

And again : —

> " God cheats men into living on by hiding
> How blest it is to die."[2]

---

[1] " Scire mori sors prima viris, sed proxima cogi."
Phars. IX. 211.

[2] " Victurosque dei celant, ut vivere durent,
Felix esse mori." — *Phars.* IV. 520.

God certainly seems to have succeeded in concealing the charms of death from this pseudo-Stoic, who was as unworthy of his family as of his age, and who was not ashamed to try to claim credit for a great death after exhausting all the devices of turpitude to avoid it.

Quintilian said of the "Pharsalia" that it was perhaps rhetoric rather than poetry, — an excellent criticism, which might well be applied to certain modern poets. Admirable as are the "Lays of Ancient Rome" and "Lalla Rookh," we feel that the main ingredient in the handiwork of Macaulay and Moore is not poetry, but rhetoric, when we compare them with "Christabel" or "Maud;" and the same will be the result of a comparison between the "Pharsalia" and the "Aenëid." Quintilian's criticism on the "Pharsalia."

Lucan, as has been observed by Mr. Crutwell, has not the reverence of Virgil for the gods, nor the antagonism of Lucretius; he does not rise above a flippant and shallow scepticism. Hence he is hampered in the use of the supernatural, and is obliged to have recourse to witches, demons, ghosts, and visions. The real strength of this epic poem without a hero is in the rhetorical skill displayed in those parts of it where rhetoric is really appropriate, as for instance in the magnificent reflections on the death of Pompey. It is his matchless powers as a rhetorician and a phrasemonger[1] Lucan's religious feelings. His rhetoric.

[1] Quintilian calls him *sententiis clarissimus.*

that have made a poem, perused throughout by few, such a fruitful source of quotations which have become household words : like " In se magna ruunt," " Stat magni nominis umbra," " Victrix causa deis placuit sed victa Catoni," " Nulla fides regni sociis," " Multis utile bellum," " Nil actum credens dum quid superesset agendum." But it is

Exaggera- this gift which has often betrayed him
tion. into wild exaggeration, as in the episode, over three hundred lines long, of the African serpents and the deaths which they inflicted,[1] and in the loathsome banquet of the carrion birds and beasts on the field of Pharsalia, which reminds one of a horrible passage in Byron's " Siege of Corinth," beginning, —

> " And he saw the lean dogs 'neath the wall
> Hold o'er the dead their carnival."

Lucan is a perfect type of Silver Poetry, because

Lucan a per- his strong point is his power of descrip-
fect type of
Silver tion. For it is in their descriptions that
Poetry. the Gold and Silver Ages present to us a most marked contrast. The Golden Age is subjective, and detail is subservient to a spiritual de-

---

[1] One cannot but smile at the absurd exaggeration of such expressions as *unum pro corpore volnus.* Still more ridiculous is his description of the difficulties attending the burial of the victims of the serpents, who swelled so much that their graves would rise into mountains. But perhaps his wildest hyperbole is when he cautions the emperor to keep the centre of the heavens when added to the stars, lest his weight should overbalance the firmament.

lineation; description is rather a sketch than a picture, and addresses itself more to the mind than to the eye. The Silver Age revels in objective detail, and dwells more on repulsive than attractive qualities, for the former are more obvious to a less keen insight. Beauty, except to the eye of genius, is uniform, while ugliness presents, even to a commonplace observation, a multitude of different features, and a wide field for detailed elaboration. M. Nisard has well illustrated this contrast by comparing Virgil's Sibyl in the sixth book of the "Aenëid" and Lucan's in the fifth of the "Pharsalia." Virgil paints, Lucan anatomizes. The same will be the result of putting side by side a picture of a shipwreck by each poet. A faculty for minutely describing natural objects, to which may be added erudition (if that is a good quality in a poet), constitutes the chief merit of Lucan, and perhaps the only merit of the "Thebaid" and "Achilleid" of Statius, the "Argonautica" of Valerius Flaccus, the "Punica" of Silius Italicus, and the "Aetna" whose author is unknown.

The other poet of the reign of Nero, if poet he can be called, is Seneca the younger. Seneca. No fewer than six Senecas have been postulated at different times in the history of literature, but we have no evidence whatever that there were more than two, — the father, who wrote works on rhetoric; and the son, who not only cultivated his father's favorite studies, but was the author of several tragedies, which, there is reason to believe,

were never put upon the stage. Martial congratulates Corduba on having produced two Senecas,
meaning doubtless the rhetorician and the tragic
poet. Sidonius Apollinaris speaks of one Seneca
who cultivates "scabrous" Plato, while the other
"makes the stage of Euripides shake beneath his
tread."[1] Opinions differ widely not only concerning the merits of the tragedies as a whole, but also
concerning the relative excellence of each as compared with the others. One critic calls the "Oedipus" "a great work," "a precious jewel," while the
"Troades" he pronounces utterly worthless; and
of the "Octavia" he says, "If it is not the work
of a child, I am a child myself." Another calls
the "Troades" divine, the "Octavia" below it,
but still excellent; while the "Oedipus" in his
judgment is so lacking in all inspiration that it
can hardly be reckoned among tragedies at all.
Teuffel writes, "The *praetexta* entitled ' Octavia '
is certainly not by Seneca." On the question of
the merits of the tragedies as works of art there
can hardly be two opinions. They were
evidently written for the arm-chair, not
the stage, but even as such they are
worthless as studies of the human mind. The

Effect of
Stoicism on
his plays.

---

[1] " Quorum alter colit hispidum Platonem,
Orchestram quatit alter Euripidis."

The extreme infelicity of the epithet *hispidum* as applied to
Plato almost prepares us for the metrical monstrosity in the
next verse.

philosophy of Seneca reappears in his plays.   The
oft-quoted lines,[1] —

> "Where you were your birth before,
>   There you 'll be when you 're no more," —

afford a good example of the kind of moralizing
which prevails in his plays.   Their key-note is
Stoicism.   No virtues are found in them but the
virtues of the schools.   All the softer traits of humanity disappear.   Modesty, pure love, filial affection no longer have any interest, but must make
way for the virtues that can strut and rant.
Love in Seneca is sensual and shameless.   The
Phaedra of Euripides[2] struggles against
the burden that is laid upon her, but Aph-
rodite is greater than she.   She speaks

Compared with Euripides.

of her mother Pasiphaë with pity, and, though
dissuaded by her nurse, persists in her resolve to
die.   The Latin Phaedra exults in her passion for
Hippolytus, envies the monstrous love of Pasiphaë,
and pretends a resolution to die, that she may
deceive her nurse and gain her as an accomplice.
And while laboriously unfolding the unnatural
aberrations of a distorted passion, Seneca ima-
gines that he is doing what Euripides did and
analyzing a woman's heart.   In the same way he
transforms the loving yet patient Deianira of
Sophocles into a furious virago, and Antigone into

---

[1] " Quaeris quo jaceas post obitum loco,
    Quo non nata jacent."

[2] *Hippol.* 337 ff.

a special pleader, who discusses with her father Oedipus the question how far his relations with his mother can be held to involve real guiltiness. The death of Polyxena in Euripides, put beside that of Iphigenia in Aeschylus and his imitator Lucretius, shows a great lowering of tone. But in Euripides we have only to complain that Polyxena is too collected when she thinks how she must arrange her robes so as to fall with decency and decorum; in Seneca, Polyxena rivals Cato in her stoical contempt of death, and dashes herself to the ground, invoking mother Earth's vengeance on her sacrificers. There is the same exaggeration in his male characters. His Hercules dies in the attitude of a gladiator ; and his Oedipus has only to be set beside that of Sophocles, and it will at once be seen how completely all refinement has left the portrait.

Though Petronius Arbiter has transmitted to us a good deal more prose than verse, I may perhaps include in this review of the poetry of the Decline one who has left us a poem on the Civil War in three hundred verses, which good authorities have pronounced to outweigh in the critical balance the whole of the " Pharsalia," [1] and a fragment of five-and-sixty

Petronius Arbiter.

---

[1] Mr. Heitland, in his very able introduction to Mr. Haskins' excellent edition of the *Pharsalia*, regards this little poem as thrown off half in rivalry, half in imitation of Lucan, like our *Rejected Addresses*, though less definitely intended for ridicule.

lines on the " Capture of Troy," containing the
Laocoön episode, and balked (it has been said)
of its place among the masterpieces only by
the inevitable comparison with the incomparable
" Aenëid." I own that I have not formed so high
an opinion of these poems, or of the other metrical
jeux d'esprit scattered through the " Satyricon,"
but I gladly embrace the opportunity of making a
few observations on one of the most singular lega-
cies to us from the ancient world. Whether this
strange medley (resembling in some respects the
Satura Menippea) was written as a satire on Nero
or Tigellinus, or on the other hand was merely a
study in the social life of the writer's time, and who
that writer was, and where he lived, — these are
questions which have been often asked and have
received various answers. The belief long prevailed that the author of the " Satyricon " was the
consul Petronius, of whose life and character Tacitus has given us such a brilliant sketch in the
" Annals," [1] and who, according to that historian,
while his life-blood, in obedience to the tyrant's
mandate, was flowing from his veins, wrote a full
account of the profligacy of Nero and his court,
and sent it under his seal to the emperor. And it
was maintained that we have in the " Satyricon,"
a part of which is extant, this very document.
But it is absolutely extravagant to suppose that
even the fragment of the " Satyricon " which we
possess (and there is good reason to believe that it

[1] XVI. 18, 19.

is not a tenth part of the whole work) could have been composed and dictated in a single day by a man bleeding to death. Besides, the " Satyricon " is not such a work as the death-bed *chronique scandaleuse* of the consular victim of Nero's tyranny must have been. What character in the fragment could possibly stand for the tyrant, and why should the writer have been careful to veil his invective behind so impenetrable a screen, when, destined not to survive his work, he might have made all the debauchery and cruelty of the imperial monster burn naked in letters of fire before the eyes of his countrymen ? But I have already said too much on a subject on which I should not have touched, were it not that histories and dictionaries of literature still treat this extravagant hypothesis as tenable. Mr. Crutwell's excellent " History of Roman Literature " rightly repudiates it. Petronius has been placed in the time of Augustus, Tiberius, Nero, Marcus Aurelius, Severus, Zenobia, Constantine, Julian, and has even been identified with a bishop of Bologna who died and was canonized in the fifteenth century. If *he* was the author of the " Satyricon," we cannot help feeling a want of confidence in the efficacy of the intercession of St. Petronius.

The chief interest of the " Satyricon " for us is His work an excellent picture of social life. the specimen which it affords us of everyday manners and conversation under the Empire. We find all the usual features of the *sermo volgaris*, and what especially strikes

us is, that familiar discourse at this period reproduces the archaic language of the comic drama
far more conspicuously than even the familiar
correspondence of Cicero. We meet the characteristic irregularities of gender, such as *vinus,
fatus, caelus, schemae;* old forms like *lacte* for
lac and *frunisci* for *frui;* anomalies of verbal in-
flexion, as *mirat, vagat, pudeatur;* and late uses
of words, as *querela,* " a quarrel," *latrocinium,*
" larceny," *largus* and even *ambitiosus* in the
sense of " abundant." Again, as in Cicero's letters, we meet conversational phrases presenting
a curious similarity to the slang of to-day, —
urceatim pluere, " to rain bucketfuls ; " *olla male
fervet,* " it is hard to keep the pot boiling ; " *fides
male ambulans,* "tottering credit ; " *habet haec res
panem,* "there's money in this ; " *prae litteras* (sic)
fatuus, " mad after books." Broadly, the Latinity
is on the verge of Low Latin, a fact which must
be insisted on because the purity of the Petronian
Latinity has often been praised. Even Lipsius
has styled Petronius epigrammatically, but surely
erroneously, *auctor purissimae impuritatis.*

As the " Satyricon " is not in the hands of many,
and indeed ought by no means to be
recommended for general perusal, I may
perhaps bring before you a specimen of
the conversation at Trimalchio's table,

Specimen of the " Satyri-con " from this point of view.

which will show how little this feature of social
life has undergone any real change since the days
of the Roman Empire. I pass over the more

serious table-talk in which Cicero and Publilius
Syrus are compared, ghost stories are told, and
impromptus thrown off, as well as the pretentious
monologues in which Trimalchio amusingly displays his ignorance of mythology, history, and
science. These passages are too formal for my
purpose, which is to exhibit in a free and abridged
translation the ordinary give-and-take of commonplace conversation between average and undistin-
guished guests during the temporary absence of
the host from the room.[1]

" As his departure delivered us from his usurpation of the
talk, we tried to draw our neighbors into conversation.
'What is a day?' cried Dama, after calling for a larger
glass. 'Nothing. Before you have time to turn round it is
night. One should therefore go straight from the bedroom
to the dining-room. And what a regular freezing we have
been having of late! I could scarcely get hot in my bath.
However, a hot drink is as good as a greatcoat. I've had
some stiff ones [*staminatas*], and I am about full; it has got
into my head.' Here Seleucus broke in with, ' I don't take
a bath every day. Constant washing wears out the body as
well as the clothes; but when I 've put down my good posset
of mead, I can tell the cold go hang. However, I could not
have bathed to-day in any case, as I had to attend a funeral.
Poor Chrysanthus, you know, a nice fellow, has just slipped
his wind [*animam ebulliit*]. It was only the other day he

---

[1] *Sat.* XLI.–XLVI. The conversation is so steeped in
the slang of the period that I have added the Latin in some
cases. Without the Latin I might be suspected of exaggerating the colloquial character of the language. I have followed the text of Bücheler, under whose hands Petronius
emerged from chaos into cosmos. The interpretation is
nearly always that of Friedländer's admirable edition.

said how d' ye do to me. I can fancy I am talking to him
now. Ah, we are only air-balloons, summer flies; this life's
a bubble. And it's not as if he hadn't tried the fasting
cure. For five days neither bit nor sup passed his lips, and
yet he's gone. Too many doctors did for him, or else it was
to be. A doctor's really no use except to feel you did the
right thing. An excellent funeral it was, superior bier and
trappings, and the mourners first class.' He was becoming a
bore, and Phileros interrupted him with ' Oh, let us leave
the dead alone. He's all right. He had a decent life and
a decent death. What has he to complain of? He rose
from the gutter, and was once so poor that he would have
picked a farthing out of a midden with his teeth. But he
grew like a honeycomb. I suppose he has left behind him a
cool 100,000, and all in hard cash. To speak the truth —
for, as you know, I wear my heart upon my sleeve [*linguam
caninam comedi*] — he was a rough-spoken fellow, quarrel-
someness personified [*discordia non homo*]. Now his brother was a fine, friendly, open-handed gentleman, and kept a
good table. At first everything went ugly with him [*malam
parram pilavit*], but his first vine-crop pulled him together
[*recorrexit costas*]; he sold his wine for whatever he chose
to ask. But what really kept his head above water [*mentum
sustulit*] was that legacy, when he walked into a good deal
more than was left him. That was why that blockhead
Chrysanthus quarreled with his own brother, and left away
his money to some Tom, Dick, or Harry [*nescio cui terrae
filio*]. It's an ill turn when a man turns his back on his own.
He took all his slaves told him for gospel [*habuit oracularios
servos*], and they played the deuce with him. Credulity is
fatal, especially for a business man. However, he got far
more than he deserved; Fortune's favorite, lead turned to
gold under his hands. And how many years do you think
he had on his back? Seventy and more, I should say. But
he was as hard as nails [*corneolus*], and carried his age
splendidly, — as black as a crow. Ah, I knew him long, long
ago, when he did something smack, something grow to.

He had a general kind of taste [*omnis minervae homo*].
Well, he enjoyed himself, and I for one don't blame him.
It's all he takes to the grave with him.'

"'How you go on talking,' said Ganymedes, 'about what
has nothing to do with the heavens above or the earth beneath, and no one troubles his head about the supply of
food. I declare I could not buy a mouthful of bread this
day. It's the drought, and now we have had a year's fast.
Bad luck to the Aediles, they have an understanding with
the bakers: "*Scratch me and I'll scratch you* [*serva me, ser-
vabo te.*]" So it's the folk in a small way [*populus minutus*]
bear the brunt, while the topsawyers have high jinks all the
time [*isti majores maxillae semper saturnalia agunt*]. Ah,
if we had the giants now that we had when I came back
from Asia! How well I remember Safinius! He lived near
the Old Arch when I was a boy: a regular pepper-box,
he'd knock sparks out of the ground under his feet [*piper
non homo, is quacunque ibat terram adurebat*]. And so in
his time food was cheap as dirt. You'd get for an *as* a loaf
that two men could not eat; now you get a thing the size of
a bull's eye. Ah, things are going from bad to worse every
day. This place is growing downwards like a cow's tail
[*retroversus crescit tanquam cauda vituli*]. But I'm hanged
if I don't think it is all the irreligion of the age; no one fasts
or cares a jot for Jupiter. Time was when our ladies used to
go in their robes with tossed hair, bare feet, and pure hearts,
and pray for rain, and it used to rain bucketfuls at once, and
they all came back like drowned rats. But now we have lost
our religion, and the fields are feeling the effect of it.'
'Easy, easy,' said Echion, a shoddy merchant; 'there are
ups and downs, as the peasant said when he lost his speckled
pig: to-morrow may bring what we have n't to-day, — that's
the way the world jogs along [*sic vita truditur*]. There would
not be a better country than this in the world, only for the
men that are in it. It is in a poor way now, but so are others.
We must n't be too particular. The sky's above us all [*ubi-
que medius caelus est*]. If you lived somewhere else, you

would say that here the pigs were going about ready roast, crying *Who'll eat me?* ' "

The conversation then turns on a flirtation between a certain lady and her slave, and the meanness of Norbanus, who provided such wretched gladiators that they had no chance against the wild beasts. Before Trimalchio returns, the shoddy merchant, warmed with wine, has plucked up spirit to invite the great *littérateur* Agamemnon to his poor abode, promising to show him his son, who is an infant phenomenon for brains, and would be very industrious, only he is " clean gone on pet birds " (*in aves morbosus*). He tells Agamemnon his son is now in four times (*quattuor partes dicit*), by which he means that he can divide by four, for it was the division, not the multiplication, table that was taught to Roman boys, who had to learn, not what was four times twelve, but what was the fourth, the half, three fourths, of twelve.

We have nowhere a more vigorous sketch of a purse-proud millionaire than in Trimalchio, who never buys anything, as there is nothing which is not produced on some one or other of his estates, many of which he has never seen ; who asks, "What is a poor man ? " and who punishes the slave for picking up a silver dish which had fallen on the floor, and gives orders that it shall be thrown out with the rest of the sweepings of the hall. The fragment is no doubt full of impurities, and it depicts a society not only utterly depraved, but strangely

General estimate of the " Satyricon."

coarse under a superficial refinement. Yet it treats love, or perhaps we should rather say gallantry, with far more feeling than any poet of the Silver Age, and it stands alone in Latin literature for the dramatic skill with which the characters are made to speak each in the tone and style which befits his position and education. This is a completely modern note, and we are often reminded of the dexterous touch of George Eliot when we listen to the silly prattle of the less cultivated *convives*. Ganymedes, for instance, gives three separate and quite unconnected reasons, — the drought, the incompetence of the Aediles, and the irreligion of the age, — each of which alone is said to account for the dearness of provisions ; and Seleucus explains the death of Chrysanthus by the hypothesis that he had too many doctors, " or else it was to be," — just such a fatuity as would have been put into the mouth of Mr. Brooke by George Eliot, who is never richer in her dramatic coloring than when she is portraying intellectual poverty and logical inconsequence. But we must dwell no more on a work which, though full of instruction and deserving far more attention than it has received from English scholarship, is certainly more interesting for the pictures of society than for the poetry which it contains.

With Statius and Martial, their rise and their decline, is closely connected an institution so characteristic of the Roman Empire that a few observations concerning it will not be out of place here.

The habit of consulting the taste of one's friends about one's poetry was as old at least as Horace, who tells how he used to show his work to his friend Varus, who would say to him, "Revise that, I pray, and that;" and Tarpa seems in his time to have been a general referee on literary questions. But the public calling together of one's friends to pronounce on a newly written poem was the invention of Asinius Pollio, whose taste even in boyhood was so warmly commended by Catullus. Public readings were encouraged by Augustus. In this, as in other matters, we recognize in Ovid a link connecting the Golden with the Silver Age. Ovid, like Lucan, loves publicity and display. Horace and Virgil crave quiet and privacy. The practice of reciting fell into disuse in the literary barrenness of the principate of Tiberius; but under Nero, and again under Domitian, it revived and flourished. We read in a letter of Pliny's that "for the whole of April there was hardly a day without a public reading." One Crispinus was the great manager and arranger of these *réunions*, which reach their high-water mark in the time of Martial, and of Statius, of whom Juvenal tells us that when he named a day for a public reading he threw all Rome into a state of delight. A sign of lessened interest in public recitations appears in the change of name given to them when they began to be called *ostentationes* (ἐπιδείξεις) instead of *recitationes;* and Pliny [1] mentions an amusing *contretemps* which

[1] *Ep.* VI. 15.

perhaps marks the epoch when their popularity was beginning to wane. One Passienus Paulus began to recite a poem in which he had assumed permission to address his friend Javolenus Priscus. The recitation commenced with the words, " Thou bidd'st me, Priscus," [1] but unfortunately his friend Priscus was present, and, being a plain person who held by matter of fact in all things, he interrupted the reciter with, " Excuse me, I did nothing of the kind ; there must be some mistake." The example of Priscus was thereafter followed by persons who were bored by the recitations, and interrupted them with the suggestions of a pretended simplicity. On another occasion chance was on the side of the audience. During a public reading in the house of Capito, a chair occupied by a very corpulent member of the audience began to emit ominous groans and creakings which portended imminent ruin. When finally it collapsed under its load, and when the occupant, who had been fast asleep, woke up declaring that he had just closed his eyes to concentrate his attention on the poem, but had never been asleep at all, the peals of laughter were so loud and long that Capito was obliged to announce that the rest of the reading would be postponed to another day. The whole tale as told by Pliny reminds us how some little foibles of humanity have survived unchanged from the days of Domitian, and that then as now the charge of having fallen asleep was likely to be repudiated with

[1] *Prisce, jubes.*

STATIUS

an indignation often not felt under far more serious
imputations. We read, moreover, that it was the
habit of rich men to send their servants to represent them at such functions, just as they now
sometimes commission empty carriages to do vi-
carious mourning at funerals. These servants, no
doubt, especially if they were Greeks, were skillful
in devising means of interrupting the performance,
or miching from it to the nearest tavern. Plain-
tive is the lamentation of Pliny over the decline
of the institution, and frequent are his assurances
that he never failed to respond to an invitation to
such a *séance*, and that "all who loved letters" —
by which he means all who encouraged recitations
— were ever sure of his sympathy and applause.

For such a purpose no one could have higher
qualifications than Statius, who was, of
all the Roman poets, the most ready and
versatile. Like Ovid and Pope, "he lisped in numbers, for the numbers came." He writes private little notes to his wife and daughter in verse, — that
wife Claudia who so fondly adored her husband
ever since the day when she saw him crowned with
the wreath of victory at the Alban games, and who
would not allow him to leave the scene of wider fame
and louder plaudits for Naples, where he would fain
be again, and where he thinks [1] he would get a husband for his beautiful and clever daughter (Claudia's step-daughter) whom he loves so much, and
who is withering on the virgin thorn in a city of

Statius.

[1] *Silv.* III. 5.

venal tenderness, and of marriage without love, but never without dowry. Words seem to have come to Statius before thoughts. It is a question, says M. Nisard in his brilliant account of the Statii *père et fils*, whether there are innate ideas, but he seems to have had innate verses. His father had won crowns in the Nemean, Isthmian, and Pythian festivals at Naples, and probably half a dozen faded wreaths were all that he left to his son, except a valuable goodwill in the poetic business. His father had lived through the troublous times when Vitellianists and Vespasianists were at each other's throats. One day the Capitol was burned. This was fortunate for him, because it gave him a subject for a poem, which he had written and dedicated to the emperor before the ashes were cold. He was moreover in the habit of giving lessons in Greek, and teaching their ritual to the Julian and Sibylline priests, the Augurs, and the Luperci. Thus he was able to introduce his son to influential patrons, and Statius the younger Poet to the at once became poet-laureate to the aristocracy. aristocracy. The loss of a wife, a dog, a parrot, found in him a ready chronicler ; orders were executed with punctuality and dispatch ; and the building of a palace was not a theme too high for him, or the purchase of a turbot too low. Statius was of course a flatterer, not only of the emperor but of his favorites, freedmen and sons of freedmen, for whom he invented pedigrees. He had the alternative of kissing the emperor's feet, like Martial, or of sharing the fate of Lucan and Seneca. The emperors would have been glad if all the people had but one throat out of which the life might be squeezed; but, failing that, they found it their interest to flatter the people, while they forced proud nobles into the arena, and mingled the blood of a Paulus Aemilius with that of a German slave. The court poet is betrayed in the lukewarmness of Statius' eulogy[1] on his brother-poet Lucan. The frigid mythology which we find in this piece runs through all his poetry, which from childhood to age never took one step in advance. The commonplaces of rhetoric are the Alpha and Omega of his art.

It is customary to represent Martial as the most debased of flatterers, who licked the feet of the living Domitian and spat on his corse. This view is not altogether wrong. General opinion is seldom wholly mistaken, but often needs qualification, and here it needs much. He undoubtedly exaggerates habitually anything good that may be found in the living Domitian, and studiously conceals his faults; but that he insulted the dead emperor is not true. What are his allusions to Domitian after his death? He writes to Nerva : —

Martial.

> " In troublous times the heavy hand of might
> Could not divert thee from the path of right."[2]

[1] *Silv.* II. 7.

[2] " Sub principe duro
Temporibusque malis ausus es esse bonus."

This and a few other equally moderate utterances
are the grounds on which the indictment rests.[1]
Surely we have not here one who tramples on a
Often mis- fallen oppressor, but rather one who
represented. feels that by former expressions he has
forfeited the right to be as severe as the case war-
rants.　Pliny[2] ascribes sincerity to Martial, and
we must remember that the epigram, the form
which he chose as the vehicle for his thoughts,
almost excludes the softer feelings.　His condemnation of Nero[3] is certainly neither vehement
nor abundant.　A military despotism is the worst
sort of tyranny, because it kills the sentiments
which are the very life of a civilized society.　"It
created around itself the quiet of the graveyard,"
says Teuffel : "servility alone was allowed to
speak."　We cannot help feeling for the poet
Poorly re- when we find how little material benefit
warded for he reaped from the prostitution of a great
his flatter- genius to the poor business of a court
ies.
poet.　It is pathetic to see him licking the hand
which pushes him away, and blessing the emperor

[1] XII. 15. 9 is equally temperate, but V. 19. 5 and XII. 6.
4 are stronger.　The fierce couplet —

> "Flavia gens, quantum tibi tertius abstulit haeres :
> Paene fuit tanti non habuisse duos" —

is included in the "Spectaculorum liber" (32).　It is due to a
Schol. on Juv. IV. 38, and it is not certain that it is by Martial.
[2] *Ep*. III. 21.
[3] It is decided enough, but not very earnest, as in VII. 34. 4 :

> "Quid Nerone pejus ?
> Quid thermis melius Neronianis ?"

for the kind tone in which he refuses his petition : —

"If this be the smile with which help is refused, what must
be the smile when he gives?"[1]

He got little but empty honors, which made his poverty the more galling, because they imposed upon him some little dignity to maintain. To set against thousands of petitions we have not a single acknowledgment of a pecuniary favor. He seems to have received from the emperor a wretched little house in the country, the roof of which was not water-tight, and the garden of which did not supply him with sufficient vegetables for his frugal table.[2] He exults over the present of a new *toga* from Parthenianus,[3] but feels that he can hardly live up to such a garment, and begs for a common one to save it.[4] Always the beggar's whine; and his delight when he receives an alms shows how rare was such a piece of luck. Always indigence, which often betrays itself in the cynicism of his epigrams, as in that one[5] where he cries : —

"My parents in their folly taught me letters,"[6] —

an unfilial exclamation wrung from him by the success of a contemporary shoemaker. Martial, like the other Roman poets, tells us hardly anything of his youth.

Meagre details of his life.

[1] "Si negat hoc voltu, quo solet ergo dare?"
[2] VII. 31. 36. [3] VIII. 28.
[4] IX. 50. [5] IX. 74.
[6] "At me litterulas stulti docuere parentes."

We know, however, that he came from Bilbilis to Rome at the age of one-and-twenty, in the reign of Nero, and lived there till he was six-and-fifty. He wrote nothing under Nero, nor under Galba, Otho, Vitellius, Vespasian, those emperors whose reigns were counted by weeks, and four of whom sat in the Palace of the Caesars during ten months, "as if," in the words of Plutarch, "they were players in a booth, going on to the stage and anon off again." When he left Rome after a sojourn of thirty years, so little had he made by being a court poet that his friend Pliny had to discharge the cost of his return to his native Bilbilis. The twelfth book, which was written there, is full of melancholy and regret for Rome. We do not know whether his life reached the limit of five-and-seventy years which he coveted, but he seems to have outlived his enjoyments, ambitions, and hopes.

He has left us fourteen books, containing nearly Estimate of fifteen hundred epigrams. We could well his poetry. dispense with about two thirds of them, but the residue is precious. We have in Martial a matchless picture of Rome. Nowhere else do we find one so strong, so spirited, so filthy, even so mean, for now nothing is on a great scale in Rome except vice. Though the vehicle of his thoughts is so adverse to the expression of sensibility, yet we have distinct signs of it in his poetry, as when he declares that the birthday of his beloved Quintus conferred on him a greater boon than his own; that a gift to a friend is the only thing that is out of the

reach of chance, and money given away in presents
is the only abiding wealth. His sincere and exquisite pictures of the delights of country life could not
have been drawn by a man of shallow heart; and
we cannot help feeling that he was on the whole a
good man, who, in the forty-seventh epigram in the
fifth book, enumerates the ingredients of a happy
life. His impurities would now forbid the application to him of any such title, but we must remember that expressions which shock us now did not
seem shocking to his contemporaries. He even
boasts that young girls can read him without
danger; and indeed his books are a pathological
museum of vice, and his foul epigrams, like Zola's
novels, disgust rather than corrupt. Respectable
men in Rome avowed their admiration of him, and
he challenges his readers to find anything foul in
his life, unchaste though his verses may be and
are.

Statius and Martial never mention each other's
names, no doubt because they were rival
beggars compelled to offer their literary
wares to an emperor who was no judge
of them, and who had to be approached through
illiterate eunuchs and freedmen. M. Nisard compares certain poems in which Statius and Martial
have treated the same theme, and is disposed to
award the palm to Statius. A favorite eunuch
named Earinus had cut off his hair and dedicated it to Aesculapius. Martial deals with this
incident in four sportive little epigrams in the

ninth book, chiefly dwelling on the unsuitable-
ness of the name to the Latin metres. Statius
devotes to it a poem [1] nearly as long as Wordsworth's immortal " Ode on Immortality," with
elaborate mythological machinery. One cannot
help thinking that victory, with such a subject and
achieved by so laborious a method, is itself defeat.
The result is much the same when we observe
how each deals with another theme, a bronze statue
of Hercules which had been owned by Alexander
the Great, Hannibal, and Sulla, and was now the
property of a Roman virtuoso, Novius Vindex.[2]
A better principle of comparison would be to observe how high each can rise, and how low he can
sink. Martial is often profoundly touching. He
sometimes seems to mock his own sensibilities and
those of his readers. As Heine sometimes seems
ashamed of possessing human feelings, and, revers-
ing the well-known Terentian phrase, delights in
showing how alien to him is all that is human by
putting a piece of cold cynicism beside some profound and pathetic reflection ; so Martial, having
touched the most exquisite note in Byron's

> " O snatch'd away in beauty's bloom," —

we mean the last couplet,

> " And thou who bidd'st me to forget,
>   Thy cheeks are wan, thine eyes are wet," —

concludes a noble poem with some lines of the

[1] *Silv.* III. 4.
[2] Mart. IX. 44, 45; Stat. *Silv.* IV. 6.

foulest indecency. But he rises high though he chooses to stoop low. Statius never approaches the "pure serene" in which Martial sometimes is willing to float for a while,[1] and how miserably low he can fall will be evident to any one who reads the creeping Sapphics [2] in which he apostrophizes the condition of childlessness as "to be avoided by every effort," —

"Orbitas omni fugienda nisu."

Taking into consideration the absurdity of personifying and apostrophizing the condition of childlessness, the grotesque feebleness and almost offensive tastelessness of the expression, and the imbecility of the sentiment, I should be disposed to pronounce this the very worst line in Latin poetry, though others in the same poem run it close in the race for this distinction, especially the very next verse, in which childlessness is described as "buried with no tears" (*orbitas nullo tumulata fletu*), as if a father could enjoy the thought of his children weeping over his bier.

The worst line in Latin poetry.

Every one interested in Latin literature is familiar with the excellent chapter (the 64th) in Merivale's "History of the Romans under the Empire," in which he

Merivale on the Flavian epoch.

---

[1] Perhaps the best piece of Statius is the prayer for sleep in *Silv.* V. 4, with which should be read a fine description of the abode of Sleep in *Theb.* X. 84 ff.

[2] *Silv.* IV. 7.

contrasts the Flavian with the foregoing literary epochs, and points out the influence of the professorial system established throughout the Empire by Vespasian. Dean Merivale remarks that the Flavian era was an age of positive thought, that the nymphs and heroes of Statius were copied from the courtiers of the Palatine, and the Medea of Valerius Flaccus was a virago of the imperial type, a Lollia or Agrippina. If Valerius Flaccus and Silius Italicus had allowed their work to express more freely the spirit of their age, they would have been far more interesting and valuable to us now. But they seem to have resisted it strenuously, and to have tried to use again the old poetic framework which was worn out and should have been abandoned. It was a great mistake when Silius Italicus, applying the supernatural machinery of the Aenëid to a historical narrative, made Volturnus, sent by Aeolus at the prayer of Juno, blind the eyes of the Romans at Cannae, and when he depicted Venus as plunging the Poeni into sloth at Capua.

It would be useless even to attempt to characterize the later verse-writers like Prudentius, whom Bentley strangely called the Virgil and Horace of the Christians, but of whom no more can justly be said than that he is the least bad among the Christian versifiers, though inferior to some of them, for instance to Juvencus, in the use of the language. But there is one very late poet of whom a word may be

Later verse-writers.

said. Claudian's position in literature is unique. It is remarkable enough, as has been observed, that after three centuries of torpor the Latin muse should have revived in the reign of Honorius; surprising that this revival should have been brought about by a foreigner, an Oriental; but most amazing of all that a justly won and enduring reputation should be founded on court poems, installation odes, and panegyrics on inconsiderable people in an uninteresting age. Gibbon says: " He was endowed with the rare and precious talent of raising the meanest, of adorning the most barren, and of diversifying the most similar, topics." We may, perhaps, fitly conclude this lecture with a translation from Claudian in prose from the graceful pen of Professor Jebb, my predecessor in this Lectureship, whose taste, learning, eloquence, and judgment were, I feel sure, duly appreciated last year by this audience. It is an extract from the poem on the consulship of Stilicho, A. D. 400, a eulogy on the Empire of Rome. It is a splendid expression of what ought now to be the ambition and aspiration of at least one great empire and one great republic: —

" She, she alone, has taken the conquered to her bosom, and has made men to be one household with one name, herself their mother, not their empress, and has called her vassals citizens, and has linked far places in a bond of love. Hers is that large loyalty to which we owe it that the stranger walks in a strange land as if it were his own; that men can change their homes; that it is a pastime to visit Thule, and to expose mysteries at which we once shuddered; that we

drink at will the waters of the Rhone and the Orontes; that
the whole earth is one people." [1]

[1] " Haec est in gremium victos quae sola recepit,
   Humanumque genus communi nomine fovit
   Matris non dominae ritu, civesque vocavit
   Quos domuit, nexuque pio longinqua revinxit.
   Hujus pacificis debemus moribus omnes
   Quod veluti patriis regionibus utitur hospes;
   Quod sedem mutare licet; quod cernere Thulen
   Lusus, et horrendos quondam penetrare recessus;
   Quod bibimus passim Rhodanum, potamus Orontem:
   Quod cuncti gens una sumus."

APPENDIX.

A VERY interesting account of the translators of Virgil into verse, up to his own time, was given by the late Professor Conington in the "Quarterly Review" for 1861.[1] The most remarkable versions since that time have been first, of course, Conington's own translation of the "Aenëid" into the octosyllabic measure so successfully used by Sir Walter Scott in his metrical romances; and, more recently, the versions by Mr. William Morris, Canon Thornhill, and Lord Justice Sir Charles Bowen. Mr. Morris has adopted the long fourteen-syllabled metre of Chapman's "Homer," which had already been employed by an early translator of Virgil, Thomas Phaer (1558–1573). I must own that I was disappointed with his "Aenëids of Virgil." One did not find in it that deftness of phrase-making and that easy command of rhythm which distinguish "The Earthly Paradise," and many of the sonnets of one to whom one unhesitatingly accords a place in the small and distinguished company of living poets. In the "Aenëids of Virgil" he was unfortunate in the choice of a subject. His chief gift is to be able to throw round his theme a kind of archaic halo, an old epic atmosphere, which is so skillfully generated that the reader wanders enchanted with his new guide through Hellenic and Alexandrine mythland. But this old-world tone, so invaluable to a translator of Homer, or even of Apollonius Rhodius, is entirely unsuitable to Virgil, who, in dealing with lan-

[1] No. 219, pp. 73–114.

guage, is abreast of his age, or even in front of it; whose chief characteristics are a delicate intricacy of expression and a terse pointedness, the corruption of which generated the stilted poetry of silver Latinity; whose style, in fine, far more readily suggests a comparison with Mr. Ruskin or Matthew Arnold than with Sir Thomas Malory or Spenser. Hence the sense of incongruity inspired by such Wardour-Street English as *eyen* and *clepe*, and by such lines as, —

"That thence a folk, kings far and wide, most noble lords of fight,
   Should come for bane of Libyan land : such web the Parcae
      dight;"[1]

or

   "Unto the fatherland of storm, full fruitful of the gale,
      Aeolia hight, where Aeolus is king of all avail."[2]

I will give as a sample of his work the fine speech of Dido[3] after she has resolved to destroy herself, and I will put beside it the same passage from the two other most recent versions : —

                              "Ah, Jove ! and is he gone ?
   And shall a very stranger mock the lordship I have won ?
   Why arm they not ? Why gather not from all the town in chase ?
   Ho ye ! Why run ye not the ships down from their standing place ?
   Quick, bring the fire ! shake out the sails ! hard on the oars to sea !
   What words are these ? Or where am I ? What madness changeth
      me ?
   Unhappy Dido ! now at last thine evil deed strikes home.
   Ah, better when thou mad'st him lord — lo whereunto are come
   His faith and troth who erst, they say, his country's house gods
      held,
   The while he took upon his back his father spent with eld ?
   Why ! might not I have shred him up and scattered him piecemeal
   About the sea, and slain his friends, his very son, with steel,
   Ascanius on his father's board for dainty meat to lay ?
   But doubtful, say ye, were the fate of battle ? Yea, O yea !

   [1] *Aenëid*, I. 21, 22.   [2] I. 51, 52.   [3] IV. 590–629.

What might I fear, who was to die — if I had borne the fire
Among their camp, and filled his decks with flame, and son and
  sire
Quenched with their whole folk, and myself had cast upon it all!
    .   .   .   .
Lo this I pray, this last of words forth with my blood I pour,
And ye, O Tyrians, 'gainst his race that is, and is to be,
Feed full your hate! When I am dead send down this gift to me:
No love betwixt the peoples twain, no troth for anything!
And thou, Avenger of my wrongs, from my dead bones outspring,
To bear the fire and the sword o'er Dardan-peopled earth
Now or hereafter; whensoe'er the day brings might to birth.
I pray the shore against the shore, the sea against the sea,
The sword 'gainst sword—fight ye that are, and ye that are to be!"

Put beside this the version of Sir C. Bowen, which, in
its plain, manly, straightforward vigor, affords a strong
contrast to the artificial simplicity of Mr. Morris's verses,
and indeed would be in many respects adequate except
for the metre : —

" Father of Earth and of Heaven! and shall this stranger, she cries,
  Wend on his treacherous way, flout Dido's realm as he flies?
  Leaps no sword from the scabbard? Is Tyre not yet on his trail?
  None of ye warping the ships from the dockyards, hoisting the sail?
  Forth with the flame and the arrow! To sea and belabor the
    main!
  Ah, wild words! Is it Dido? Has madness troubled her brain?
  Ah, too late, poor Dido! The sin comes home to thee now!
  Then was the hour to consider, when thou wast crowning his brow.
  Look ye! The faith and honor of him who still, as they say,
  Carries on shipboard with him his Trojan gods on the way!
  Bore on his shoulders his aged sire! Ah, had I not force
  Limb from limb to have torn him, and piecemeal scattered his
    corse
  Over the seas? His crews to have slain, and, banquet of joy,
  Served on the father's table the flesh of Iulus the boy?
  Even were chance in the battle unequal, — death was at hand.
  Whom had Dido to fear? I had borne to his vessels the brand,

Filled with flames each deck, each hold, — child, people, and sire
Whelmed in a blazing ruin, and flung myself on the pyre !
This last prayer as my life ebbs forth I pour with my blood ;
Let not thy hatred sleep, my Tyre, to the Teucrian brood :
Lay on the tomb of Dido for funeral offering this !
Neither be love nor league to unite my people and his !
Rise ! thou Nameless Avenger from Dido's ashes to come,
Follow with fire and slaughter the false Dardanians home !
Smite them to-day, hereafter, through ages yet unexplored,
Long as thy strength sustains thee, and fingers cling to the sword !
Sea upon sea wage battle forever !   Shore upon shore,
Spear upon spear !   To the sires and children strife evermore ! "

The same passage as translated by Canon Thornhill
well illustrates the extreme vigor of his work, whilst it
labors under the characteristic defect of diffuseness : —

" Shall he then go ?   Go, and our kingdom left
Insulted, mocked, to point a rover's scoff !
What, lieges, ho ! — Will they not arm and out,
All Carthage, quick ?   Not chase the faithless foe ?
Nor pluck those laggard vessels from the docks ?
Away ! forth fire and sword ! ply sail and oar ! —
Yet hold ; what words are these ?   where, what this place ?
What madness whirls my brain ?   Ah, wretched queen,
Needs guilty deed to touch thy dainty sense ?
Late wail'd what 's done ; wise hadst thou rued in time,
When heart and sceptre at thy giving lay.
Mirror of knighthood's truth ! and this is he,
The world-famed prince that ever with him bears
His country's god about ! the model son,
Who on his back did safe from foes bear off
The helpless burden of his aged sire !
Might not this hand — fool, to forbear the deed ! —
Have shred his mangled carcase to the waves,
Slain friends and followers, yea, done to death
Ascanius' self, and at the father's board
Have served him up his murdered boy to boot ?
True, 't were to fight at risk ; but what of that ?
Self-doom'd to death, whom — what — had I to fear ?

No; I had fired their fleet, each gangway filled,
And, smothering deck with flame, slain sire and son,
With all the cursed brood extinct, and crowned
The blazing ruin with myself and mine!

　.　　.　　.　　.　　.　　.　　.　　.　　.　　.

Such wish take he from me, this parting curse
Here with my streaming blood to Heaven I pour,
Then, Tyrians, you with endless feud still vex
His seed, breed, kind, — yea, all shall ever trace
His caitiff line; with this meet tribute still
Present your Dido's tomb.　Be love nor league
Your hostile realms betwixt!　O from our dust —
Hear, righteous Heaven, the prayer! — some Champion start,
Some bold Avenger, doomed with fire and sword
To hunt those Trojan vagrants through the world,
Be it to-day, to-morrow, or whene'er;
No time unmeet shall will and means supply;
Fight shore with shore opposed, wave fight with wave,
Fight all — who — what — or are, or e'er shall be!"

The several renderings of this passage seem to me about as characteristic of the merits and defects of the several authors as any one could have chosen. One might have selected more favorable specimens of the powers of Sir Charles Bowen and Canon Thornhill.

Here is a passage [1] in which the former very skillfully reproduces that sympathy which the face and voice of Nature awaken in the poet : —

" Come, Galatea, where in the waves can a merriment be?
　Here are the golden blooms of spring; earth bountiful, see,
　Here by the river scatters her bright-hued flow'rs evermore,
　Over the cavern hangs one poplar of silvery white,
　Lissom vines have woven a roof that shades it from light;
　Come!　Let the madcap billows in thunder break on the shore."

In the last lines of Jupiter's speech in the first book [2] the translator rises with the poet : —

[1] *Ecl.* IX. 38–43.　　　[2] *Aenëid,* I. 286–296.

" Then Caesar of Troy's bright blood shall be born
Bounding his throne by the ocean, his fame by the firmament floor
Julius hight, from Iulus, his great forefather of yore.
Thine ere long to receive him in heaven, thy fears at an end
Laden with Eastern trophies.   To him, too, vows shall ascend.
Rude Time, waxing mellow, shall lay fierce battles aside,
White-haired Faith, with Vesta, Quirinus, and Remus allied,
Rule with justice the nations, and speedily War's grim gates
Close with their iron bolts and their iron-riveted plates.
Sinful Rebellion within, an imprisoned Fury, the while
Piling her fiendish weapons, shall sit firm bound on the pile,
Hands in a thousand fetters behind her manacled fast,
Blood-red lips still yelling her thunder-yells to the blast."

I have not space for as many extracts as I would
gladly make, and I must refer you to the sombre strain
which tells of the descent into Hell,[1] beginning, —

" So unseen in the darkness they went by night on the road
Down the unpeopled kingdom of Death and his ghostly abode ; "

and to the splendid speech of Anchises at the end of
the sixth book, of which I can only quote the closing
lines : —

" Child of a nation's sorrow ! if thou canst baffle the Fates'
Bitter decrees, and break for a while their barrier gates,
Thine to become Marcellus !   I pray thee bring me anon
Handfuls of lilies, that I bright flowers may strew on my son,
Heap on the shade of the boy unborn these gifts at the least,
Doing the dead, tho' vainly, the last sad service.   He ceased."

Sir Charles Bowen has also been very successful in
couplets here and there, in which he has managed to
preserve great spirit in an absolutely literal rendering,
as for instance, —

" Far on the watery waste he beheld Troy's company driven,
Trojans crushed by the waves and the wrack and ruin of heaven ; "[2]

[1] *Aenëid*, VI. 268–281.   [2] I. 128.

and —

" Come, let us perish, and charge to the heart of the enemies' line.
One hope only remains for the conquered, — hope to resign." [1]

Canon Thornhill is perhaps most successful in Dido's
fierce denunciation of her faithless lover : [2] —

"Nor goddess gave thee birth, false-hearted wretch,
Nor Dardanus thy miscreant kind begot,
But thou from flinty Caucasus wast hewn,
Congenial grain ! and tigers gave thee suck.
Yes, why mince words, and wait for baser wrong?
What ! see me weep, nor heave one kindly sigh !
Moved he those eyes? shed he one answering tear?
Yea, was e'en pity to my pangs denied ?
But why note this or that, or how award
The palm for worst where barbarous all alike?
Ay me ! not man alone — not Juno now,
Nor Jove himself, hath ruth of wretches' wrong !
Yes, yes ; no trusting more of Earth or Heaven.
This ingrate I, what time our angry waves
Flung out the needy waif upon these shores,
Not housed alone and fed, but bade him share —
Ah, fool ! — my throne and state, and snatched withal
His shattered barks and starving crews from death.
Ha ! that way madness lies — my brain 's afire !
'T is Phoebus now — 't is now some Lycian seer —
Anon — and special sent of Jove himself —
E'en Heaven's own herald cleaves his aëry way
To bear the dread command.   Yes, fitting task,
Belike, for god's employ ! such cares — 't is apt ! —
Must ruffle Heaven's repose !   But I, good sooth,
Nor court thy stay nor deign thy lies refute."

This very spirited rendering of the Dublin scholar
is, it must be owned, affluent to diffuseness, containing
ten lines more than the Latin, and it will be noticed
that there is a heightening of the tone which almost

[1] *Aenëid*, II. 353.   [2] IV. 365–380.

amounts to exaggeration. "Wretch," "miscreant," "barbarous," are not in the Latin, and *dicta* is not *lies;* on the other hand, "that way madness lies" is very happily adopted from "King Lear." Conington, with his shorter measure, uses one line less. I quote his rendering to show that, with all his skill, in a really impassioned passage his ambling metre drags him down : —

> "No goddess bore thee, traitorous man:
> No Dardanus your race began ;
> No ; 't was from Caucasus you sprung,
> And tigers nursed you with their young.
> Why longer wear the mask, as though
> I waited for some heavier blow ?
> Heaved he one sigh at tears of mine ?
> Moved he those hard impassive eyne ?
> Did one kind drop of pity fall
> At thought of her who gave him all ?
> What first, what last ?   Now, now I know
> Queen Juno's self has turned my foe :
> Not e'en Saturnian Jove is just :
> No faith on earth, in heaven no trust.
> A shipwrecked wanderer up and down,
> I made him share my home, my crown :
> His shattered fleet, his needy crew
> 'From fire and famine's jaws I drew.
> Ah, Furies whirl me ! now divine
> Apollo, now the Lycian shrine,
> Now Heaven's own herald comes, to bear
> His grisly mandate through the air !
> Aye, gods above ply tasks like these ;
> Such cares disturb their life of ease. —
> I loathe your person, scorn your pleas."

Both Sir Charles Bowen and Canon Thornhill are thoroughly trustworthy in point of scholarship.   Both show a careful and judicious use of the admirable com-

mentary of Conington and Nettleship, and in the case
of the former one can discern an independent power of
insight and apprehension. Hence the misconceptions
of the earlier translators have disappeared from the
work of the Lord Justice and the Canon. Thus, in
"Aenëid," IV. 11, Conington makes it quite clear that,
when Dido exclaims,

"Quem sese ore ferens! quam forti pectore et armis!"

she is expressing her admiration of the stout chest and
broad shoulders of Aeneas;[1] so Enid, as she looks on
her sleeping lord, cries, —

"O noble breast and all-puissant arms!"

In accordance with this interpretation, which is certainly right, Sir Charles Bowen renders, —

"Who is the stranger come to our palace halls as a guest?
Princely his bearing, — a hero's arms and a hero's breast."

And Canon Thornhill : —

"What face and mien — did'st mark? — and bearing high,
What noble breast and stalwart might of arm!"

No doubt Lord Tennyson had this passage in his
mind when he wrote the lines which I have quoted
from "Enid and Geraint;" the poet saw the real meaning of a passage which was misapprehended by the
earlier commentators, who made *armis* "deeds of arms,
warlike achievements." In "Cymbeline" (IV. 2, 308),
Imogen, in her grief, dwells even more forcibly on physical endowments : —

"The garments of Posthumus!
I know the shape of 's leg; this is his hand;
His foot Mercurial; his Martial thigh;
The brawns of Hercules."

[1] *Armis* comes from *armus*, "a shoulder," not from *arma*.

The pretty phrase, *radiisque retexerit orbem*,[1] is as prettily turned by Sir C. Bowen into "uncurtains the land;" and *vir gregis ipse caper*[2] really gains point as "our sultan goat." But he is completely surpassed by the Dublin translator in turning

> "Ast ego quae divum incedo regina."[3]

Nothing could be better than

> "I who queen it through these courts of heaven."

How poor beside this is Sir C. Bowen's —

> "I who in high heaven move as a queen;"

and Conington's —

> "I who through heaven its mistress move;"

and Morris's —

> "I who go for the queen of the gods."

Canon Thornhill is, I think, guided by a true instinct in appropriating, when it is ready to his hand, some happy classicism of Tennyson or Milton. For instance, —

> "This way and that dividing the swift mind"

is far better than Sir C. Bowen's —

> "Hither and thither he hurries his thought;"

aetheria lapsa plaga is exactly "stoop'd from his aëry tour;" *toto praeceps se corpore ad undus mersit* very probably suggested "throws his steep flight," and may therefore fairly be restored to its owner. Less obvious, but as pleasing, is Canon Thornhill's adoption of Shake-

---

[1] *Aenëid*, IV. 119.   [2] *Ecl.* VII. 7.   [3] *Aenëid*, I. 46.

speare's "a pliant hour" for *mollissima fandi tempora*,[1] and, for another passage,[2] of Milton's

> " Towards heaven's descent doth slope his west'ring wheel."

He would have done well to apply the same principle oftener.   Virgil's delicate expression, —

> " Solane perpetua moerens carpere juventa,"[3] —

has no closer parallel than Shakespeare's " withering on the virgin thorn."

Again, in " Aenëid," IV. 530, —

> " Aut pectore noctem
> Accipit,"

the translators have failed to take advantage of Lord Tennyson's musical echo, —

> " She ever failed to draw
> The quiet night into her blood."

But the chief defect of both these excellent works lies in the metre; and the metre is all-important in reproducing the effect of the original poem.   "Art thou that Virgil? " — the question of Dante — must be put to every adventurous spirit who attempts to clothe Virgil in the garb of a new tongue.   And we must answer No, if an unsuitable metre is chosen, or a suitable metre is inadequately handled.

The Dublin translator has chosen the metre which is, perhaps, better fitted than any other, except perhaps the heroic couplet, to give the impression of the Latin hexameter ; but my readers will have seen already that

[1] *Aenëid*, IV. 293.
[2] "Devexo interea propior fit vesper Olympo." — VIII. 280.
[3] IV. 32.

he has not mastered that most elusive of arts, the power to make blank verse sing. It is impossible by any analysis to fix the quality or qualities which make the " Idylls of the King" poetry, while the " Epic of Hades" is merely measured prose. Mr. Worsley, in his preface to his " Iliad," attempts to tell us what blank verse means : " An essential condition to its existence is, that not the line only, but the whole sentence and paragraph, should really scan. A series of blank lines, though each line in itself may be full of merit, is no more blank verse than good bricks are of necessity a good structure."

Now the Dublin scholar often gives admirable lines, but his translation as a whole has the cadence of the " Epic of Hades " — to which, be it observed, he points as one of the models of English blank verse — rather than that of " Paradise Lost" or " Tithonus." Dr. Symmons, who early in the last century essayed with poor success to surpass Dryden in the use of his own weapon, the heroic couplet, speaks of blank verse " as only a laborious and doubtful struggle to escape from the fangs of prose ; " adding that, " if it ever ventures to relax into simple and natural phraseology, it instantly becomes the prey of its pursuer." Dr. Johnson must have been under the influence of a somewhat similar feeling when he advised poets who did not think themselves capable of astonishing, but only aimed at pleasing, to condescend to rhyme. Dr. Henry, on the other hand, regards rhyming as a crime : " Drunkenness is an aggravation of, not an excuse for, the outrages of the drunkard ; rhyme is an aggravation of, not an excuse for, the outrages of the rhymester." The Dublin Canon is far from clipping the wings of his ambition in the fashion suggested by Dr. Johnson. His aim is often to astonish, and he has not failed in sometimes achieving it. He is never dull or bald, and we can hardly say as much for any other blank-verse translation of Virgil, from that of the ill-fated Earl of Surrey to the recent version by Mr. Rickards and Lord Ravensworth. But Canon Thornhill has one grievous sin. He is diffuse, and Virgil is the most condensed of poets. Now, he who essays "the poet's chiming close" has some excuse for diffuseness. Rhyme is a mocking fiend, a wicked Siren, who allures her victims into her toils and then enjoys their struggles. Rhyme can plead no justification for herself. There never was and never will be any reason why thought should express itself in words which produce a certain assonance at certain intervals. Yet, as was said of dicing in ancient Rome, it will ever be forbidden and ever practiced. Diffuseness is one of the witch's imps. It will always be true, as was said by the witty author of "Hudibras," that

> "Those who write in rhyme still make
> The one verse for the other's sake ;
> For one for sense and one for rhyme
> They think 's sufficient at one time."

This is the genesis of the second verse in the couplet by which Dryden translated *tantaene animis caelestibus irae* : —

> "Can heavenly minds such high resentment show,
> *Or exercise their spite in human woe ?*"

The same may be said of the last lines in Pope's "Iliad : "—

> "Such honors Ilion to her hero paid,
> *And peaceful slept the mighty Hector's shade.*"

And the same imp, when Johnson had expressed admirably in one verse a well-known Juvenalian gnome,[1] —

> "Slow rises worth by poverty oppressed,"

hitched on a tag of pitiful bathos : —

> " *This mournful truth is everywhere confessed.*"

But the wielder of blank verse is without excuse for diffuseness ; yet we find that in the passage above, on
which we compared Sir C. Bowen, Canon Thornhill,
and Mr. Morris, the Latin being twenty-five lines in
length, Mr. Morris has twenty-six verses, Sir Charles
Bowen twenty-seven, and Canon Thornhill forty-one.
No doubt his measure is shorter than theirs, but Conington, with his shorter octosyllabics, has two verses
less, and Mr. Rickards, using the same metre, gives only
thirty-one verses. The version by Mr. Rickards and
Lord Ravensworth has the merits as well as the defects
which arise from a recoil from exuberance. It may
fairly claim to be the most condensed translation of the
" Aenëid " which has appeared. Of course the hexameter, which averages fifteen syllables, cannot always
be compressed into a ten-syllabled line ; but their rendering goés as far as possible in this direction. Lord
Ravensworth defies all comers to turn into one heroic
verse the last line in the description of the shield of
Aeneas : [2] —

> "Indomitique Dahae et pontem indignatus Araxes,"

or the less ambitious

> " Troës, Agyllinique, et pictis Arcades armis." [3]

[1] "Haud facile emergunt quorum virtutibus obstat
Res angusta domi." — *Sat.* III. 164.
[2] *Aenëid*, VIII. 728.   [3] XII. 281.

" Blank verse really deserving of the name," writes
Conington in his preface, " I believe to be impossible,
except to one or two eminent writers in a generation."
With this opinion I heartily agree. Of Englishmen
during the last generation, probably not one but Tennyson and Mr. Swinburne could produce blank verse
which would be a worthy counterpart of

" The stateliest measure ever moulded by the lips of man."

Of the metre which Conington himself has adopted,
the less said the better. It has spoiled an admirable
performance. Inextricably entangled as it is in our
minds with three subjects, — the biting invective of Swift
and Butler, the Oriental love-tales of Byron, and the
Border warfare of Scott, — it would offend us even if,
in itself and apart from associations, it was fitted to be
an equivalent for the varied and long-drawn roll of the
" Aenëid." But it is absolutely in itself unsuitable.

" I admit," says the Bishop of Derry,[1] " that Scott
can do wonders with the octosyllabic line, when the
trumpet of battle is in his ears, or when his spirit gallops
with the hunter in the storm of chase along the hills.
I admit that Byron has sometimes breathed into it the
tempest of his passion, and Wordsworth the chastened
wisdom of his meditative morality. But I maintain that
there are incurable defects in the measure for a long and
serious poem. It cannot be sustained at a high pitch.
Its fatal facility is a perpetual temptation."

Dr. Henry protests with characteristic impetuosity
against setting Virgil a-chorusing with Hieland caterans.
We must own our participation to some degree in the

---

[1] In a lecture given as one of a series of Lectures on Literature
and Art delivered in Dublin in 1868.

feeling which makes Dr. Alexander so eloquent and Dr. Henry so indignant. Every metre has its own peculiar associations. The *terza rima* of Dante and the *ottava rima* of Pulci belong, in the phrase of Schiller, to different jurisdictions. Would any sane man think of turning " Childe Harold " into the measure of " Hudibras," or the " Battle of Chevy Chase " into the Spenserian stanza? Scott contended that, certain superfluous words being omitted, the first two verses of Pope's " Iliad " would run better in octosyllabics, thus : —

> " Achilles' wrath, to Greece the spring
> Of woes unnumbered, Goddess, sing."

But the omitted words are not superfluous. They perform a most important function in retarding the metre, and bringing in with the heroic couplet a dignity which is lost in the octosyllabic scurry. If the Muse appeared in answer to such an invocation, she should come with the tripping step of a slipshod waiting-maid answering a bell. But what shall we say of the metre which Sir Charles Bowen has employed? I cannot help feeling that here, too, a fine piece of work has been spoiled by the metre. Sir Charles pleads for it that it is the Latin hexameter shorn of a syllable, since Coleridge's line, —

> " In the hexameter rises the fountain's silvery column," —

would become, if the final dissyllable were replaced by a single syllable, —

> " In the hexameter rises the fountain's silvery spray."

Against this plea one would be disposed to urge that the hexameter is not a metre at all unless it is scanned by quantity, and the English hexameter does not even suggest rhythm except to those who are familiar with

Greek and Latin poetry, and these it offends.   So that
to me at least it seems that there is nothing gained by
an approximation to the so-called English hexameter.
Moreover, the dropping of the final syllable altogether
revolutionizes the whole character of the metre, which,.
after the change, ceases to suggest the hexameter at all.
Each metre has its own character, its own expression,
which it *may* preserve under considerable modification,
but to which the slightest readjustment *may* prove fatal,
just as a slight injury may completely change the expression of a human face, which a much more serious
lesion might leave unaltered.   We feel that we have an
iambic line of the Miltonic form in Tennyson's —

> "Ruining along the illimitable inane,"

though it would be hard to mark the five beats.   We
might many times read or recite —

> " And Sorrow's faded form and Solitude behind "

without observing that it was a Greek *senarius* wanting
a *caesura*.   Let us take an English line with the measure and *caesura* of a Greek *senarius*, and it does not
strike our ear as being metrical, if unaided by rhyme.

> " And know by heart the congress of the nightly stars "

is a line in the late Professor Kennedy's translation of
the " Agamemnon."   It is in the very model of a Greek
senarius, but it seems to our ear mere prose.   Now, just
as the twelve-syllabled iambic verse must in English
fall into two equal parts, as in —

> " And Sorrow's faded form | and Solitude behind,"

so the verse which Sir Charles has chosen is either no
metre at all, or it is the metre which Swinburne has

used so grandly in the "Song in Time of Revolution : " —

> " The heart of the rulers is sick, and the High Priest covers his
> head,
> For this is the song of the quick which is heard in the ears of the
> dead."

Each line falls into two parts, and Swinburne has emphasized this essential quality in the metre by marking the end of the first part as well as the second with a rhyme. This rule is observed by Sir Charles Bowen, whether it be by chance or design, in many, perhaps most, of his lines, but it ought never to be violated. His poem would then be written in anapaestic measure, and would not attempt, as it vainly does in its present form, to remind the reader of the measure of the " Aenëid." Here are some verses which we should find it difficult to scan. We may say of them with Touchstone : " This is the very false gallop of verses : why do you infect yourself with them ? " —

" Thither crossed the Achaeans and hidden on its desolate beach." [1]

" Slowly at last by the Ithacan's thunders driven to divine." [2]

" Blindly to enter the havens that appear so nigh on the main." [3]

Very disagreeable, too, are the frequent introduction of the triple rhyme, and the alternation of the rhyme when the ear is accustomed to the couplet. Sometimes [4] we meet the distant rhyme-recurrences of a sonnet.

> " Imperio laeti parent et jussa facessunt " [5]

is not a very striking verse, but it ought to find a place in the translation. On the other hand, Sir Charles is

[1] *Aenëid*, II. 24.   [2] I. 128.   [3] III. 382.
[4] VI. 607–613.   [5] IV. 295.

not justified in importing into a passage a sentiment
not to be found there.

" Nor shall I ever tire of remembering Dido the sweet "

is far more loving than

" Nec me meminisse pigebit Elissae." [1]

One would have welcomed such a symptom of tenderness in the Man of Destiny, but no such soft word ever
passed his cold lips. Still less did he say, when he
appealed to his deserted mistress in the Shades : [2] —

" Tarry, and turn not away from a face *that on thine would dwell ;
'Tis thy lover thou fliest*, and this is our last farewell ! "

What he said was : —

" Siste gradum, teque adspectu ne subtrahe nostro ;
   Quem fugis ? Extremum fato quod te alloquor hoc est."

Projecere animas is rendered " strewed their lives on
the sands," but this is only the tribute exacted by
rhyme, and must be classed with " the mazy lev'ret,"
" earth's soft arms," and " the stars of the blue Aegean,"
which Messrs. Butcher and Lang resent in the metrical
versions of Homer. As we are dealing with matters
of detail, we may add that " Ascan " seems to us a
dangerous experiment. Robert Andrews (1766) gave us
Daphny, Philly, Thyrse, Lyke (for Lycus), and Jutna (for
Juturna), but his precedent has been rightly neglected.
To estimate broadly the work of Lord Justice Bowen,
one would say that he has produced in his translation
a work of high literary art, and that his finished scholarship, sound judgment, and perfect taste would have
achieved an ideal translation if he had chosen a better

[1] *Aeneid*, IV. 335.   [2] VI. 465.

metre, and been more uniformly careful in the handling of it.

Of recent critical and exegetical labors on Virgil, by far the most important work is Dr. Henry's " Aenëidea." Dr. James Henry was elected a scholar of Trinity College, Dublin, in the year 1817, and graduated in 1819. For some years he practised as a physician in Dublin, but before he reached middle life he abandoned the practice of his profession, and devoted all his leisure and most of his ample means to the prosecution of Virgilian inquiry. Like Varro, " the most learned of the Romans," he pursued the footsteps of Aeneas whithersoever his fated wanderings had led him. Styx only with nine-fold coil set a bound to the feet of this enthusiastic follower of the Trojan hero. The first fruit of his labors was a translation of the first two books of the " Aenëid " into blank verse, published in Dublin in 1845. This was followed by a rather *bizarre* transcript of the sense of the first six books in highly diversified measures under the quaint title of " Six Photographs of the Heroic Times " (Dresden, 1853). The inquiries requisite for the execution of that task produced " Notes of a Twelve Years' Voyage of Discovery in the First Six Books of the Aenëis " (Dresden, 1853). This volume was brought out in German in an abridged form in the Göttingen " Philologus " in 1857, under the title " Adversaria Virgiliana." Probably he would have continued to use that medium of publication if the editor of the " Philologus " had not protested against Dr. Henry's omission of all accents and breathings in his Greek quotations. The editor offered to supply the accents and breathings himself, but Dr. Henry was obdurate; he would have none of " those schoolboy scratchings, those grotesque and disfiguring *additamenta* of the grammarians." Fleckeisen, on his side, was (very properly) inflexible, and the "Adversaria" ceased to appear. Dr. Henry, in his preface to the "Aenëidea," thus describes the subsequent course of his studies : —

" My love for the subject, instead of diminishing, increased with years, how much owing to the mere influence of habit, how much to the approbation with which my labors, imperfect as they were, had been received by competent judges both in England and on the continent of Europe, and especially in Germany, how much owing to a consciousness of the daily increasing facility with which I brushed away, or imagined I brushed away, from my author's golden letters some of the dust accumulated on them during the lapse of nearly twenty centuries, I shall not take it on me to say. But certain it is, that it is only with increasing love and zeal I have since 1857 not merely re-wrought the whole of the old ground, but taken in the entirely new ground of the last six books, and increased the previously very imperfect collection of *variae lectiones* by the insertion in their proper places of those of all the first-class MSS. carefully collated by myself and daughter in two journeys made to Italy for the express purpose, and of ten, being all that were of any importance, of the Paris MSS."

The first volume of the "Aenëidea" was published in 1873, the second in 1878, under the editorship of the late John F. Davies, M. A., of Trinity College, Dublin, and Professor of Latin in Queen's College, Galway. It is a monumental work. Disfigured as it is by much eccentricity of typography and style, by many more or less irrelevant (though generally eloquently and brilliantly written) digressions, by exaggerated acerbity of tone, and some undue obtrusion of the writer's personality, it forms, nevertheless, perhaps the most valuable body of original comment and subtle analysis which has ever been brought together for the illustration of a Latin poet. All the MSS. of Virgil written in capitals he has collated from beginning to end, some of them — the Vatican fragment, the Roman, the Palatine, and the Medicean — twice over. Of the second class of MSS., those not written in capitals, he has collated the Laurentian, Vatican, Paris, and Dublin, from beginning to end, the others only after the end of the sixth book. But it is in his interpretation and illustration that he has done such inestimable work. Having command of an extremely vigorous and affluent style of English, he is able to put in the most forcible and attractive form the discoveries achieved by his keen insight and cultivated taste ; but he is unfortunately a revolutionary by constitution, and too often steps out of his path to have a tilt with some usage or belief which seems to offend him, chiefly because it is long established and generally respected. His commentary on the first verse of the " Aenëid," which he strenuously maintains to be, —

> " Ille ego, qui quondam gracili modulatus avena,"

runs to 104 pages, being interrupted by a *parergon* of 28 pages in smaller type, in which he assails the first thirteen lines of Conington's verse translation. This rather ponderous *jeu d'esprit*, with its cumbrous dramatic machinery, whereby Priscian, Zumpt, Bopp, and Lindley Murray are introduced as interlocutors, would go far to induce a reader of taste to close the volume, especially when he found Dr. Henry railing at Conington in a dozen verses, beginning, —

"I do not like thee, Juno fell,
The reason why I know full well,"

for using " fell " to render *saevae* in the fourth verse of
the " Aenëid," and then seriously giving " vixen " as a
more suitable epithet. But the reader would have reason to regret it if he allowed this buffoonery to drive
him away from such a treasure-house of learning. The
first volume (864 pp.) finishes the first book, the second
(861 pp.) takes us to the end of the fourth. The third
contains the commentary as far as the tenth book, and
a fourth volume concludes the work.

The criticism of Virgil has, as a rule, flowed in an
easy channel with little alteration of the text, and the
originality of editors has shown itself in refinement of
exegesis. The edition of Ribbeck, however, affords a
notable exception to this rule, and is not adapted to inspire us with a respect for German taste and judgment,
however much we may admire German erudition. Perhaps his most demonstrably absurd conjecture is on
cumulatam morte remittam,[1] a passage of recognized
difficulty, where, reading *monte* for *morte*, and quoting
the proverbial *magnos promittere montes* in its defense, he
puts into the mouth of Dido an expression which, if
justifiable at all, would be worthy only of some swagger-
ing Palaestrio or Geta of the comic stage. " To promise
huge mountains " might be an intelligible though rather
vulgar proverbial expression, meaning to make promises
as " big as mountains," while "to send one away
crowned with the reward of a mountain " would most
probably be ludicrous in the highest degree to the ear
of a contemporary of Virgil. Conington remarks that
there is nothing so hazardous as to try to manipulate a

[1] *Aenëid*, IV. 436.

familiar proverb by varying the expression, and that half the blunders made by foreigners in essaying a strange tongue turn on experiments of that kind. An Indian Baboo,[1] describing the sorrow felt by the family at the death of the subject of his memoir, wrote, "The house presented a second Babel, or a pretty kettle of fish." Ribbeck's *cumulatam monte remittam* would probably have appeared as ludicrous to an Augustan Roman as the English of Mookerjee seems to us. Still more amusing is his conjecture on "Aenëid," XII. 55, —

> "At regina, nova pugnae conterrita sorte,
> Flebat, et ardentem generum moritura tenebat,"

where, by changing *moritura* to *monitura*, he makes the Queen-mother Amata cling to Turnus, not full of the presage of impending death, but primed with a lecture!

---

[1] *Memoir of the late Honorable Justice Onoocool Chunder Mookerjee*, by Mohindro Nauth Mookerjee, his nephew; Calcutta, 1876. This delightful specimen of Baboo English was largely noticed by the London press on its appearance. Here are a few more choice specimens of his style : "His first business on making an income was to extricate his family from the difficulties in which it had been lately enwarped, and to restore happiness and sunshine to those sweet and well-beloved faces on which he had not seen the soft and fascinating beams of a simper for many a grim-visaged year." "This was the first time that we see a Pleader taking a seat in the Bengal Legislative Council solely by dint of his own legal weapon ; and he was an *au fait*, and therefore undoubtedly a transcendental lucre to the Council." "Justice Mookerjee very well understood the boot of his client, for which he would carry a logomachy as if his wheel of fortune depended upon it, or even more than that." "His elevation created a catholic ravishment throughout the domain." "When a boy he was filamentous, but gradually in the course of time he became plump as a partridge." Let editors think of Mookerjee when they propose to introduce the language of every-day life into an epic in a foreign tongue.

On certain others of Ribbeck's textual corrections, *capsos* for *captas*[1] and *aliam* for *illam*,[2] I will quote the criticism of Dr. Henry, as it quite coincides with my own judgment, and gives withal a characteristic sample of his manner : —

"But what's this? The waste and barren syrtis of Ribbeck's orthographical varieties is passed, and yonder before us opens the splendid mirage of his conjectural emendations. I see island-dotted seas and lakes . . . and Ribbeck gigantic in the midst, building — no, not temples, not castles, but *capsi* for those twelve wild swans you see, wheeling round and round high above him in the air, and not minding either him or his *capsi*. Is he deaf, and does n't hear their singing? Or is it possible he does n't know that singing swans never live in *capsi?* And now the *capsi* are finished, and the swans have flown away, and Ribbeck, nothing daunted, is as intent on a search for Aeneas's twentieth ship, as he was just now on building *capsi* for twelve wild swans. . . . No matter how the MSS. cry out *Uno ore,* 'You lie, you lie!' and 'Shame! shame!' it is the twentieth, not the nineteenth ship of Aeneas which is devoured by the vortex, and Virgil wrote, not *illam* but *aliam*."

[1] *Aeneid,* I. 396.   [2] I. 116.

INDEX

The Index is intended to supplement the Table of Contents. Subjects to be found readily there are not mentioned in the Index, which records chiefly references to persons.